HOW TO UNDERSTAND
AN ACT OF PARLIAMENT

HOW TO UNDERSTAND AN ACT OF PARLIAMENT

D J Gifford PhD (Cantab)
John Salter MA (Oxon)

Cavendish
Publishing
Limited

First published in Great Britain 1996 by Cavendish Publishing Limited,
The Glass House, Wharton Street, London WC1X 9PX
Telephone: 0171-278 8000   Facsimile: 0171-278 8080

British Library Cataloguing-in Publication Data.

Gifford, Understanding an Act of Parliament.
1. Great Britain. Parliament. House of Commons – Rules and
2. Legislative bodies – Great Britain 3. Parliamentary practice – Great
Britain
I. Title II. Salter
328.4.1077

ISBN 1 85941 206 8

Printed and bound in Great Britain by
Biddles Ltd, Guildford and King's Lynn

PREFACE

There is a very real need today for people to know how to approach an understanding of the numerous Acts of Parliament and other forms of legislation that affect so many aspects of their daily lives. The age in which we live is an age of rapidly increasing governmental control. That control has extended into every walk of life. For all of us there is legislation of one type or another that affects the things we can do and controls how we can do them. From the broadcaster to the manufacturer, from the sales staff to the company secretary, there are Acts of Parliament and statutory instruments that must be complied with if penalties are to be avoided.

There was a time when only the lawyer had to know how to understand an Act of Parliament. That time has long since passed. Today there are many walks of life in which the knowledge of how to understand an Act of Parliament is essential. In the professional field the accountant, the architect, the engineer, the chartered surveyor, the chief executive of a hospital or a geriatric complex, and the town planner must have a good working knowledge of the special rules that govern the reading of legislation; they must know how to understand legislation and how to use it. In the commercial field this knowledge is of growing importance for the landlord, the manager, the company secretary, the shopping centre manager, the developer, the estate agent and the builder. In the field of government this knowledge is perhaps most important of all – and it is of importance not merely for those in the public service but for those in the creative field of local government.

An Act of Parliament is not something that can be read like a book. That is not just because the Act of Parliament is heavier reading, as indeed it usually is. It is because over the years the law has developed special rules that govern the reading of the Act of Parliament. Every Act of Parliament must be read in the light of those rules, and the person who attempts to read an Act of Parliament without a working knowledge of the more important rules of interpretation may fall into error. That error may be expensive.

The rules which govern the reading and interpretation of an Act of Parliament also govern the reading and understanding of legislation in all the other forms that legislation takes today. They govern the reading and understanding of the maze of subordinate legislation whether made by central or local government or by other statutory authorities. Such subordinate legislation is made today in growing profusion in the administration of an increasing number of statutes.

The object of this book is to explain the more important of the rules that govern the reading and understanding of legislation, and to do so as far as possible in ordinary everyday language. The reader who studies and understands those rules will gain more from the reading of legislation whether reading an Act of Parliament or any other form of legislation. The reader will not, however, become an expert in the science of interpreting legislation and must therefore expect to have to turn to members of the legal profession for help in solving the many complications that arise in the course of modern legislation. The more legislation grows the greater is the service which the legal profession can and does give to the community through its interpretation of the legislation and through its unravelling of the tangled legislative knots.

T C Beirne School of Law,   D J Gifford
University of Queensland

Denton Hall,   John Salter
5 Chancery Lane,
Clifford's Inn,
London

CONTENTS

TABLE OF CASES

EUROPEAN UNION CASES

TABLE OF STATUTES

GLOSSARY

Act
a law which has been made by Parliament – an Act of Parliament (also called a statute)

Amending Act
an Act passed by Parliament to alter another existing Act of Parliament.

Assent
the approval given to an Act of Parliament by the reigning King or Queen.

Bill
the draft of a proposed Act of Parliament (the term 'Bill' is used to describe the draft before Parliament has passed it and it receives the royal assent as an Act).

Code
a law passed by Parliament with the intention of giving a comprehensive coverage of the law on a particular subject matter and replacing the previous law relating to that subject matter.

Consolidating Act
an Act passed to bring into one Act of Parliament an original Act together with all the amendments that have been made to that original Act by various amending Acts of Parliament, or an Act passed to bring into one Act of Parliament provisions which have previously been scattered in various earlier Acts which it repeals.

Division
if an Act of Parliament is divided into parts those parts may themselves be subdivided into divisions each of which is likely to contain a number of related sections.

Enactment
an Act

Hansard
the publication in which are recorded the speeches made in Parliament.

Heading
words appearing at the top of a part or division of an Act of Parliament, they approximate to the chapter heading in a book; or words which are the first line of each section and are specific to it.

Legislation
law made by a body which has power to make law – the term is often used to refer to the Acts of Parliament, but it can also be used to refer to law made by persons or bodies whose law-making powers are given to them by Act of Parliament.

Long title
the longer of the two titles which are given to an Act of Parliament, the long title sets out some indication of the scope of the Act. See also **Short title**.

Marginal note
marginal notes appear as notes set in the margin of the Act. They set out (not always accurately) an indication of the matters dealt with in the section or subsection against which the marginal note appears.

Paragraph
a portion of a subsection.

Part
for an Act of Parliament the part corresponds to the chapter of a book.

Precedent
a decision by the High Court of Justice or by the Court of Appeal, the House of Lords or the Privy Council.

Pt
an abbreviation for 'part'.

s	an abbreviation for 'section'.
Schedule	a provision of an Act of Parliament appearing at the end of the Act, it is most commonly used to prescribe a form that is to be used in administering the Act or to prescribe rules for carrying some provision of the Act into effect. It corresponds to an appendix in a book.
Section	every Act of Parliament is divided into sections which are numbered consecutively and which approximate to the verses of a book of the Bible.
Short title	the short name of the particular Act of Parliament for easy reference. See also **Long title** in this glossary.
Sidenote	another name for a marginal note.
ss	an abbreviation for 'sections'.
Statute	another name for an Act of Parliament.
Subordinate legislation	a law which is made by some person or body other than Parliament and acting under the authority of an Act of Parliament.
Subsection	a section may itself be subdivided into provisions which are known as 'subsections' and which are themselves numbered numerically within the section.
Title	each Act of Parliament has two titles – the long title and the short.

CHAPTER 1

HOW AN ACT OF PARLIAMENT IS MADE

What an Act of Parliament is

An Act of Parliament (or, to give it its other name, a statute) is part of the law of the land. It is in fact law made by Parliament. If Parliament wants to make a law on some matter on which there is no law, or if Parliament wants to alter the existing law, it does so by making an Act of Parliament. The Act of Parliament is the way in which Parliament sets out its decisions on what the law is to be.

If heads of business or heads of departments wish to lay down some rule for their staff they can set it out in a written notice or they can tell the staff by word of mouth. Parliament, however, consists of a large number of elected representatives who are known as 'Members of Parliament'. Members of Parliament as such cannot make law on their own as individuals. Parliament is a body which consists of a large number of Members but which can only act as a body.[1]

How an Act of Parliament begins

The first of our Acts of Parliament was what is known today as the Statute of Merton. It took its name from the Surrey village in the priory of which Parliament met to pass the Act. It became part of the law of England in 1235, and some of it is still part of the law in England today.[2]

The king of England at the time when the Statute of Merton was passed was Henry III. In those early days, and for some hundreds of years afterwards, many of the Acts of Parliament came into being because they were suggested by the reigning king himself. For example, when King Henry VIII wanted to divorce Katherine of Aragon in order to marry Anne Boleyn, a special Act of Parliament was passed to let him do so. As Parliament said, that Act was passed so that

> the lawful matrimony had and solemnized between your Highness and your most dear and entirely beloved Queen Anne shall be established and taken for undoubtful true sincere and perfect ever hereafter.[3]

Two years later King Henry VIII persuaded Parliament to pass another Act to say that

> the same marriage between your Highness and the late Queen Anne shall be taken deemed reputed and judged to be of no force strength virtue or effect[4]

because, as Parliament said,

---

1   As to speeches in Parliament and reports, see Chapters 26 and 27.
2   See *Jowitt's Dictionary of English Law* (2nd edn, Sweet & Maxwell, London, 1977) p 1178. For other Acts of Parliament passed in the 13th century and still part of the law of England in the 20th century see Fay, *Discoveries in the Statute Book* (Sweet & Maxwell, London, 1939) p 9.
3   Act of Succession 1534, quoted in Fay, *Discoveries in the Statute Book*, p 64.
4   Quoted in Fay, *Discoveries in the Statute Book*, p 65.

the lady Anne, inflamed with pride and carnal desires of her body, putting apart the Dread of God and the excellent benefits received of your Highness ... most traitorously committed and perpetrated divers detestable and abominable treasons.[5]

One of the most notorious of the Acts of Parliament that came into being because it was suggested by the king was another of the Acts suggested by King Henry VIII. It was passed in 1531. In that year the Bishop of Rochester's cook put poison in a large quantity of porridge that was cooked for the bishop's household and for the poor of the parish. Many people became ill after eating the porridge and one person died. Henry VIII, who was very fond of his food, was no doubt alarmed at this risk of poisoning, and a special Act was rushed through Parliament. It provided that a poisoner must be boiled to death. It was even applied to poisoning that was carried out before the Act had come into force, and so the bishop's cook was the first poisoner boiled to death.

Another poisoner known to have been boiled to death was a servant girl who poisoned her husband in 1531,[6] and there seem to have been at least two others.[7] The Act has since been repealed.

Although for a long time the king was supreme, the day came when Parliament itself gained the greatest power. From that day the number of Acts of Parliament that came into being because the king suggested them became less and less; and today it must be seldom, if at all, that an Act of Parliament comes into being because the reigning king or queen suggests it.

A person in the street might think that most Acts of Parliament come into being because some Member of Parliament suggests them. That is far from being the case. Of course there are cases in which a Member of Parliament sees the need for a new Act of Parliament and persuades Parliament that that new Act should be made. That Member of Parliament may not even be a member of the party that is in power in Parliament at the time. There are various Acts of Parliament in force today that have been brought before Parliament by a member of Parliament who was in the opposition. The way in which Parliament works, however, makes it more difficult for a proposal for an Act of Parliament to be brought forward by a member of the opposition than it is for the same proposal to be brought forward by a member of the party that is in power, and especially by a member of Cabinet. Indeed, the pressure of government business has become such that a Member of Parliament who is not a minister may have great difficulty in having a Bill that is proposed by him or her (known as a Private Member's Bill) even considered by Parliament.

Parliament works through a government and an opposition.[8] The government consists of a large number of Members of Parliament who are known as backbenchers, and a smaller number who comprise the executive.

---

5   Quoted in Fay, *Discoveries in the Statute Book*, pp 77–78.

6   See Fay, *Discoveries in the Statute Book*, pp 77–78 (the Act was repealed in 1547).

7   See Megarry, Sir Robert, QC (formerly Megarry V-C) *Miscellany-at-Law* (5th imp, Stevens & Sons Limited, London, 1975) pp 334–35.

8   There may, of course, be other parties and independent Members of Parliament (who are not members of any party) who have not committed themselves to support either the government or the opposition.

Senior ministers form the Cabinet. Various Acts of Parliament begin when Cabinet decides that Parliament must take action to meet some need in the community or to protect the state against something that is affecting it. For example, a Cabinet which is concerned at the damage which heavy trucks cause to roads may cause Parliament to enact legislation creating special road taxes.

Another way in which an Act of Parliament can begin is by a decision made by a political party. Some political party may adopt a policy which can be put into effect by the making of an Act of Parliament. The decision to adopt that policy may be made by the executive of a political party, or by Members of Parliament belonging to that party and meeting at a party meeting in the party room, or it may be made at a conference attended by a large number of the members of that party. In such a case that decision may result in an Act of Parliament being made. Of course, not every policy adopted by a political party is necessarily enacted into law immediately that party gains office – if at all.

It is not only a political party that may make decisions that result in Parliament passing an Act. Pressure for the making of Acts of Parliament to alter the law affecting companies can come from the business community. Lobbyists, too, may exert pressure to alter the law. There are, of course, other groups, too, which can persuade Parliament to change the law. The councils which have to give effect to our local government law naturally come to know the defects in it. When some defects in the law affecting local government become known to a council that council may seek the change in the law that it needs to overcome the defect.

There is a strong tendency today for the Cabinet to decide to appoint what is probably most commonly known as a Royal Commission or a board of inquiry to inquire into a particular matter. Other commissions may be appointed upon a continuing basis. Boards and commissions produce reports. Those reports in many instances are pigeonholed but in some instances form the basis for the enactment of new legislation or subordinate legislation.

The most important source of new Acts of Parliament today is the government department. Senior members of the public service play an important part in the starting of new Acts of Parliament. The department which has to enforce an Act of Parliament of course becomes aware of the defects in the Act. The senior officers of the department are therefore in a position to suggest what new Act of Parliament should be made in order to cure the defects, and they also know what new powers should be given to the department in order to gain full effect for the Act. Indeed, the advice which the head of a government department may offer to Cabinet may go even further, and it may include suggestions for the making of completely new Acts of Parliament to cover new situations. Unfortunately, it is possible for this position of influence to be abused – as followers of the 'Yes, Minister' series will be aware. The department may obtain legislation which benefits it, or benefits some pressure group, without necessarily benefiting the public.

How the Act of Parliament is prepared

Although there are many ways in which an Act of Parliament can get its start, the actual writing (or, as it is called, the drafting) of the Act of Parliament is almost always carried out by a public servant in the parliamentary department the members of which have the duty of drafting Bills. They have a difficult task. The number of Acts, and statutory instruments and other forms of subordinate legislation, that they are called upon to draft is increasing rapidly, and the Acts and subordinate legislation are becoming more and more technical in their nature. It is not easy to do this sort of work in a hurry, and it is never easy to prepare Acts or subordinate legislation dealing with technical matters. It is not surprising, therefore, that legislation has phrases that can be interpreted in two or more different ways, and it is not surprising that there is often room for real doubt about the true meaning to be given to some particular portion of an Act of Parliament.[9]

One of the difficulties in drafting the modern Act of Parliament is that so often that Act deals with something of a technical nature that is beyond the ordinary everyday experience of the person who is writing the Act. The departmental officer concerned may think that he or she has made the drafter fully aware of the problems with which the Act is intended to deal, and the drafter may think that he or she is fully aware of those problems. When the Act comes to be enforced, however, it often becomes apparent either that there has been a misunderstanding or that there is some aspect of the matter which has not been thought of by the departmental officer or by the drafter. It is easy to criticise, but it is hard to draft. The fact that something has been overlooked may cause comment, but it is much easier to see the omission after it has been discovered in practice than it is to guard against that omission when drafting the Act of Parliament itself. The fact that these omissions do occur, however, adds to the difficulty of reading the finished Act of Parliament which all too often has to be made to work in circumstances of which the drafter was unaware.

How the Act is considered in Parliament

The fact that an Act of Parliament has been drafted does not of course make it part of the law. There is still much to be done before it becomes law. At that stage, therefore, it is not called an Act; it is called a Bill.

Except in the case of a Bill which has been prepared for a member of the party which is in opposition in Parliament, the usual practice is to place the Bill before Cabinet for approval before it is brought before the Members of Parliament as a whole.

When a Bill is brought before Parliament itself it is considered three times by each House of Parliament[10] – or, to use the phrase which Parliament uses, it is given three readings. In addition to those three readings Parliament may refer the Bill to a Parliamentary committee to examine it and report back to Parliament before the Bill progresses further, and the right to refer a Bill to such

---

9   This room for doubt is not limited to Acts of Parliament, and it is certainly not limited to laws prepared by a public servant in office for that purpose.

10   In very limited circumstances the House of Commons can enact legislation without the approval of the House of Lords.

a committee is not confined to one House of Parliament: either House may refer the Bill to a committee for examination.

The fact that a Bill is brought before Parliament does not mean that it must become part of the law. Even if the Bill is brought before Parliament by the party which is in power in Parliament, Parliament as a whole may decide not to make that Bill part of the law.

It is said that at one time the English Parliament had to consider a Bill which provided that

> all women of whatever age, rank or profession, whether maid or widow, who shall after this Act impose upon and seduce into matrimony any of His Majesty's subjects by means of scents, paints, cosmetics, artificial teeth, false hair, bolstered hips, high-heeled shoes, or iron stays, shall incur the penalties against witchcraft, and the marriage be declared null and void.[11]

Parliament did not make that Bill part of the law of the land!

Even if Parliament accepts the idea that the Bill should become part of the law of the land it may decide to make changes in the Bill. The usual time at which these changes are made is when the Bill is receiving its second reading. The changes made at that stage may be quite large ones. Sometimes changes may be made because the pressure of public opinion forces the Cabinet to change its policy. Other changes may be made because the department or other body which will have to administer the Act discovers defects in it and so puts forward amendments to the Bill. Changes may also be made because the Members of Parliament themselves are not prepared to accept the Bill in the form in which it is brought before them. Of course there are many Bills that are passed as Acts of Parliament without any changes, but there is always the possibility of changes being made when any Bill is brought before Parliament.

The British Parliament consists of the House of Lords and the House of Commons. If a Bill is brought before the Parliament the Bill must normally be passed by both Houses before it becomes an Act of Parliament. In practice it receives all three readings in one House before it is sent to the other. Of course the House which receives the Bill after it has already been considered by the other House of Parliament is not bound to accept the Bill in the form in which the other House of Parliament has accepted it. The second House of Parliament may decide that changes should be made. If that happens, the Bill must be sent back to the first House of Parliament for further consideration. If the two Houses of Parliament cannot agree upon the changes which should be made to the Bill, there is a special system to try to overcome the difference of opinion between the two Houses of Parliament. In that case each House of Parliament appoints a small number of its Members to represent it. These Members are known as managers. The managers of the two Houses then meet together to see if they can agree upon the changes that should be made in the Bill. As a result, the Bill, if it finally becomes an Act of Parliament, may be in a form that is very different to the form that was intended by the Member of Parliament who first brought it before Parliament.

---

11 Quoted in Fay, *Discoveries in the Statute Book*, pp 196–97.

How the Act of Parliament comes into force

When the Bill has been passed by Parliament it has still to be approved by the Queen before it can come into force. Some Acts of Parliament come into force as soon as they have been approved by the Queen, but others come into force at some later date. The actual date on which an Act of Parliament comes into force is considered in Chapter 9.

Once an Act of Parliament has come into force it will ordinarily continue to be in force indefinitely: 'A statute once passed is deemed to be perpetual unless and until it is repealed by some later Act of Parliament.'[12] However, Parliament may insert an express provision into the Act providing for that Act to cease to have effect after a specified period or on the happening of a specified event but such a provision cannot preclude Parliament from subsequently changing its mind and providing by an amending Act or other later Act that that earlier Act is to continue in force either for a longer period or a shorter period, or perpetually.

Acts obtained by fraud

Once the Act comes into force the way in which it was obtained becomes irrelevant. Even if Parliament were misled by fraudulent misrepresentations or otherwise to pass an Act which it would not have passed if it had known the true position, the Act has full force and effect unless and until Parliament repeals it: in this regard 'the court will not inquire into what passed in the course of the passage of the Bill through Parliament'.[13]

---

12 *Hebbert v Purchas* (1871) LR 3 PC 605, HL at 650.
13 *British Railways Board v Pickin* [1974] AC 765, HL, Lord Cross of Chelsea at 802 .

CHAPTER 2

THE SPECIAL RULES FOR UNDERSTANDING ACTS OF PARLIAMENT

Ambiguity in Acts of Parliament

Difficulties can arise in understanding an Act of Parliament because of an oversight by the drafter, a misprint, or even a mistake as to the law as it existed when the Act was made by Parliament – difficulties which are considered in Chapters 30 and 31. However, the difficulties to understanding an Act of Parliament are not limited to difficulties such as those. Parliament is passing an increasingly greater number of Acts, and government departments are finding a need for an increasingly greater number of statutory instruments. The more Acts are required, the greater is the pressure upon the drafter. The greater, therefore, is the risk of lack of clarity in the wording of the Acts of Parliament. One confused piece of drafting called forth the following comment:

> We should have much more confidence in deciding this case if the court or counsel were able to provide a clear and really cogent explanation of why that alteration [of the Act] is made, and what purpose it is sought to achieve. The court finds it difficult to determine precisely what was the purpose in the draftsman's mind, and counsel have not been able to assist us either.[1]

Lord Wilberforce in a case decided in the House of Lords complained of an Act that

> The ... Act, as is common with land acquisition and works legislation, contains a farrago of sections, loosely pinned together from various precedents, which have neither internal clarity nor mutual consistency. In face of this, the normal tools of interpretation fail to operate: attempts to construe the Act as a whole lead to perplexity: to attribute a consistent meaning to particular words ... leads to absurdity: to try to ascertain the intention of Parliament leads to conflicting conclusions. In fact, golden rules must yield to instruments of baser metal. One can only search for the occasional firm foothold and cautiously proceed from there.[2]

In another case Lord Wilberforce complained that 'the section is a labyrinth, a minefield of obscurity'.[3]

Judges' criticisms of the drafting of Acts of Parliament

Because of the pressure under which the drafting of Acts of Parliament has to be carried out the task of the drafter is a hard one. Indeed, as one leading writer has pointed out,

> In a sense, the scales are heavily weighted against the draftsman: if he has made himself plain, there is likely to be no litigation and so none to praise him, whereas if he has fallen into confusion or obscurity, the reports will probably

---

1   *R v Swabey (No 2)* [1973] 1 WLR 183, Lord Widgery CJ at 184 (Courts-Martial Appeal Court).
2   *Argyle Motors (Birkenhead) Ltd v Birkenhead Corpn* [1975] AC 99, HL, Lord Wilberforce at 129.
3   *Vandyk v Oliver* [1976] 2 WLR 235, HL at 240.

record the results of the fierce and critical intellects of both bar and bench being brought to bear on his work.[4]

Certainly the meaning of words used in the Acts of Parliament has often been difficult to find, and the judges have frequently criticised the drafting of Acts of Parliament. For example, a judge has complained that 'it has taken us a long period of acute concentration to disentangle the conceivably relevant passages from an accumulation of complicated terminology'.[5] In a case decided in the House of Lords it was held that the interpreting of a section of another English Act[6]

> involves the consideration of provisions which are, I think, of unrivalled complexity and difficulty and couched in language so tortuous and obscure that I am tempted to reject them as meaningless.[7]

The Acts of Parliament dealing with the position of landlords and tenants have been the subject of a great deal of criticism by the judges. They have been called 'a byword for confused draftsmanship'.[8] One writer, himself an eminent judge, has collected some of that criticism:

> In this 'extraordinary and unique legislation', 'the Acts were passed in a hurry, the language used was often extremely vague', and the language 'resembles that of popular journalism rather than the terms of the art of conveyancing'. 'It is a patchwork legislation, has not been framed with any scientific accuracy of language, and presents great difficulties of interpretation to the courts that have to give practical effect to it.' As MacKinnon LJ observed, 'anybody may be forgiven for making a mistake' about 'the hasty and ill-considered language' of 'this chaotic series of Acts', that 'welter of chaotic verbiage which may be cited together as the Rent and Mortgage (Interest) Restrictions Acts 1920 to 1939'. In one case Scrutton LJ said: 'I regret that I cannot order the costs to be paid by the draftsman of the Rent Restrictions Acts, and the members of the legislature who passed them, and are responsible for the obscurity of the Acts.' 'If the judges now had anything to do with the language of Acts they are to administer, it is inconceivable that they would have to face the horrors of the Rent and Mortgage (Interest) Restrictions Act – horrors that are hastening many of them to a premature grave.'[9]

Another eminent textbook writer quotes a judge[10] as saying:

> It is a public scandal that the Board of Trade have not seen fit to present the effect of rules and orders affecting the furniture trade in a form in which the ordinary, skilled, intelligent man may understand them... It is intolerable that a community, the vast percentage of which is anxious to obey the law, should be faced with a jumble of orders which are quite unintelligible. It is saddled with the

---

4   Megarry, Sir Robert, QC (formerly Megarry V-C), *Miscellany-at-Law* (5th imp, Stevens, London 1955) p 349.

5   *Zarcyznyska v Levy* [1979] 1 WLR 125, Kilner Brown J at 128 (Employment Appeal Tribunal).

6   Section 46 Finance Act 1940.

7   *St Aubyn v Attorney-General* [1952] AC 14, HL, Lord Simonds at 30.

8   *Joint Properties Ltd v Williamson*, [1945] SC 68, Lord Normand, Lord President at 74.

9   Megarry, Sir Robert QC (formerly Megarry V-C), *Miscellany-at-Law* (5th imp, Stevens, London, 1955) p 352.

10 Stable J.

burden of employing an infinite number of people in the perfectly hopeless task of trying to find out what these things really mean.[11]

As an example of drafting that is hard to understand a textbook writer quotes the following order:

The Control of Tins, Cans, Kegs, Drums and Packaging Pails (No 5) Order, 1942 (a), as varied by the Control of Tins, Cans, Kegs, Drums and Packaging Pails (No 6) Order, 1942 (b), the Control of Tins, Cans, Kegs, Drums and Packaging Pails (No 7) Order, 1942 (c), the Control of Tins, Cans, Kegs, Drums and Packaging Pails (No 8) Order, 1942 (d), and the Control of Tins, Cans, Kegs, Drums and Packaging Pails (No 9) Order, 1942 (e), is hereby further varied in the Third Schedule thereto ... by substituting for the reference 2A therein the reference '2A (1)' and by deleting therefrom the reference 2B.

This Order shall come into force on the 25th day of August 1943, and may be cited as the 'Control of Tins, Cans, Kegs, Drums and Packaging Pails (No 10) Order, 1943', and this Order and the 'Control of Tins, Cans, Kegs, Drums and Packaging Pails (Nos 5–9) Orders 1942 may be cited as the 'Control of Tins, Cans, Kegs, Drums and Packaging Pails (No 5–10) Orders, 1942–43' .[12]

As the textbook writer adds,

An explanatory note mercifully informs us: 'The above Order enables tin plate to be used for tobacco and snuff tins other than cutter lid tobacco tins.'[13]

Unfortunately, the fact that a statute has to be read and obeyed by persons without any knowledge of law and without the benefit of a higher education does nothing to ensure that it will be in plain language. The importance of the legislation to the community as a whole does not guarantee clarity. Town planning legislation has been criticised repeatedly by judges in England of which examples are the description of it as 'somewhat complex and at times bewildering legislation'[14] and

as has been forcefully pointed out to me in this appeal, in this area of legislation, whichever way one goes seems to result in some instances in reaching absurd results.[15]

In recent years an attempt has been made at 'plain English' drafting. Admirable as a concept, it has undoubtedly conferred some benefits. The redrafting of insurance policies has both shortened the policy documents and made them much more intelligible. Unfortunately, however, the same advantage has not been gained in the drafting of Acts of Parliament. The abandoning of language which has already been interpreted by the courts can actually lead to an increase in uncertainty and consequently to further litigation. The problems of 'plain English' drafting of statutes are increased when the legislation is intended to operate in a technical field with its own complex

---

11 Allen, Sir Carleton Kemp, *Law and Orders* (2nd edn, London, Stevens & Sons, 1956) p 175.

12 Quoted in Allen, Sir Carleton Kemp, *Law and Orders* (2nd edn, London, Stevens & Sons, 1956) p 176.

13 Allen, Sir Carleton Kemp, *Law and Orders* (2nd edn, London, Stevens & Sons 1956) p 177.

14 *Bolton Corpn v Owen* [1962] 1 QB 470, Lord Evershed MR at 482 (Court of Appeal).

15 *Camden London Borough Council v Secretary of State for the Environment* [1988] 86 LGR 775, Farquharson J (later Farquharson LJ) at 780.

concepts and jargon. Another problem is that in some instances at least legislation has been enacted in part in 'plain English' and in part in its traditional form, a duality that of itself can raise difficulties in interpretation.

Legislation by reference

There is one short cut that drafters of Acts of Parliament have taken from time to time. Instead of setting out in full in the new Act of Parliament everything that is to apply to the particular matter, the drafter takes the short cut of incorporating in the new Act of Parliament various provisions contained in other Acts of Parliament. Of course, since a short cut is being used, the drafter does not set out those provisions in full in the new Act but merely refers to the provisions in the other Acts as being incorporated in the new Act. This is known as legislation by reference. It raises difficulties of its own. Often there is difficulty in applying to the new Act the provisions of the older Acts which were written for a different purpose.

Again when Parliament says that two Acts are to be read as one (a common form of legislation by reference) the two Acts must be read together as if all the provisions of both Acts were really contained in one single Act of Parliament – the whole of the provisions must be read

> as if [they] had been contained in one Act unless there is some manifest discrepancy making it necessary to hold that the later Act has, to some extent, modified something found in the earlier Act[16]

The rule has been clearly stated by Lord Esher MR who said:

> If a subsequent Act brings into itself by reference some of the clauses of a former act, the legal effect of that, as has often been held, is to write those sections into a new Act just as if they had been actually written in with the pen or printed in it.[17]

The two Acts are treated as if they were in fact only one Act and as if all the provisions in that one Act had been passed by Parliament at one and the same time.[18]

As long ago as 1875 a select committee of the British Parliament described legislation by reference as making an Act so ambiguous, so obscure, and so difficult that the judges themselves could hardly assign a meaning to it, and the ordinary citizen could not understand it without legal advice.[19] Legislation by reference has been repeatedly criticised by the judges for more than a century.[20] In England the judges three times over a period of 25 years repeated exactly the same criticism of legislation by reference, referring to 'the difficulties and obscurity which arise from legislation by reference to and incorporation of other

---

16 *Canada Southern Rly International Bridge Co* (1883) 8 App Cas 723, Earl of Selborne LC at 727 (Privy Council).

17 *Re Wood's Estate* (1886) Ch D 607, CA at 615.

18 *Re Wood's Estate* (1886) Ch D 607, CA at 615.

19 See *Craies on Statute Law* (7th edn, by Edgar, SGG, Sweet & Maxwell, London, 1971) p 29.

20 See, for example, *R v Eaton* (1881) 8 QBD 158 at 160; *Knill v Towse* (1889) 24 QBD 186 at 195.

statutes.'[21] It has been well said that 'It is a great pity that simplicity and clarity, which ought to be the chief aim of parliamentary draftsmen are so often sacrificed ... to a most pernicious fetish – legislation by reference'.[22]

The need for special rules for the reading of Acts of Parliament

The difficulties that can arise in trying to find the true meaning of an Act of Parliament are numerous indeed. An Act of Parliament by its very nature is not something that can be read like a novel. It is something in which each word must be carefully examined. The rights of the private individual may depend upon which of two or more possible meanings is given to the words of the Act. Even the question whether or not a person is to be sent to prison can depend upon what meaning the court gives to ambiguous words used in an Act of Parliament.[23] It is important, therefore, to do whatever can be done to see that courts adopt as uniform an approach as possible to the reading of ambiguous Acts of Parliament. To try to achieve that uniformity the courts have developed a series of rules which they have applied over the years:

> From early times courts of law have been continuously obliged, in endeavouring loyally to carry out the intentions of Parliament, to observe a series of familiar precautions for interpreting statutes so imperfect and obscure as they often are.[24]

It is those rules with which this book is concerned. The use of the rules helps readers of an Act of Parliament to find what the Act really means. Readers must, however, always bear in mind that what they are trying to do is not to carry out some school exercise but to find the real meaning of the Act. As a very distinguished judge has said:

> Then rules of construction are relied upon. They are not rules in the ordinary sense of having some binding force. They are our servants not our masters. They are aids to construction, presumptions or pointers. Not infrequently one 'rule' points in one direction, another in a different direction. In each case we must look at all relevant circumstances and decide as a matter of judgement what weight to attach to any particular 'rule'.[25]

This does not mean that judges are free to substitute their own ideas of what Parliament should have said for what Parliament has in fact said in its legislation. Even in respect of statutory provisions troubled by doubt or ambiguity there are rules of interpretation that judges are expected to apply.

---

21 *Willingdale v Norris* [1909] 1 KB 57, DC, Walton J at 66 quoted in *Hart v Hudson Bros Ltd* [1928] 2 KB 629; and again quoted in *Phillips v Parnaby* [1934] 2 KB 299.

22 *Re Goswami* [1969] 1 QB 453, unanimous decision of the Court of Appeal at 461.

23 *Fawcett Properties Ltd v Buckingham County Council* [1961] AC 636, HL at 671.

24 *Nairn v University of St Andrews* [1909] AC 147, HL, Lord Loreburn LC at 161.

25 *Maunsell v Olins* [1975] 1 All ER 16, HL, Lord Reid at 18.

CHAPTER 3

THE ELEMENTS OF AN ACT OF PARLIAMENT

Introduction

Before considering the special rules that are used in reading an Act of Parliament it is necessary to know the various elements that make up the Act of Parliament and the particular rules that apply to each of those elements.

The elements of an Act of Parliament

The following are the more important elements that may be found in an Act of Parliament:

> number of the Act
> long title of the Act
> enacting words
> short title of the Act
> date on which the Act comes into force
> preamble
> statement of principle
> sections, subsections and paragraphs
> parts and divisions
> headings
> definitions
> schedules
> provisos
> punctuation

Most of these elements of an Act of Parliament are dealt with in separate chapters in this book, as are also the coat of arms and regnal year, and the marginal notes.

CHAPTER 4

THE COAT OF ARMS AND THE REGNAL YEAR

The form of the coat of arms and regnal year

There is no rule of law that requires an Act of Parliament to have the coat of arms and the regnal year printed on it. The form used in Britain used to display the coat of arms and have the regnal year below it. Today the regnal year is no longer used. Instead under the coat of arms there is the name of the statute and the number of the Act in the statutes passed in the particular calendar year, thus:

1995 CHAPTER 30[1]

The effect of the coat of arms

It is usual for a coat of arms to appear at the beginning of an Act of Parliament. However, the fact that it does appear (or that it does not appear) at the beginning of an Act of Parliament does not in any way affect either the meaning or the legal effect of that Act of Parliament.

The regnal year

The regnal year is, of course, not the calendar year: it is the year of the reign of the particular king or queen. The regnal year is very often printed in Latin. An example of this printing of the regnal year is:

ANNO UNDECIMO

ELIZABETHAE SECUNDAE REGINAE

The word 'anno' means 'in the year'. The word following 'anno' is the Latin word for the number of the year of the reign. In the example given above that word is 'undecimo' which means 'eleventh'.

Like the coat of arms, the printing of the regnal year had no legal effect. The Act is just as much an Act of Parliament and is just as much part of the law of the land if the regnal year is not printed on it. Indeed, this was recognised by the practice of omitting both the coat of arms and the regnal year when issuing consolidations of the Act and the amendments Parliament had made to it.[2]

---

1 Landlord and Tenant (Covenants) Act 1995.
2 See, for example, the Supreme Court of Judicature (Consolidation) Act 1925.

CHAPTER 5

THE NUMBER OF THE ACT

The nature of the number

Every Act of Parliament receives a number. Each Parliament has its own numbering. The system used by the British Parliament formerly was to start the numbering again at the beginning of each session of the sittings of Parliament, and is now to start it again at the beginning of each calendar year.

The form of the number

The form of the number of course differs according to the system in use at the particular time when the statute is enacted.

When the British Parliament started the numbering of its Acts anew with the beginning of each new session of Parliament its number referred to the regnal year. For example, the number of the Slaughter of Animals Act 1958 was printed as follows:

(7 ELIZ 2 CH 8)

However, the sessions of Parliament do not always coincide with the regnal year. It often happens that the session of Parliament starts towards the end of one year of the reign and extends into the next year of the reign. When that happened the number of the Act under the former British parliamentary system referred to both years of the reign. Thus for example, the number of the Local Government Act 1958 is:

(6 & 7 ELIZ 2 CH 55)[1]

The English system in use today is different. The number of the Finance Act 1981 is printed as follows:

1981 CHAPTER 35

The effect of the number

The number given to an Act of Parliament has no legal effect. It does not affect the meaning of the Act of Parliament in any way. It is merely an easy way of finding the Act of Parliament: when the Acts are bound into a volume, they are usually printed in their numerical order.

---

1   In the example given, 'ELIZ' is short for Elizabeth and 'CH' is short for chapter. '6 & 7 ELIZ 2 CH 55' therefore means the 55th Act (or 'chapter') in the parliamentary session in the sixth and seventh years of the reign of Queen Elizabeth II. In more recent Acts instead of 'CH' the abbreviation used is c.

CHAPTER 6

THE LONG TITLE OF THE ACT

The form of the long title

The long title appears under the number of the Act. The long title of the Local Government Act 1958 is:

> An Act to make further provision, as respects England and Wales, with respect to grants to local or police authorities, with respect to the rating of industrial and freight-transport hereditaments and of transport, electricity and gas authorities, with respect to the making of changes in the area, name, status and functions of local authorities, and with respect to local government finance and elections; to amend the law in England and Wales and in Northern Ireland as to the making by trustees of loans to local and other authorities; and for purposes connected with the matters aforesaid.

Another example of the long title is that of the English Employer Liability (Defective Equipment) Act 1969:

> An Act to make further provision with respect to the liability of an employer for injury to his employee which is attributable to any defect in equipment provided by the employer for the purposes of the employer's business; and for purposes connected with the matter aforesaid.

Not all Acts of Parliament, however, have long titles as lengthy as the two examples set out above. An example of a briefer long title is to be found in the English Gas Levy Act 1981 which reads

> An Act to impose on the British Gas Corporation a levy in respect of certain gas.

The long title as part of the Act

The first Acts of Parliament did not have titles. The first time that an Act of Parliament was given a title was about 1495.[1] Even when the long title came to be added to each Act of Parliament as a matter of course, as it did from about 1513,[2] the long title was not regarded as part of the Act of Parliament itself. Today, however, the position is different: the long title is part of the Act of Parliament.[3]

---

1   *Chance v Adams* (1696) 1 Ld Raym 77 at 78; 91 ER 948. *Words and Phrases Judicially Defined* (1st edn, Butterworths, 1943), vol 1, p 50, gives the date as 1496. *Maxwell on the Interpretation of Statutes,* (12th edn by Langan, P St J, Sweet & Maxwell, London 1969), p 40, gives the year as 'about the 11th year of Henry VII' (that is, 1496). *Craies on Statute Law* (7th edn, Sweet & Maxwell, London, 1971), p 190 quotes the date as 1495 but refers in a footnote to an Act passed eight years earlier.

2   *Craies on Statute Law* (7th edn, by Edgar, SGG, Sweet & Maxwell, London, 1971) p 190.

3   *Fielden v Morley Corpn* [1899] 1 Ch 1, CA, Lord Lindley MR at 4; affd [1900] AC 133, HL.

Using the long title to find the meaning of the Act

The long title is the first of the elements of an Act of Parliament that can be used to find the meaning of the Act, and generally its scope.[4] It can also be used to remove ambiguity.[5] Another use is to ascertain the purpose for which the statute has been enacted.[6] Indeed, as Lord Simon of Glaisdale has said in the House of Lords the long title 'is the plainest of all the guides to the general objectives of a statute'.[7]

Generally, the long title is not used to find the meaning of the Act unless the particular section of the Act that is being read is one which could have two or more different meanings. If the meaning of the section is clear, it should not be altered by reading the long title.

If any section of the Act contains words which have two or more meanings, the reader of the Act may use the long title to help him or her choose between those meanings, for 'it is legitimate to use it for the purpose of interpreting the Act as a whole and ascertaining its scope'.[8]

An Irish case gives an example of the way in which the long title is used to remove doubt as to the meaning of a section. In that case the section which the court had to consider might be read as applying to carts whether they were used for hire or whether they were used for private purposes, or it might be read as only applying to those carts which were used for hire. The long title of the Act was

An Act to consolidate and amend the laws relating to hackney and stage carriages, also job carriages and horses and carts let for hire within the police districts of Dublin.[9]

The court chose the meaning which only applied the section to carts used for hire, and it did so because it said that was the effect of reading the section in the light of the long title. Chief Justice Lefroy said:

Now the title of the Act ... shows that the legislature intended to make regulations with respect to carriages and other vehicles let for hire. It is quite true that, although the title of an Act cannot be made use of to control the express provisions of the Act, yet if there be in these provisions anything admitting of a doubt, the title of the Act is a matter proper to be considered, in order to assist in the interpretation of the Act, and thereby to give to the doubtful language in the body of the Act a meaning consistent rather than at variance with the clear title of the Act.[10]

---

4   *East & West India Dock Co v Shaw Savill & Albion Co* [1888] 38 Ch D 524.

5   *Pattinson v Finningley Internal Drainage Board* [1970] 2 QB 33.

6   *Knowles v Liverpool City Council* [1993] 1 WLR 1428, HL, Lord Jauncey of Tullichettle at 1431.

7   *Black-Clawson International Ltd v Papierwerke Waldhof-Aschaffenburg AG* [1975] AC 591, HL at 647.

8   *Vacher & Sons Ltd v London Society of Compositors* [1913] AC 107, HL, Lord Moulton at 128.

9   Dublin Carriages Act 1853.

10 *Shaw v Ruddin* (1859) 9 Ir CLR 214 at 219.

CHAPTER 7

THE ENACTING WORDS

The use of enacting words

Not all Acts of Parliament have enacting words. There was a period when Acts did not use them. Modern Acts, however, do have them.

If enacting words are used they are usually set out below the long title of the Act.

The form of the enacting words

The actual words normally used are:

> Be it enacted by the Queen's most Excellent Majesty, by and with the advice and consent of the Lords Spiritual and Temporal, and Commons, in this present Parliament assembled, and by the authority of the same, as follows:

However, different wording is used if the statute is to involve public expenditure, and even in respect of those Acts the words appearing as enacting words in one such Act may be different from those in another such Act even in the same year. Thus the enacting words of the Consolidated Fund Act 1981 (assented to on 19 March 1981) read

> Most Gracious Sovereign,
>
> WE, your Majesty's most dutiful and loyal subjects, the Commons of the United Kingdom in Parliament assembled, towards making good the supply which we have cheerfully granted to Your Majesty in this Session of Parliament, have resolved to grant unto Your Majesty the sums hereinafter mentioned; and do therefore most humbly beseech Your Majesty that it may be enacted, and be it enacted by the Queens' most Excellent Majesty, by and with the advice and consent of the Lords Spiritual and Temporal, and Commons, in this present Parliament assembled, and by the authority of the same, as follows:

yet on the very same day the enacting words used for the Gas Levy Act 1981 used different terminology, namely

> Most Gracious Sovereign,
>
> WE, Your Majesty's most dutiful and loyal subjects, the Commons of the United Kingdom in Parliament assembled, towards raising the necessary supplies to defray Your Majesty's public expenses, and making an addition to the public revenue, have freely and voluntarily resolved to make the provision hereinafter mentioned; and do therefore most humbly beseech Your Majesty that it may be enacted, and be it enacted by the Queen's most Excellent Majesty, by and with the advice and consent of the Lords Spiritual and Temporal, and Commons, in this present Parliament assembled, and by the authority of the same as follows:

Each of the examples quoted above is used in respect of a statute passed by the House of Commons and by the House of Lords. There are, however, special circumstances in which, the House of Lords having rejected a financial Act, the House of Commons can pass the Act without the Lords' concurrence, and the enacting words in that rare instance are

Be it enacted by the Queen's Most Excellent Majesty, by and with the advice and consent of the Commons in this present Parliament assembled, in accordance with the provisions of the Parliament Acts 1911 and 1949, and by the authority of the same, as follows:

The effect of the enacting words

The enacting words do not affect the meaning of the Act in any way. Different words could be used, or no enacting words at all, without affecting the meaning or the binding effect of the Act.

CHAPTER 8

THE SHORT TITLE

The nature of the short title

As its name indicates, the short title is normally a brief one. For example, although the long title of the European Assembly Elections Act 1981 contains 43 words and appears as follows:

> An Act to amend the provisions of Schedule 2 to the European Assembly Elections Act 1978 with respect to the supplementary reports affecting Assembly constituencies to be submitted by the Boundary Commission for any part of Great Britain following reviews of parliamentary constituencies.

the short title (of only five words) reads as follows:

> European Assembly Elections Act 1981[1]

The place where the short title is to be found

The practice of the British Parliament is to place the short title at the end of the Act of Parliament immediately before the schedules. Thus the short title of the Housing Act 1957 appears in s 193(1) of that Act. A typical section setting out a short title is:

> 84 – (1) This Act may be cited as the Criminal Justice (Scotland) Act 1980.

The reader, it should be noted, has been confronted with 60 pages of statute before reaching the short title, and even then finds the short title as one subsection of a section comprised of seven subsections.

The use of the short title

The short title is the most convenient way of referring to an Act of Parliament. There is much less chance of a mistake if an Act of Parliament is referred to by its short title than there is if it is referred to by its number, since the possibility of an error in the printing, or of misrecollection, can more readily arise in the case of a number than in the case of a title.

The legal effect of a short title

Justice is not a coin in the slot machine. Indeed, if the courts were worked upon a coin in the slot basis they would not be able to give justice. One result of the legal system we have, however, is that judges can hold differing views upon those parts of the law in which there is as yet no clear rule. The use that is to be made of the short title in finding the meaning of an Act is in one of those as yet uncertain parts of the law.

---

1   Section 2 European Assembly Elections Act 1981.

Whilst it is clear that the long title can be used to find the meaning of a section which is capable of two or more meanings,[2] there is no clear rule with regard to the use of the short title.

Judges of high standing have said that the short title cannot be used to find the meaning of a section which could have two or more meanings. Lord Moulton said:

> The title of an Act is undoubtedly part of the Act itself, and it is legitimate to use it for the purpose of interpreting the Act as a whole and ascertaining its scope. This is not the case with the short title, which in this instance is 'The Trade Disputes Act 1906'. That is a title given to the Act solely for the purpose of facility of reference. If I may use the phrase, it is a statutory nickname to obviate the necessity of always referring to the Act under its full and descriptive title. It is not legitimate, in my opinion, to use it for the purpose of ascertaining the scope of the Act. Its object is identification and not description.[3]

In a case decided shortly afterwards Lord Moulton repeated this view:

> Attention was called to the short title of the Act, namely the 'Telegraph (Arbitration) Act 1909', and it was urged that this gave countenance to the contention that the reference was merely an arbitration. With regard to this I adhere to the opinion which I expressed in my judgment in the case of *Vacher & Sons Ltd v London Society of Compositors*, namely, that, while it is admissible to use the full title of an Act to throw light upon its purport and scope, it is not legitimate to give any weight in this respect to the short title which is chosen merely for convenience of reference and whose object is identification and not description.[4]

Lord Justice Kennedy has expressed the same view:

> I lay no stress upon the language of s 2(2): 'This Act may be cited as the Vexatious Actions Act.' In the first place, although the use of the word 'actions' except in reference to civil proceedings is now obsolete, it is just possible that the parliamentary draftsman may have had in mind the fact that in a passage of *Bacon's Abridgement*, which was cited to us by counsel, is to be found the statement that 'actions are divided into criminal and civil'. In the second place, in two recent cases in the House of Lords there have been expressions of opinion on the part of the Lord Chancellor and Lord Moulton against the use of its short title as an aid to the interpretation of the statute.[5]

Lord Justice Buckley (later Lord Wrenbury) was of the same opinion:

> As to title, the matter is governed by the title placed at the head of the Act, and that is 'An Act to prevent abuse of the process of the High Court or other courts by the institution of vexatious legal proceedings'. That is the governing title. The fact that for the purpose of identification only, and not of enactment also, authority is given to identify the statute by a particular name, in which the word 'action' occurs, is, I think, immaterial. The words 'This Act may be cited as the Vexatious Actions Act 1896' effect nothing by way of enactment. They do no more than create a name and whether it is as a matter of description accurate or not is immaterial. In support of this view I refer to that which Lord Haldane LC

---

2   See Chapter 6.

3   *Vacher & Sons Ltd v London Society of Compositors* [1913] AC 107, HL at 128–29.

4   *National Telephone Co Ltd v Postmaster-General* [1913] AC 546, HL at 560.

5   *Re Boaler* [1915] 1 KB 21, CA at 35.

said in *Vacher & Sons Ltd v London Society of Compositors* as regards the title 'Trade Disputes Act 1906', and that which Lord Moulton said in the same case, and to that which the latter said further in *National Telephone Co v Postmaster General*.[6]

The reference made by the two Lords Justice to the view of the Lord Chancellor is to his statement that

> it is true that it is provided that the Act may be cited by the short title of the Trade Disputes Act 1906. But the governing title is that which introduces the statute as an Act to provide for the regulation of trade unions and trade disputes.[7]

The opposite view, namely that the short title can be used to clarify the meaning of a section the effect of which is uncertain, has been expressed by judges of equally high standing. Lord Selborne said:

> I cannot but say that the mere fact that the Act of Parliament ... is called 'The Superannuation Act 1859', and is referred to here by that title, goes a long way to repel the narrow and technical interpretation which the argument of the appellants seeks to put upon that word 'superannuation'. The legislature thought that all the cases of pensions provided for by the Act came within the sense of the word 'superannuation', as conveniently and popularly used, sufficiently to make that short title a good general description of all that was done by the Act.[8]

Mr Justice Scrutton[9] said:

> Section 2 of the Act contains a subsection: 'This Act may be cited as the Vexatious Actions Act 1896.' This has certainly, in my mind, supported the conclusion to which I have come ...

> Maxwell, *The Interpretation of Statutes* (5th edn), p 67, summarises the authority thus: 'It is now settled law that the title of a statute may be referred to for the purpose of ascertaining its general scope.' I agree that the court should give less importance to the title than to the enacting part, and less to the short title than to the full title, for the short title being a label, accuracy may be sacrificed to brevity, but I do not understand on what principle of construction I am not to look at the words of the Act itself to help me to understand its scope in order to interpret the words Parliament has used by the circumstances in respect of which they were legislating. It is by no means conclusive, but it is striking ...[10]

When judges differ it is not easy to say what rule the courts will finally adopt. On the one hand, the short title is set out in a section of the Act itself. On the other hand, the fact that the short title is designed to be brief must obviously affect its value as a means of finding the meaning of the Act. Perhaps the true view is to be found in the last of the quotations set out above, namely that the short title can be used to find the meaning of a section that is not clear but that it has far less value for that purpose than has the long title.

Particular care must be taken if an Act has both a long title and a short title. It cannot be assumed that the two will always be compatible; and, if they are not, it is the long title that should be used if help is needed to interpret the Act.

---

6   *Re Boaler* [1915] 1 KB 21, CA at 27.

7   *Vacher & Sons Ltd v London Society of Compositors* [1913] AC 107, HL at 114.

8   *Middlesex Justices v The Queen* (1884) 9 App Cas 757, HL, Earl of Selborne LC at 772.

9   Later Scrutton LJ.

10 *Re Boaler* [1915] 1 KB 21, CA at 40–41.

CHAPTER 9

WHEN AN ACT COMES INTO FORCE

The date on the Act of Parliament

After the long title, each Act of Parliament has a date. The following example is from the Redundancy Fund Act 1981:

> An Act to increase the limit imposed by section 198(2) of the Employment Protection (Consolidation) Act 1968 on the aggregate amount which may be borrowed by the Secretary of State for the purposes of the Redundancy Fund.
>
> [19th March 1981]

What the date on the Act of Parliament means

After a Bill has been passed by Parliament it must be submitted for approval or rejection by the Queen. The Queen's approval to the Act is known as the royal assent. The date shown on the Act of Parliament is the date upon which the Act received the royal assent.

The date on which the Act comes into force

If the Act does not set out any date on which it is to come into force, the ordinary rule is that it comes into force on the day on which it receives the royal assent.[1]

Parliament of course has power to set out in the Act that the Act will come into force on some day other than the day on which it receives the royal assent. Parliament can say that the Act is to come into force on some day later than the day on which it receives the royal assent, and Parliament also has power to say the Act is to be read as if it had come into force even before it has been passed by Parliament.[2]

If Parliament chooses to provide for the Act to come into force on some day after the day on which it receives the royal assent, it may either specify a particular date or it may empower some person or body to decide on the date on which the Act is to come into force or on the various days on which various parts of the Act are to come into force. A typical example states:

> (2) This Act shall come into force on such date as the Secretary of State may appoint by order made by statutory instrument; and different dates may be so appointed for different provisions or different purposes.
>
> (3) Any order under subsection (2) above may make such transitional provision as appears to the Secretary of State to be expedient in connection with the provisions thereby brought into force.[3]

---

1 Section 4(*b*) Interpretation Act 1978.
2 Section 4(*a*) Interpretation Act 1978. See also the definition of 'commencement' in Schedule 1 of that Act which provides that '"commencement" in relation to an Act or enactment, means the time when the Act or enactment comes into force'.
3 Section 84(2)–(3) Criminal Justice (Scotland) Act 1980.

Bringing the Act into force on a later day

Parliament quite often uses the idea of bringing an Act into force on some day later than the day on which the Act receives the royal assent. When Parliament decides that an Act is to come into force on some day later than the date on which the Act receives the royal assent it does so by setting that fact out in the Act itself.

The idea of delaying the coming into force of an Act of Parliament is one that can be used for various reasons. One reason is that the Act may be quite a long one, and it would take some time to print copies for members of the public to buy. Another reason may be that the Act of Parliament leaves something to be dealt with by subordinate legislation to be made under the Act, and Parliament thinks it wise to delay the coming into force of the Act until such time as the subordinate legislation has been made. Another reason may be that the new Act replaces an old one and makes some major changes that people must learn of before the new Act can be successfully brought into force. Whatever the motive may be in the particular case, Parliament never has to give a reason for delaying the coming into force of the Act: all it has to do is to set out in the Act that the date on which it starts to operate is a date after the date on which it receives the royal assent. If it does so, the Act cannot be applied until that date is reached, and, if something is done before that date which would have been an offence had the Act been in force, the Act cannot operate in respect of it.[4]

Parliament can also decide that some parts of the Act are to come into force on one date and other parts are to come into force on another date. Indeed, it could even decide that particular sections of an Act are to come into force on one date and the remainder of the Act is to come into force on another date.

If an Act is one that is to come into force on a date to be proclaimed, the person reading the Act must inquire to find out whether or not it has been proclaimed. In one case it was sought to prosecute someone under an Act that had not been proclaimed. The court described the prosecution as resembling 'nothing so much as pulling a bell-handle without a bell at the end'.[5] Of course, the prosecution failed.

Treating an Act as having been in force from a day before the date on which it was passed

Parliament has power to treat an Act as having been in force from a date before the day on which it was enacted. Such an Act is known as a retrospective Act. The way in which to read retrospective Acts is a topic of its own and is dealt with in Chapter 39 of this book.

---

4   This is so even if the question arises on the hearing of an appeal and the date of the hearing of that appeal is after the Act has come into force: *Wilson v Dagnall* [1972] 1 QB 509, CA.

5   *R v Kynaston* (1926) 19 Cr App R 180, Lord Hewart CJ at 181.

The date on an Act reprinted after it has been amended

Statutes are amended by Parliament from time to time. Indeed, some statutes are amended very frequently. Sometimes the amendments are not even in an Act of the same name as the statute being amended. To try to make the statute law easier to ascertain, Parliament has now provided for the issue of what are known as reprints. A reprint is a copy of the Act that incorporates in it all the amendments made by Parliament and in force up to the date on which the reprint was prepared. Such a reprint may be on paper, or on a computer disc, or both. The reprint system is therefore different from the system that has so far been discussed in this chapter. An Act published as a reprint does not have a date after the long title. Ordinarily it has a date at the top of the first page of the reprint, and that is the date on which the Act was prepared for printing: it is the date up to which amendments to the Act have been incorporated in the reprint.

The fact that the reprint incorporates the original Act and the amendments that have been made to it means that various provisions in the reprint can have come into force at different times. It is usual, therefore, to set out in the reprint the dates when the various amending Acts which are incorporated in it came into force.

The reprint system is valuable but it has its dangers. Although it is unusual for errors to occur it is possible that some amendment to the Act has been omitted from the reprint. If that occurs the provision or provisions that are omitted must be treated as if they were inserted in the reprint and continue to be of full force and effect.

A further problem inherent in the reprint system is that further amendments to the Act may occur after the date of the most recent reprint. This is a problem more likely to arise in respect of printed reprints than in respect of those on a computer disc.

CHAPTER 10

THE PREAMBLE

The nature of the preamble

The preamble is a preliminary statement which usually sets out the reasons for making the Act of Parliament and the scope of the Act. The preamble does not often appear in a modern Act of Parliament. When a preamble does occur it can be a useful guide to interpretation of the Act as is well illustrated in a statute the short title of which is the Courts of Justice Building Act 1865:

> Whereas a Bill has been or is about to be introduced into Parliament in the present session, by the short title of 'The Courts of Justice Concentration (Site) Act, 1865', and the purposes intended to be carried into effect by such Bill are the acquisition of a site capable of affording accommodation to the Superior Courts of Law and Equity, the Probate and Divorce Courts, the High Court of Admiralty, and the various offices belonging to the same, and to such other courts for the administration of justice, and offices connected therewith, as may be required:
>
> And whereas it is expedient to make provision for the cost of acquiring such site, and of the erection thereon of suitable buildings, with all proper furniture and conveniences, for such courts and offices; and also to make provision for such other changes incident to and consequential on the removal of the existing courts and offices from the site now occupied by them as are herein-after mentioned:
>
> And whereas it is expedient that the cost of erecting the said Courts of Justice should be borne as follows:
>
> 1st. By money to be provided by Parliament, to the extent of the value of property surrendered, and of relief to the public by the cessation of rents now charged to the public:
>
> 2dly. By a contribution of one million stock, part of a sum of one million two hundred and ninety-one thousand six hundred and twenty nine pounds ten shillings and fivepence three pounds per cent stock, now standing in the books of the Bank of England to the credit of an account intituled 'Account of securities purchased with surplus interest 'arising from securities carried to account of monies placed out for 'the benefit and better security of the suitors of the High Court of 'Chancery,' which has arisen from the profit of investments, made under the authority of Parliament at the risk of the public, of unemployed cash balances paid into the High Court of Chancery on account of individual suitors, and which is herein-after referred to as the Surplus Interest Fund:
>
> 3dly. By the taxation of suitors of the courts, other than the Court of Chancery, to be accommodated in the said building:
>
> And whereas it is expedient that the monies required from time to time for carrying into effect the purposes of the said Site Act and this Act should be defrayed in the first instance out of monies to be provided by Parliament:
>
> And whereas the capital of the aforesaid Surplus Interest Fund is ultimately liable to make good any deficiency which may occur in the general cash balance remaining in the Court of Chancery from time to time for payment of the sums due to the suitors of the said court, and the same is, with other funds in Chancery, also charged with the payment of certain compensations in the nature of life annuities and other temporary charges; and it is expedient that provision

should be made for such liabilities and charges in the manner herein-after appearing:

One of the commonest cases in which Parliament still uses a preamble today is what is known as a private Act which is one that affects the interests of individuals, or of particular localities, or of a statutory body such as a council, and do not involve matters of public or parliamentary policy. Ever since 1850 statutes have been treated as public Acts unless they contain an express provision to the contrary.

Another example, from the Merchant Shipping (Minicoy Lighthouse) Act 1960, recites:

> Whereas the lighthouse on Minicoy Island (in this Act referred to as 'the lighthouse';) between the Laccadive and Maldive Islands, is a colonial light within the meaning of the Merchant Shipping (Mercantile Marine Fund) Act, 1898, but has, since the second day of April, nineteen hundred and fifty-six, been administered by the Government of India:

> And whereas it is expedient that the lighthouse and the sums held in the General Lighthouse Fund in connection therewith should be transferred to the Government of India

The preamble as part of the Act of Parliament

If Parliament does include a preamble in an Act, the preamble is treated as part of the Act itself. It is somewhat similar in its effect to the long title.

The preamble when the meaning of the Act is clear

There is an understandable reluctance to refer to the preamble as an aid to interpretation of an Act if the provision in the Act that is being considered is one with a plain meaning. Generally speaking, therefore, if the meaning of the section is plain, it will not be altered by the preamble: 'If an enactment is itself clear and unambiguous, no preamble can qualify or cut down the enactment.'[1]

The preamble will not have the effect of extending the meaning to be given to the substantive sections of the Act if their plain meaning is narrower than the words of the preamble itself. Indeed, the preamble can have the effect of restricting the meaning of the Act.[2]

The use of the preamble to find the meaning of a section

If an Act contains a preamble and some section in that Act could bear two different meanings, the preamble can be used to find the true meaning of that section although it is not as useful for this purpose as the sections of the Act. An interesting example of the use of the preamble in this way is to be found in a

---

1 *Powell v Kempton Park Racecourse Co* [1899] AC 143, HL, the Earl of Halsbury at 157.
2 *Halsbury's Laws of England* (4th edn, Butterworths, London) vol 44, para 815, fn 5.

case concerning bankruptcy. The court had to find the meaning of a section which provided that

> if at any time hereafter any person shall become bankrupt and at such time shall by the consent and permission of the true owner have in their possession, order, and disposition any goods or chattels ... the commissioners shall have power to sell and dispose of the same for the benefit of the creditors.[3]

The owner of some diamonds delivered them to a Mr Levi who was to sell them for him. Mr Levi subsequently became bankrupt, and the creditors claimed to be entitled to seize the diamonds. They claimed that the words in the section ('*any* goods or chattels') were wide enough to refer to the diamonds. The court, however, decided that the section was one which could bear different meanings, and it therefore read the section in the light of the preamble. The preamble used the words:

> And for that bankrupts frequently convey over *their* goods and yet continue in possession and dispose of them.

The court therefore held that the meaning of the section was limited by the words '*their* goods' in the preamble.[4]

A preamble, where there is one, can be useful as directing the reader to the purpose of the Act.

---

3 Sections 10–11 Bankrupts Act 1623 (21 Jac 1 c 19), (England).

4 *L'Apostre v Le Plaistrier* (1708), cited in *Copeman v Gallant* (1716) 1 P Wms 314 at 318; 24 ER 404 at 406.

CHAPTER 11

THE STATEMENT OF PRINCIPLE IN AN ACT

What the statement of principle of an Act is

In those instances in which an Act of Parliament has a statement of principle it is included in the Act to give the reader a statement of what Parliament considers were the purposes it sought to achieve by passing that Act.

The statement of principle is part of the Act

Since the statement of principle is contained in a section of the Act it must be treated not as a preamble or a long title but as a substantive part of the Act.

Where to find the statement of principle

If an Act does have a statement of principle – the reader will find many that do not – it is reasonable to expect to find it at or near the beginning of the Act. However, there is no requirement that it be placed in any particular part of the Act or that an Act have such a section at all. If the Act does have a statement of principle it could be applicable to part only of the Act and therefore set out in that part, or it could indeed be anywhere in the Act.

How to use the statement of principle

One of the major principles used in statutory interpretation is the purposive approach.[1] If a section in an Act is ambiguous, and one possible interpretation of that section is in accordance with Parliament's purpose in passing the Act while an alternative interpretation would not achieve that purpose, the first interpretation is to be preferred. In applying this principle of interpretation it may be of assistance that Parliament has stated its purpose in a statement of principle rather than leaving that purpose to be deduced by the court.[2]

Traps to using the statement of principle

The most obvious trap to a statement of principle is that only some Acts have one. However, even if there is no statement of principle in the Act being interpreted it is still possible to interpret it according to what the court finds to be the purpose of the Act.[3]

Another trap which may not be so obvious is that there may be matters dealt with in the substantive sections of the Act which do not fall within the statement of principle. The longer the Act is, the greater is the likelihood of

---

1   See Chapter 25.

2   Note, however, that a statement of principle can have the opposite effect.

3   This is known as the purposive approach and is considered in Chapter 25.

provisions falling outside the scope of the statement of principle and that likelihood could be increased if the Act proves to be one that is amended frequently by Parliament. Probably in order to try to meet the problem, some statements of principle are expressed in such wide terms as to be difficult to apply.

CHAPTER 12

SECTIONS, SUBSECTIONS AND PARAGRAPHS

Sections

As a matter of convenience Acts of Parliament are divided into numbered sections. The sections are numbered consecutively. Generally in this system the numbering starts at the beginning of the Act and continues in unbroken sequence to the end of the Act. The following are three sections comprising the Consolidated Fund Act 1981:

1 The Treasury may issue out of the Consolidated Fund of the United Kingdom and apply towards making good the supply granted to Her Majesty for the service of the year ending on 31st March 1980 the sum of £34,297,072.18.

2 The Treasury may issue out of the Consolidated Fund of the United Kingdom and apply towards making good the supply granted to Her Majesty for the service of the year ending on 31st March 1981 the sum of £2,166,168,000.

3 This Act may be cited as the Consolidated Fund Act 1981.

Subsections

To make the provisions of an Act easier to refer to, the sections themselves may be divided into smaller segments which are known as subsections. The following is an example of a section divided into three subsections:

83 – (1) Schedule 6 to this Act shall have effect for the purpose of the transition to the provisions of this Act from the law in force before the commencement of those provisions and with respect to the application of this Act to things done before the commencement of those provisions.

(2) The enactments specified in Schedule 7 to this Act shall have effect subject to the amendments there specified, being minor amendments or amendments consequential on the provisions of this Act.

(3) The enactments specified in Schedule 8 to this Act (which include certain spent provisions) are hereby repealed to the extent specified in the third column of that Schedule.

Paragraphs

The subsections may themselves be divided into smaller segments which are known as paragraphs. The following is an example of a section divided into subsections one of which is divided into three paragraphs:

6 – (1) The Secretary of State may make such grants or loans to any body, as he considers appropriate for the purpose of assisting in –

(a) the promotion of the practice of engineering;

(b) the encouragement and improvement of links between industry, or any part of industry, and bodies or individuals concerned with education;

(c) the encouragement of young persons and others to take up careers in industry, or in any part of industry, and to pursue appropriate educational courses.

(2) Any grants under this section may be made on such conditions, and any loans under this section may be made at such rates of interest, as the Secretary of State may with the approval of the Treasury determine.[1]

The paragraphs are those portions of the section which are introduced by the symbols (a), (b) and (c) in the example quoted above.

Paragraphs of an Act may themselves be divided into sub-paragraphs, and those sub-paragraphs may even be divided further.

The effect of the setting out of the Act in numbered sections, subsections, and paragraphs

The fact that an Act of Parliament is set out in sections, subsections (and, sometimes, paragraphs) is a matter of convenience, but its only legal effect arises if there is a conflict between two sections in the one Act.

Conflicting sections in the one Act

If two sections in the one Act of Parliament are in conflict with each other, the traditional rule is that the person seeking to find their meaning should first look to the nature of each of those sections. If one makes a general provision on the matter and the other deals with the matter specifically, the specific section will prevail over the general one:

> The rule is, that whenever there is a particular enactment and a general enactment in the same statute, and the latter, taken in its most comprehensive sense, would overrule the former, the particular enactment must be operative, and the general enactment must be taken to affect only the other parts of the statute to which it may properly apply.[2]

If the case of conflict is one in which both the sections are general sections or both are specific ones, and if it is impossible to reconcile the two sections, the traditional principle applied by the courts is that the section which appears later in the Act prevails over the earlier section.[3]

These principles are the same as those a court will apply to a conflict between two statutes. That conflict is dealt with in Chapter 36.

Although the traditional principle has the authority of the Privy Council[4] the Court of Appeal has now rejected it and has adopted instead the purposive basis of interpretation[5] without adverting to the fact that the purposive basis may not solve the problem.

---

1   Industry Act 1981.
2   *Pretty v Solly* (1859) 426 Beav 606 at 610; 53 ER 1032, Romilly MR (later Baron Romilly MR) at 1034; *Barker v Edger* [1898] AC 748, PC at 754.
3   *Wood v Riley* (1867) LR 3 CP 26.
4   *Barker v Edger* [1898] AC 748, PC at 754.
5   *Re Marr* [1990] Ch 773, CA.

The way in which sections, subsections, paragraphs and subparagraphs are referred to

Earlier in this chapter an example was given of a section divided into subsections and paragraphs. One of the paragraphs could be referred to in writing in the usual abbreviated form as follows:

s 6(1)(a).

However, in spoken form that becomes:

section six, subsection one, paragraph a.

CHAPTER 13

PARTS AND DIVISIONS

The nature of parts and divisions

In the longer Acts of Parliament it is quite common to find a number of sections treated as a group. That group is known as a part.

If the number of sections in a part is sufficient to justify doing so, that part may itself be divided into smaller groups of sections and those smaller groups are known as divisions.

An idea of the way in which an Act is divided into parts and divisions may be gained from the Local Government Planning and Land Act 1980:

PART I   LOCAL GOVERNMENT – RELAXATION OF CONTROLS
PART II   PUBLICATION OF INFORMATION BY LOCAL AUTHORITIES
PART III DIRECT LABOUR ORGANISATIONS
          Works Contracts
          Functional Work
          Accounting Provisions
          Financial Provisions
          Supplementary
          General
PART IV   LOCAL GOVERNMENT ALLOWANCES
PART V   RATES
          Valuation
          Fish Farms
          Reliefs
          Recovery of Rates
          Unused and Unoccupied Property
          Miscellaneous

Another approach adopted by the British Parliament is to achieve the same result as parts by a series of central headings that do not actually use the word 'Part'. Thus, in the Industry Act 1981 there are headings respectively to ss 1–2, 3–4, 5, and 6–7. An example is afforded by ss 5 and 6 and their respective headings:

Redundancy payments

5 In section 2(4) of the Shipbuilding (Redundancy Payments) Act 1978 (which gives the Secretary of State power to amend any scheme made under that Act by extending the period in relation to which the scheme operates from two years to four years) there is added, at the end –

> ', and may by order further amend any such scheme by substituting six years for the said period of four years.'

Miscellaneous

6 (1) The Secretary of State may make such grants or loans to any body, as he considers appropriate for the purpose of assisting in –

(a) the promotion of the practice of engineering;

The effect of dividing an Act into parts and divisions

If an Act is divided into parts and divisions the courts will ordinarily assume that the dividing of the Act in that way is intended to indicate that the group of sections in the part or in the division relates to a particular subject. The courts will not read a section in one part or division as relating to a subject matter that is dealt with in another part or division of the Act unless it is clear from the wording of the section that it must be read in that way and that the section has therefore been placed in the wrong part or division. If, however, it is clear from the section that it has been included in an inappropriate part or division, the section will be given its full clear meaning irrespective of the part or division in which it is placed.

CHAPTER 14

HEADINGS

The use of headings

When an Act is divided into parts the custom today is to put a heading to each part. Similarly, when the sections within a part are divided into divisions the custom is to put a heading to each division.[1] Curiously, the use of headings in Acts of Parliament did not start until 1845. In Acts passed thereafter the headings can be said to 'constitute an important part of the Act itself'.[2] When an Act does have headings, any of the sections under such a heading must be interpreted in the light of all the sections under that heading.[3]

A statute may have not only headings but subheadings, and even the subheadings can be used 'to resolve any ambiguities'.[4]

The effect of headings when the meaning of an Act is clear

As a general rule the heading to a part or division will not be used to alter the clear meaning of a section. If the meaning of the section is plain, it will generally be given that plain meaning even if that meaning differs from the meaning that one would expect from reading the heading:

> The law is quite clear that you cannot use such headings to give a different effect to clear words in the section, where there cannot be any doubt as to their ordinary meaning.[5]

As Lord Justice Harman has held, 'If there were no doubt at all about the meaning of the paragraph ... it would not be right to overrule it by the heading'.[6]

The effect of headings when the meaning of a section is not plain

When it is not clear from the words of the section how broadly it is to apply, a heading to the part or division of the Act in which that section appears can be used to help to determine the scope of the section, the correct way of interpreting the provision being 'to read it in conjunction with the heading and make the two consistent if possible'.[7]

---

1 See Chapter 13.
2 *Eastern Counties Rlys v Marriage* (1860) 9 HLC 32, Channell B at 41; 11 ER 639, HL at 643.
3 *Inglis v Robertson* [1898] AC 616, HL.
4 *Sovmots Investments Ltd v Secretary of State for the Environment* [1976] 2 WLR 73, Forbes J at 86; affd, after intermediate reversal in part, [1979] AC 144, HL.
5 *R v Surrey Assessment Committee* [1948] 1 KB 29, Lord Goddard CJ at 32.
6 *Qualter, Hall & Co Ltd v Board of Trade* [1962] Ch 273, CA at 287.
7 *Qualter, Hall & Co Ltd v Board of Trade* [1962] Ch 273, CA, Harman LJ at 287.

Similarly, when a section has two or more possible meanings, the heading to the division or part in which that section appears can be used as a means to find out which of those possible meanings should be given to the section.[8] When the meaning of a section is not plain the heading is treated by the courts as if it were a preamble to the part or division above which it appears; and it has, indeed, been said that these headings are capable of 'affording ... a better key to the constructions of the sections which follow them than might be afforded by a mere preamble'.[9]

The effect of a heading when there is only one section under it

Even if there is only one section appearing under the heading, the heading is used to find the true meaning of that section if there is doubt about the meaning of the section.

---

8 *Hammersmith Rly v Brand* (1869) LR 4 HL 171, HL.

9 *Eastern Counties Rlys v Marriage* (1860) 9 HLC 32, Channell B at 41; 11 ER 639, HL at 643.

CHAPTER 15

MARGINAL NOTES

The nature of marginal notes

Marginal notes (or, as they are sometimes called, sidenotes) appear, as their name indicates, in the margin of the Act of Parliament. They are not part of the Act itself.

The form of a marginal note

The marginal note is intended to give a brief indication of the matters dealt with in the section or subsection against which it appears. Sometimes the marginal note is expressed as a very brief indication of the subject matter of the section against which it appears. A typical example of this terse type of marginal note is:

Financial provisions
82 There shall be defrayed out of money provided by Parliament any increase attributable to the provisions of this Act in the sums payable out of such money under any other Act.[1]

In other cases the marginal note purports to summarise the contents of the section:

Right of certain past Members and widows or widowers of such Members to payments out of House of Commons Members' Fund.

1 – (1) The trustees of the House of Commons Members' Fund shall make periodical payments out of the Fund to persons who–

(a) are eligible or treated as eligible by virtue of this section as past members or as the widows or widowers of past members; and

(b) have at any time after the passing of this Act applied to the trustees for such payments.

(2) A person who is not disqualified for payments under this section is eligible to receive such payments –

(a) as a past member, if he satisfies the conditions of this section as to service and qualifies by reason of age or infirmity;[2]

Parliament and the marginal notes

The marginal notes may perhaps give Members of Parliament a quick indication of the scope of the Bill. Since, however, the marginal notes do not form part of the Act, they are not amended by Parliament even if the sections against which they appear are amended. As Lord Justice Bagallay has said: 'I never knew an amendment set down or discussed upon the marginal notes to a clause. The House of Commons never has anything to do with a marginal note.'[3]

---

1 Section 82 Industry Act 1981.
2 Section 1(1)–(2) House of Commons Members' Fund and Parliamentary Pensions Act 1981.
3 *Attorney-General v Great Eastern Rly* (1879) 11 Ch D 449, CA at 461.

The dangers of marginal notes

Marginal notes can be very misleading to the reader of an Act of Parliament.[4] This danger of being misled can arise from several different causes.

Although it is the usual practice to place a marginal note against every section of the Act, this does not always happen.

Whilst it occasionally happens that a section of an Act has no marginal note, the lack of a marginal note occurs quite often in the case of the subsections. In s 1 Local Government Planning and Land Act 1980 the first subsection has a marginal note but sub-ss (2) (3),(4) and (5) do not.

Sometimes the marginal note can be misleading because it only indicates some of the matters dealt with in the section or subsection against which it appears. For example the marginal note which appears against s 1 Criminal Justice (Scotland) Act 1980 refers to the power of a constable to require a suspect to identify himself but it says nothing about the power of the constable to require the person to remain with him while he verifies the suspect's name and address.

> 1 – (1) Where a constable has reasonable grounds for suspecting that a person has committed or is committing an offence at any place, he may require –
>
> *Suspect or potential witness may be required by constable to identify himself.*
>
> (a) that person, if the constable finds him at that place or at any place where the constable is entitled to be, to give his name and address and may ask him for an explanation of the circumstances which have given rise to the constable's suspicion;
>
> (b) any other person whom the constable finds at that place or at any place where the constable is entitled to be and who the constable believes has information relating to the offence, to give his name and address.
>
> (2) The constable may require the person mentioned in paragraph (a) of sub-section (1) above to remain with him while he (either or both) –

A person who relied upon the marginal note might well be led to believe that the constable was going beyond his powers in requiring the suspect to remain with him: such a person could well believe that the constable was trying to achieve an arrest without admitting it and, acting under the belief that the statutory requirements had been satisfied that person would refuse to remain and thereby would be led by the marginal note to commit an offence for which he could be prosecuted. So misleading a marginal note reminds us of the complaint of Lord Justice Bramwell (later Lord Bramwell) that some marginal notes are grossly inaccurate.[5]

Sometimes the marginal notes can be even more misleading. Quite a number of examples can be given of marginal notes which are quite different from the

---

4   *Argyle Motors (Birkenhead) Ltd v Birkenhead Corpn* [1975] AC 99, HL, Lord Wilberforce at 131.

5   *Attorney-General v Great Eastern Rly Co* (1879) 11 Ch D 449, CA at 460. See also *Argyle Motors (Birkenhead) Ltd v Birkenhead Corpn* [1975] AC 99, HL, Lord Wilberforce at 131.

sections against which they appear, but the following example is sufficient to sound the warning. It is, indeed, a warning to be sounded, a warning that has been repeated many times by judges. For example, Lord Justice Sellers in the Court of Appeal has said:

> Attention was drawn to the sidenote 'power to require proper maintenance of waste land, etc'. This is a case, I think, which demonstrates how unreliable it would be, even if permissible, to pay attention to the sidenote. It seems to me to be inconsistent with the precise wording of the section itself, to which the word 'maintenance' is inappropriate.[6]

The problem as to whether marginal notes can be used to find the meaning of an Act

Over many years it had been repeatedly held by the courts that the marginal notes cannot be used as a means of finding the true meaning of a section when the meaning of that section is in doubt.[7] More recently, there has been some division of opinion amongst the judges as to the possibility of using a marginal note as an aid to interpretation.[8] It is probable that a marginal note can only be used, if at all, 'as an indication of the mischief with which the Act is dealing'.[9] Even if a marginal note can be used for that limited purpose, he or she who uses it will be treading on dangerous ground.

The value of marginal notes

Whilst marginal notes have the very real dangers that have been pointed out at some length in this chapter, they do have a limited value provided those dangers are borne in mind. For example, when Parliament takes a number of existing Acts and consolidates them into one new Act the marginal note may show the Act from which the section in the new statute has been taken.

Another possible use of a marginal note is to draw attention to other legislation the drafter considers to be relevant.

---

6   *Britt v Buckinghamshire County Council* [1964] 1 QB 77, CA, Sellers LJ at 85–86.

7   See, for example, *Thakurain Balraj Kunwar v Rae Jagatpal Singh* (1904) LR 31 IA 132 at 142; *Nixon v Attorney-General* [1930] 1 Ch 566, CA, Lord Hanworth MR at 593; *Chandler v Director of Public Prosecutions* [1964] AC 763, HL at 789. Contrary decisions (such as *Stephens v Cuckfield Rural District Council* [1960] 2 QB 373) appeared to be out of step with well-settled principle.

8   See, for example, *R v Schildkamp* [1971] AC 1, HL at 10, 20 and 28.

9   *R v Kelt* [1977] 1 WLR 1365, CA, Scarman LJ (later Lord Scarman) at 1368.

CHAPTER 16

DEFINITIONS

The need for definitions

Words are too often used loosely in ordinary speech; and, as a result, the reader comes to regard them as meaning something different from their real meaning. The word 'orphan' is an example. The ordinary person in the street would be likely to regard the word 'orphan' as meaning a person both of whose parents have died. Reference to the *Oxford English Dictionary*, however, shows that, whilst a person who has lost both parents by death is an orphan, so also is a person who has lost either parent. A person whose mother is dead but whose father is alive is, therefore, an 'orphan'.

Some words have a meaning that is hard to state with certainty. One of the most striking examples is the word 'building'. It is easy enough to say that a nine-storey office block is a 'building', but there are many borderline cases. A court has held that a movable builder's pay office made of wood and on wheels is not a building;[1] but what if it is connected to the electricity supply? In one case a greenhouse was held not to be a building,[2] but in another case it was held that it was a building.[3] The difficulty, as pointed out in various decisions of the courts, is that the question as to what is a 'building' must always be a question of degree and circumstance.[4]

When the meaning of a word is open to argument, the meaning of the section in which that word is used must itself be uncertain. To overcome difficulties of this type the drafter of an Act of Parliament uses definitions which are set out in the Act of Parliament itself. Of course the definitions set out in the Act of Parliament will only avoid argument about the meanings of the words they define if those definitions are themselves clear definitions. Drafting a clear definition is difficult, and there are definitions that create at least as much confusion as they avoid.

Another use of definitions in an Act of Parliament is to save repetition. One common use of definitions in this way occurs when it is necessary to refer to some particular board or officeholder in a number of sections in the particular Act of Parliament. If a board or officeholder has a lengthy title, it is much easier simply to refer to 'the board' or to the title of the office and to define 'the board' or that office in the Act as meaning the full title of the board or office. Similarly, many Acts of Parliament give wide powers to a Minister, and the drafter can avoid repeated references to that Minister's full title by providing a definition of Minister.[5]

---

1   *London County Council v Pearce* [1892] 2 QB 109.
2   *Hibbert v Acton* (1889) 5 TLR 274.
3   *Smith v Richmond* [1899] AC 448, HL.
4   *Moir v Williams* [1892] 1 QB 264, CA.
5   Numerous Acts have a definition of Minister.

Sometimes the definition used in an Act of Parliament is a very wide one indeed, and it includes many things that would not ordinarily be thought of as falling within the meaning of the word that has been so defined. Examine the two successive definitions of sporting event and sportsground:

'sporting event' means any physical competitive activity at a sports ground, and includes any such activity which has been advertised as to, but does not, take place; and

'sports ground' means any place whatsoever which is designed, or is capable of being adapted, for the holding of sporting events in respect of which spectators are accommodated.

The ordinary person in the street would be unlikely to think of sporting event as meaning 'activity which ... does not take place' and would be unlikely, too, to think of sportsground as meaning 'any place whatsoever which is ... capable of being adapted, for the holding of sporting events...'. Putting those two definitions together a sporting event at a sportsground includes an event which did not occur and at a place which was capable of being adapted as a sportsground but which had not been so adapted. Indeed, applying the two definitions 'any place' could refer to a church hall at which an indoor basketball match was to be played between two teams of children in the under eight category but for which no basket net or board had been provided.[6]

Another trap is that a definition is not necessarily inserted to widen the scope of the term defined: it may be inserted in the Act 'not for the purpose of enlarging the word [defined] ... but rather for clarification and avoidance of doubt'.[7]

The person who wants to read an Act of Parliament must read the definitions in that Act very carefully, and all through the reading of the Act he or she must remember which words and phrases are defined in the Act.

The definitions section

Most of the longer Acts of Parliament, and many of the shorter ones, contain a section which sets out various definitions. The practice in Acts of the British Parliament is to set these definitions out towards the end of the Act. Thus, for example, the Nurses Act 1957 has its definitions set out in s 33, and the definitions section of the Housing Act 1957 is s 189. An alternative that is used in many of the Acts of the British Parliament is to include the definitions, not in a section of the Act as such, but in a schedule.[8]

The fact that definitions are set out in a definitions section or a schedule in the Act may lead the reader of the Act of Parliament to assume that all the definitions in that Act are set out in that definitions section or schedule. There are in fact some Acts of Parliament which do put all their definitions in the definitions section or schedule, but there are other Acts of Parliament that do not do so.

---

6   The two definitions occur in s 77 Criminal Justice (Scotland) Act 1980.

7   *Knowles v Liverpool City Council* [1993] 1 WLR 1428, HL, Lord Jauncey of Tullichettle at 1433.

8   See, for example, the setting out of the definitions in Schedule 1 Interpretation Act 1978 where the definitions take five full pages.

Another trap is that some Acts have two different definitions of the one word. Of course, the fact that there are two different definitions of the one word in the one Act does not mean that those two definitions apply to that word at the same time – one is the meaning given to the word in one section and another is the meaning given to the same word in another section of the same Act. It does, however, illustrate the need to read the Act bearing in mind not only that words may be given unexpected meanings in the Act but that they may be given different meanings in different sections of the same Act.

The effect of definitions in an Act of Parliament

It is usual for Parliament to set out in the definitions section that the definitions in the Act do not apply if it is apparent from the way in which the word is used in any particular section that it is used with a different meaning in that section. For example, the opening words of a definitions section in an Act of the British Parliament[9] are:

In this Part of this Act, unless the context otherwise –

However, even if Parliament does not include a phrase like that in the definitions section, the Act still has to be read in that way: any definition set out in an Act of Parliament will be read as not applying to a particular section if that section plainly shows that the word as used in it is used in a different sense.[10] The definition contained in the Act must always yield to any contrary context in which it is used.[11] Moreover, the need to interpret a word in a sense that is different from its statutory definition may arise not only from the express words of the Act of Parliament but also by implication from the Act.

Definitions which use 'mean' or 'include' or both

When reading the definitions in an Act of Parliament it is most important to note the way in which each definition is expressed. A definition may be expressed to be one which 'means' what is stated in it, it may be one which contains the word 'includes', and it may use 'means and includes'. Each of those has, therefore, to be read in quite a different way from the ways in which the other two are to be read. A definition which uses the word 'includes' has a wider scope than one which uses 'means'. 'Including' has been held to be 'used so as to remove any doubt as to the width of the word' defined.[12] The drafter's choice of 'means' or of 'includes' is to be interpreted 'as a deliberate choice, with a deliberate consequence'.[13]

When a definition in an Act of Parliament says that the word it defines 'includes' the particular things set out in that definition, the definition itself is

---

9   Section 77 Criminal Justice (Scotland) Act 1980.

10 *Meux v Jacobs* (1875) LR 7 HL 481, HL at 493.

11 *Craies on Statute Law* (7th edn by Edgar, SGG, Sweet & Maxwell, London, 1971) p 216.

12 *Greene v Church Commissioners for England* [1974] Ch 467, CA, Lord Denning MR at 476.

13 *Lewis v Rogers* (1984) 82 LGR 670, DC at 678.

left open. A definition which uses the word 'includes' is 'not a precise definition'. Of course, it includes all the matters specifically itemised in it, but it 'does not therefore exclude other matters'.[14] The definition which uses 'includes' does not purport to be exhaustive.[15] Everything that falls within the ordinary meaning of that word still falls within the meaning of that word as it is used in that Act of Parliament.[16] In addition, the things which are specifically set out in the definition also fall within the meaning of that word as it is used in that Act. Other matters which are not set out in the definition, and which would not fall within the ordinary meaning of the word, can also fall within the meaning of the word in that Act.[17] As a general rule, when the word 'includes' is used in a definition that definition has been inserted in the Act to give that word a wider meaning than it would otherwise have.[18] Thus, it has been said that the use of the word 'includes' in a definition

> is appropriate where it is sought to apply a word in a sense which it does not normally bear, or to make it clear that the word has a meaning about which otherwise some doubt might be felt.[19]

When the definition of a word in an Act of Parliament says that the word 'means' what is set out in the definition, the definition must be read in exactly the opposite way to the way in which a definition that uses the word 'includes' is to be read. The definition which uses the word 'means' closes the meaning of the word. It limits the meaning of the word to what is set out in the definition. If the ordinary meaning of the word is different from that in the definition, the ordinary meaning is discarded for the purposes of the Act. No other things are to be added to the definition in the Act: when a statute says that a word or phrase shall 'mean' – not merely that it shall 'include' – certain acts or things, the definition 'is a hard and fast definition and the result is that you cannot give any other meaning to the word' so defined.[20]

Since 'means' and 'includes' as used in the definitions sections have such different meanings, the phrase 'means and includes' is one which inevitably raises a doubt about the proper interpretation.[21] However, it would seem that when a phrase is defined as one which 'means and includes' the matters specified in the definition, it is restricted in its meaning to what is set out in the definition – it affords 'an exhaustive explanation of the meaning which, for the purposes of the Act, must invariably be attached to these words or expressions'.[22]

---

14 *Stone v Boreham* [1959] 1 QB 1, DC, Lord Goddard CJ at 6.

15 *Commissioner of Estate and Gift Duties v Fiji Resorts Ltd* [1983] 2 AC 649, PC, unanimous decision at 659.

16 *Robinson v Barton Eccles Local Board* (1883) 8 App Cas 798, HL, Lord Selbourne at 801.

17 *Stone v Boreham* [1959] 1 QB 1, DC.

18 *Dilworth v Commissioner of Stamps* [1899] AC 99, Lord Watson at 106.

19 *Carter v Bradbeer* [1975] 1 WLR 1204, Viscount Dilhorne at 1214–15.

20 *Gough v Gough* [1891] 2 QB 665, Lord Esher MR at 674.

21 *Craies on Statute Law* (7th edn by Edgar, SGG, Sweet & Maxwell, London, 1971) p 213.

22 *Hemens v Whitsbury Farm and Stud Ltd* [1988] AC 601, HL, Lord Keith of Kinkel at 613–14.

Surprisingly, but clearly the law, even 'includes' used on its own can be interpreted as 'imperative, if the context of the Act is sufficient to show that it was not merely employed for the purpose of adding to the natural significance of the words or expressions defined. It may be equivalent to "mean and include"'.[23]

Definitions in other Acts

The fact that a word is given one meaning in one Act of Parliament does not mean that it has the same meaning in another Act of Parliament: 'The same expression, of course, may well be used in different Acts with significantly different meanings.'[24] Except in a case in which two or more Acts are to be read together as one Act,[25] a definition appearing in one Act cannot be used to interpret the same word appearing in another Act. However, a distinction must be drawn between a definition appearing in another Act on the one hand and a judicial interpretation of a word in another Act on the other hand. When a judge has interpreted a word or phrase as bearing a particular meaning that same word or phrase may well be interpreted in the same way when it appears in another Act. Judicial dictionaries provide assistance in finding the relevant cases in which words or phrases have been interpreted.

It should be noted that Parliament has passed one Act that is meant to provide definitions that are to be read into most other Acts. That Act is known as the Interpretation Act. In practice, however, that Act provides very few of the definitions that are needed to interpret an Act of Parliament.

Dictionary definitions and technical terms

The use of dictionary definitions, and the meaning to be given to technical terms, are considered in Chapter 20.

---

23 *Hemens v Whitsbury Farm and Stud Ltd* [1988] AC 601, HL, Lord Keith of Kinkel at 613–14.
24 *Re 'Fairview', Church Street, Bromyard* [1974] 1 WLR 579, Megarry J (later Megarry V-C) at 582.
25 See Chapter 35.

CHAPTER 17

SCHEDULES

The nature of a schedule

There are certain things which it is more convenient to set out in something added at the end of the Act than it is to set them out in the body of the Act itself. The system used for this purpose is that of schedules.

A common use of schedules is to specify detailed provisions for the working out of the Act.

The following is an example of a schedule:

SCHEDULE 1

Minor and Consequential Amendments of Part II of Slaughterhouses Act 1954 (Provisions Relating to Scotland)

In section 8 (provisions relating to local authority slaughterhouses), subsection (1) shall cease to have effect.

In section 10 (refusal and cancellation of registration), in subsection (3)(b) after the words 'are not' (where they first occur) there shall be inserted the words ', and are not likely within a reasonable time to be', the words from 'that any' to 'specified' (where it last occurs) shall cease to have effect, and for the words 'such premises' there shall be substituted the words 'the premises specified in the registration'; in subsection (8) for the words 'Secretary of State and any such appeal' there shall be substituted the word 'sheriff, and any such appeal shall be disposed of in a summary manner, and'; and the following provisions shall also cease to have effect–

subsections (1) and (2);

in subsection (3), paragraphs (a) and (c);

subsection (5);

in subsection (6) the words 'to the Secretary of State'.

Section 11 (compensation for closure of private slaughterhouses) shall cease to have effect.

In section 13 (power to enter premises), after subsection (5) there shall be inserted the following subsection–

(6) Nothing in this section shall authorise any person, except with the permission of the local authority under the Diseases of Animals Act 1950, to enter any premises which for the time being are, or are comprised in, an infected place within the meaning of that Act.

In section 18 (savings), subsections (2) and (3) shall cease to have effect.

In section 19 (expenses) paragraph (b) shall cease to have effect.[1]

Examples of rules set out as a schedule to an Act would be too lengthy for reprinting in this book. As an example, Schedule 1 Finance Act 1972 deals with registration for taxation purposes and contains 14 paragraphs.

---

1   Agriculture (Miscellaneous Provisions) Act 1981.

A further use of schedules is to set out lengthy provisions which persons affected by the statute can adopt if they wish to, but which they are not compelled to adopt.

Another use of schedules is to set out a scale of fees that may be charged, or to set out a lengthy technical description of some area that is defined for the purposes of the Act. Also, schedules can be used to set out the method of prosecution and the penalties for the various offences created by an Act.[2]

Other uses to which schedules have been put are repeal of other Acts or parts of Acts, amendments to particular provisions of other Acts, definitions, recording the terms of treaties or conventions or agreements, and forms the use of which is required by provisions in the Act itself.

On the facing page is an example of forms set out in the schedule to an Act of Parliament.

Forms in that broad approach are not as numerous as forms which are themselves specific, setting out details that must be completed by the person filling in the form or specific as to requirements made by the Parliament but contained in the schedule instead of in the sections of the Act.

Conflict between a section of an Act and a schedule to that Act

Where there is a conflict between the provisions contained in a section of an Act of Parliament and the provisions contained in a schedule to that same Act, the question arises as to whether the section or the schedule is to prevail. The answer to this question appears to depend upon whether the schedule sets out positive provisions, or whether it merely sets out a form. The question of the schedule which merely sets out a form is considered under **Conflict between a section of an Act and a form in a schedule to that Act** in this chapter.

If the conflict is between a section and a schedule which sets out positive provisions, the question of that conflict must, it is thought, be approached from the standpoint that the schedule is a part of the Act just as much as the section is a part of the Act:

> With respect to calling it a schedule, a schedule in an Act of Parliament is a mere question of drafting – a mere question of words. The schedule is as much a part of the statute, and is as much an enactment as any other part.[3]

If the conflict between the section and the schedule cannot be overcome, the positive provisions in the schedule must be read as overriding the provisions in the section:

---

2 This is done, for example, in the Consumer Credit Act 1974.

3 *Attorney-General v Lamplough* (1873) 3 Ex D 214, CA, Brett LJ (later Lord Esher MR) at 229.

SCHEDULES[4]

Schedule 1

Certificates as to Proof of Certain Routine Matters

1 Enactment	2 Persons who may purport to sign certificate	3 Matters which may be certified
The Road Traffic Regulation Act 1967 (c 76). The enactments specified in section 78A(3) (speeding offences generally).	The police officers who have tested the apparatus.	The accuracy of any particular – (a) speedometer fitted to a police vehicle; (b) odometer fitted to a police vehicle; (c) radar meter; or apparatus for measuring speed, time or distance, identified in the certificate by reference to its number or otherwise.
The Misuse of Drugs Act 1971 (c 38). Sections 4, 5, 6, 8, 9, 12, 13, 19 and 20 (various offences concerning controlled drugs).	Two analysts who have analysed the substance and each of whom is either a person possessing the qualifications (qualifying persons for appointment as public analysts) prescribed by regulations made under section 89 of the Food and Drugs Act 1955 (c. 16), or section 27 of the Food and Drugs (Scotland) Act 1956 (c.30), or a person authorised by the Secretary of State to make analyses for the purposes of the provisions of the Misuse of Drugs Act 1971 mentioned in column 1.	The type and classification of any particular substance, identified in the certificate by reference to a label or otherwise, which is alleged to be a controlled drug within the meaning of section 2 of the Act referred to in column 1.
The Immigration Act 1971 (c 77). Section 24(1)(a) in so far as it relates to entry in breach of a deportation order, section 24(1)(b) and section 26(1)(f) in so far as it relates to a requirement of regulations.	An officer authorised to do so by the Secretary of State.	In relation to a person identified in the certificate (a) the date, place and means of his arrival in, or any removal of him from, the United Kingdom;

---

4   Schedule 1 Criminal Justice (Scotland) Act 1980.

As Lord Sterndale MR has said:

> It seems to me that there are two principles or rules of interpretation which ought to be applied to the combination of Act and schedule. If the Act says that the schedule is to be used for a certain purpose and a heading of part of the schedule in question shows that it is *prima facie* at any rate devoted to that purpose, then you must read the Act and the schedule as though the schedule were operating for that purpose, and if you can satisfy the language of the section without extending it beyond that purpose you ought to do it. But if in spite of that you find in the language of the schedule words and terms that go clearly outside that purpose, then you must give effect to them and you must not consider them as limited by the heading of that part of the schedule or by the purpose mentioned in the Act for which the schedule is *prima facie* to be used. You cannot refuse to give effect to clear words simply because *prima facie* they seem to be limited by the heading of the schedule and the definition of the purpose of the schedule contained in the Act.[5]

Conflict between a preamble to an Act and a schedule to that Act

If an Act has a preamble and the provisions of a schedule to that Act are in conflict with the preamble the provisions of the schedule prevail: full effect is to be given in that case to the provisions set out in the schedule. This follows from the principle that a schedule is itself part of the Act which contains it.[6]

Conflict between a section of an Act and a form in a schedule to that Act

A different rule applies where the conflict is between the positive provisions of a section on the one hand and a mere form in the schedule on the other hand. In such a case the general principle is that the provisions of the section must be given their full force without being restricted in any way by the form in the schedule. A form in the schedule is a general form inserted in the Act as a matter of convenience and it cannot prevail over the words of a section in that Act:

> it would be quite contrary to the recognised principles upon which courts of law construe Acts of Parliament, to enlarge the conditions of the enactment, and thereby restrain its operation, by any reference to the words of a mere form given for convenience' sake in a schedule.[7]

---

5   *Inland Revenue Commissioners v Gittus* [1920] 1 KB 563, CA, Lord Sterndale MR at 576 (the actual decision in the case was affirmed on appeal: [1921] 2 AC 81). The Court of Appeal did not refer to this decision or to those in fns 2, 3 and 4 in Chapter 12 of this book when it rejected the principle that, if it is impossible to reconcile two provisions both of which are general or both are specific, the later in the Act prevails over the earlier: *Re Marr* [1990] Ch 773, CA.

6   *Attorney-General v Lamplough* (1878) 3 Ex D 214, CA, Brett LJ (later Lord Esher MR) at 214.

7   *Dean v Green* (1882) 8 PD 79, Lord Penzance at 89.

The rule is that

> such form, although embodied in the Act, cannot be deemed conclusive ...: we have also to consider the language of the section itself to which the schedule is appended; and, if there be any contradiction between the two, which upon fair construction there perhaps will not be found to be, upon ordinary principles the form, which is made to suit rather the generality of cases than all cases, must give way.[8]

However, the general principle cannot override the power of Parliament to so express the form as to render it imperative and therefore as taking precedence over the section of the Act.[9]

---

8   *R v Baines* (1840) 12 A & E 210 at 227; 113 ER 792, Lord Denman CJ at 799.

9   *Odgers' Construction of Deeds and Statutes* (5th edn by Gerald Dworkin, Sweet & Maxwell, London, 1967) pp 320–21.

CHAPTER 18

PROVISOS

The nature of a proviso

A proviso is something which is included in an Act of Parliament to make certain that the Act does not have the particular effect that it might have if the proviso were not included in the Act. The proviso may be inserted in the Act, for example, to preserve existing rights. It may be inserted to make sure that certain rights of the Crown are not affected by a section which does affect rights of the Crown to some extent. It may be inserted in the Act to create exemptions from the section to which it is a proviso.

The form of a proviso

Provisos frequently begin with the words 'Provided that'. However, no particular form of words is needed: it is the effect of the words used that makes them a proviso. Thus when a subsection was not worded as a proviso but was held to be 'clearly tantamount to one' it was given the effect of a proviso.[1]

The effect of a proviso

A genuine proviso is something which qualifies or modifies the section to which it is a proviso. It is, therefore, to be read in the light of that section itself. The usual effect of the proviso is to take out of the section something that would otherwise fall within it:

> When one finds a proviso to a section, the natural presumption is that, but for the proviso, the enacting part of the section would have included the subject matter of the proviso.[2]

A proviso should not be given an extended meaning: it should have no greater effect than a strict interpretation of its words requires,[3] and it should ordinarily be treated as affecting only the section or subsection to which it is annexed.[4]

Proviso inserted unnecessarily

When a Bill is being drafted or is brought before Parliament it may happen that some persons become afraid that the provisions in the Bill will affect them even although the intention is that they should not be affected by those provisions. If that happens, the Act when it is finally passed may contain a proviso stating that the particular section does not apply in the way in which those persons

---

1   *Rome v Punjab National Bank (No 2)* [1989] 1 WLR 1211, CA, Sir John May (formerly May LJ) at 1219.

2   *Mullins v Treasurer of Surrey* (1880) 5 QBD 170, DC, Lush J (later Lush LJ) at 173.

3   *Re Tabrisky* [1947] Ch 565, DC.

4   *Hill v East & West India Dock Co* (1884) 9 App Cas 448, HL.

were afraid it would apply. The proviso in such a case may have been put in because those persons' fears were correct, or it may have been put in because it was thought that there might be some basis for the fears and it was therefore thought better to make certain that the section did not apply to those persons. The fact that there is a proviso therefore does not necessarily affect the reading of the section itself. If the fears that led to the inclusion of the proviso were groundless, the proviso would obviously have no effect at all. In such a case the section is not to be read in such a way as to give effect to the proviso, but it is to be given its ordinary clear meaning without reference to the proviso:

> I am perfectly clear that if the language of the enacting part of the statute does not contain the provisions which are said to occur in it, you cannot derive these provisions by implication from a proviso.[5]

Of course, if a section of the Act is ambiguous, reference can be made to a proviso to ascertain the proper interpretation of the section; but a proviso that would lead to an irrational or unjust result must give way to the ambit of the words of the section to which it purports to be a proviso.[6]

Words wrongly expressed as a proviso

It may happen that something is expressed in the form of a proviso when it is not a proviso at all. If that happens, the words that are set out as if they were a proviso will be treated as being a separate provision of the Act and not as a proviso. Whilst in many instances it is a proviso's function to limit or qualify what preceded it 'it is the substance and content of the enactment, not its form, which has to be considered, and that which is expressed to be a proviso may itself add to and not merely limit or qualify that which precedes it'.[7]

---

5   *West Derby Union v Metropolitan Life Assurance Co* [1897] AC 647, HL, Lord Watson at 652.

6   *Director of Public Prosecutions v Goodchild* [1978] 1 WLR 578, HL, Lord Diplock at 583.

7   *Commissioner of Stamp Duties v Atwill* [1973] AC 558, PC, unanimous opinion at 561.

CHAPTER 19

PUNCTUATION

Acts of Parliament passed before 1850

In the case of Acts of Parliament which were passed by Parliament before 1850 the actual copies of the Acts which received the royal assent did not contain any punctuation. The reader of any of those Acts must therefore ignore any punctuation in the printed copy.[1]

Punctuation in Acts of Parliament passed in 1850 or later

If the real meaning of a section is clear but does not agree with the punctuation of the section, the section must be read as if it had no punctuation in it: punctuation cannot control the sense of the section if the meaning of that section is otherwise reasonably clear.[2]

A century ago it was held that punctuation could not be used to interpret a section,[3] and as recently as 1960 one eminent judge said that it is 'very doubtful' whether punctuation can be used at all in finding the meaning of a section.[4] Today however, there are various cases in which punctuation has in fact been used by the courts to find the meaning of the section[5] and it must now be taken that punctuation is to be used to interpret an Act if the meaning is not otherwise clear. As Lord Lowry has held in the House of Lords,

> not to take account of punctuation disregards the reality that literate people, such as parliamentary draftsmen, punctuate what they write, if not identically, at least in accordance with grammatical principles. Why should not other literate people, such as judges, look at the punctuation in order to interpret the meaning of the legislation as accepted by Parliament?[6]

The proper use of punctuation in the interpretation of a statute has been well put by Megarry V-C who said:

> As for [counsel for the plaintiff's] point on the comma, I accept, of course, that the day is long past when the courts would pay no heed to punctuation in an Act of Parliament: see *Hanlon v Law Society* [1981] AC 124 at 197–198 *per* Lord Lowry. Nor do I say that a mere comma can have little force; indeed, I would be the last to deny that its presence or absence may be highly significant ... Over two centuries ago James Burrow, the law reporter, in his *Essay on Punctuation* (1772, p 11), gave an illustration of the potency of punctuation in a little jingle:
>
> > 'Every lady in this land
> > Hath twenty nails upon each hand

---

1 *Inland Revenue Commissioners v Hinchy* [1960] AC 748, HL, Lord Reid at 765.

2 *Houston v Burns* [1918] AC 337, HL, Lord Finlay LC at 342, Lord Haldane at 344, Lord Shaw at 348.

3 *Duke of Devonshire v O'Connor* (1890) 24 QBD 468, CA.

4 *Inland Revenue Commissioners v Hinchy* [1960] AC 748, HL, Lord Reid at 765.

5 See, for example, *Slaney v Kean* [1970] 1 Ch 243, Megarry J (later Megarry V-C) at 252.

6 *Hanlon v Law Society* [1981] AC 124, HL, Lord Lowry at 197–98.

Five and twenty on hands and feet
And this is true, without deceit.'

Leave this unpunctuated, or with punctuation only at the end of the lines, and it seems plainly untrue. Insert a comma or semicolon at the beginning and end of the phrase 'upon each hand five', and nonsense becomes sense, albeit at the cost of some impairment of the rhythm. Yet throughout, one must remember that punctuation is normally an aid, and no more than an aid, towards revealing the meaning of the phrases used, and the sense that they are to convey when put in their setting. Punctuation is the servant and not the master of substance and meaning. Furthermore, although a pair of commas may of course be used to enclose a parenthetic phrase, there is no rule of grammar, usage or common sense that requires words so enclosed to be treated as a parenthesis.[7]

---

7   *Marshall v Cottingham* [1982] 1 Ch 82 at 88.

CHAPTER 20

THE MEANING OF WORDS NOT DEFINED IN THE ACT

The difficulty of finding the meaning of words

Even when reading an ordinary statement free from the complexities of an Act of Parliament it may be difficult to find the meaning of particular words. This difficulty may arise because the proper meaning of a word is different to the meaning the ordinary person in the street expects it to have or, more frequently, because the word has many possible meanings.[1] When the word the meaning of which has to be found is in an Act of Parliament the difficulty of finding that meaning may be increased by the complexities of the Act itself and by the possibility that Parliament has used the same word in different senses in the same Act. The rules of statutory interpretation evolved by the courts attempt to assist the reader to find a way through these difficulties and so to find the meaning of the words.

Where possible, a word is to be given a constant meaning throughout the Act

One of the rules used in reading an Act of Parliament is that a word should, if possible, be given the same meaning throughout the whole of the Act.[2] 'It is a sound rule of construction to give the same meaning to the same words occurring in different parts of an Act of Parliament.'[3]

If the word occurs twice in the one section, the rule that it is to be given the same meaning is a strong one: the rule, however, has less force when the word occurs in different sections of the Act. Indeed, if 'a word is used inaccurately in one section of a statute, it must not be assumed to have been used inaccurately when it occurs in another section of the same statute'.[4]

If it is clear that the word is not used consistently throughout the Act, the rule that it is to be treated as having a common meaning throughout the Act is of no effect. The one word has been held to have two different meanings in one and the same section of an Act.[5]

---

1   See **The need for definitions** in Chapter 16.
2   *Courtauld v Legh* (1869) LR 4 Ex 126, Cleasby B at 130. The same word is even to be given the same meaning in different Acts covering the same subject matter if they are to be read together: *Lee-Verhulst (Investments) Ltd v Harwood Trust* [1973] QB 204, CA, Stamp LJ at 218.
3   *Courtauld v Legh* (1869) LR 4 Ex 126, Cleasby B at 130.
4   *Re Moody and Yates' contract* (1885) 30 Ch D 344, CA at 349.
5   *Re Smith* (1893) 24 Ch D 672, North J at 678. As an example, s 54 Bankruptcy Act 1869 uses the word 'property' in two totally different senses.

Words in an Act of Parliament have the meaning which they bore at the date when the Act was passed

Words used in an Act of Parliament (if they are not defined in the Act) are to be read as having the meaning which they had in ordinary speech (or, if they are technical words, then as having their technical meaning) at the time when the Act was passed:

> The words of a statute must be construed as they would have been the day after the statute was passed, unless some subsequent Act has declared that some other construction is to be adopted or has altered the previous statute.[6]

What the reader of the Act has to do is to ascertain what the phrase or word meant in its ordinary popular acceptation at the date the statute was passed. However, if social conditions have changed since the legislation was passed and if the language of the enactment is wide enough to extend to those new circumstances, there is no reason why it should not apply.[7]

Since the meaning of a word does not change quickly, the rule about reading words in the light of the meaning which they had at the time when the Act was passed is generally of little assistance in the case of a comparatively recent Act.[8] However, it is possible that the rapid advance of scientific knowledge may lead to a change in the meaning given to a particular word shortly after an Act is passed: in such a case the word used in the Act is to be given the meaning that it had at the time when the Act was passed, not the current meaning and this is so even although a scientist could be confused by an understandable tendency to read the Act in its current scientific meaning.

Dictionary definitions

If the meaning of a particular word is in doubt and that word is not defined in the Act of Parliament in which it occurs, it is to be interpreted on the basis that Parliament 'intended [it] to bear its ordinary meaning'.[9] The person reading that Act of Parliament should turn to the various law dictionaries in which the legal meanings of words are set out.[10] These dictionaries include *Stroud's Judicial Dictionary*,[11] *Jowitt's Dictionary of English Law*,[12] and *Words and Phrases Legally Defined*.[13]

---

6 *Sharpe v Wakefield* (1888) 22 QBD 239, CA, Lord Esher MR at 241; affd, [1891] AC 173, HL; *Legal Aid Board v Russell* [1990] 2 QB 607, CA, Lord Donaldson of Lymington MR at 618; affd, [1991] 2 AC 317, HL.

7 *Comdel Commodities Ltd v Siporex Trade SA* [1991] 1 AC 148, HL, Lord Bridge of Harwich at 165.

8 *Assheton Smith v Owen* [1906] 1 Ch 179, CA, Cozens-Hardy LJ (later Baron Cozens-Hardy MR) at 213.

9 *Peart v Stewart* [1983] 2 AC 109, HL, Lord Diplock at 114.

10 *Haigh v Charles W Ireland Ltd* [1974] 1 WLR 43, HL, Lord Diplock at 55.

11 (Fifth edn, Sweet & Maxwell, 1986).

12 (Second edn, Sweet & Maxwell, 1977).

13 (Third edn, Butterworths, 1989).

If the word is not defined in the Act and there is no appropriate definition appearing in one of the judicial dictionaries, the reader must then turn to the ordinary standard dictionaries such as the *Oxford English Dictionary*.[14]

In using either the law dictionaries or the ordinary standard dictionaries it is necessary to be careful not to place too much emphasis upon a particular word if it has to be interpreted as part of a phrase of two or more words:

> It is often fallacious in considering the meaning of a phrase consisting of two words to find a meaning which each has separately and then infer that the two together cover the combination so arrived at. The two together may ... have acquired a special meaning of their own.[15]

Technical terms

The use of technical terms without definition in an Act of Parliament can also cause difficulty. If an Act of Parliament is one which relates to a particular trade or business, or to a particular type of transaction, and the words used in that Act are words which have a particular meaning in that trade, business or transaction, the words in the Act are to be read as having the meaning which they in fact had in that trade, business or transaction at the time that the Act came into force:

> If it is a word which is of a technical or scientific character then it must be construed according to that which is its primary meaning, namely, its technical or scientific meaning.[16]

This is so even if the technical or scientific meaning is different from the ordinary meaning of the word.[17] 'In a statute, if the legislature uses a technical term, it should ... be taken to use it in its technical sense unless it is plain that something else was intended.'[18]

The technical or scientific meaning of a word can be ascertained by using standard textbooks applicable to the particular trade, business or transaction. Evidence can be called both to assist the conclusion that the expression is used in a technical sense and to elucidate that technical meaning.

---

14 *Re Rippon Housing Order* [1939] 2 KB 838. Readers who wish to use a simplified law dictionary will find *Osborn's Concise Law Dictionary* (8th edn, Sweet & Maxwell, 1993) a useful work.

15 *Lee v Showmen's Guild of Great Britain* [1952] 2 QB 329, CA, Somervell LJ at 338.

16 *Holt & Co v Colyer* (1881) 16 Ch D 718, Fry J (later Fry LJ) at 720.

17 *Herbert Berry Associates Ltd v Inland Revenue Commissioners* [1977] 1 WLR 1437, HL, Lord Simon of Glaisdale at 1446.

18 *Methuen-Campbell v Walters* [1979] 1 QB 525, CA, Buckley LJ at 542.

CHAPTER 21

THE DIFFERENCE BETWEEN THE GENERAL RULES AND THE SPECIFIC RULES

The general rules

There are four general rules of statutory interpretation, considered in turn in the four succeeding chapters. They are the plain meaning rule, the golden rule (that manifest absurdity and injustice are to be avoided), the mischief rule and the purposive approach. These are rules of general applicability and therefore are to be contrasted with rules which apply only if the particular circumstances to which they relate occur in the Act.

Conflicts between the general and the specific rules

It is important to remember that the general rules of statutory interpretation are the basic ones. The factual circumstances for the application of one of the specific rules may apply (as, for example, the presence of a group of two or more specific words forming a class followed by a general word which would make it possible to invoke the class rule[1]) but invoking the specific rule might have the effect of defeating the purpose of the Act, and it would therefore have to give way to the purposive basis of interpretation.[2]

---

1   See Chapter 32.
2   See Chapter 25.

CHAPTER 22

THE PLAIN MEANING RULE

The names by which the plain meaning rule is known

The plain meaning rule is generally referred to as 'the plain meaning rule' but it can also be referred to as the literal rule, the ordinary meaning rule, or the grammatical rule.

The effect of the plain meaning rule

The plain meaning rule is a very simple rule. It means what it says. If the meaning of the Act is plain, it is to be given that plain meaning:

> Where the language of an Act is clear and explicit, we must give effect to it, whatever may be the consequences, for in that case the words of the statute speak the intention of the legislature.[1]

> The cardinal rule ... is that words in a statute *prima facie* bear their plain and ordinary meaning.[2]

Its words are to be given their plain and ordinary meaning applying to them the appropriate grammatical rules.

> Judicial decision cannot impose limitations upon the language of Parliament where it is clear from the words, context, and policy of the statute that no limitation was intended.[3]

Therefore,

> The first thing is to construe it according to the ordinary rules of grammar, and if a construction which satisfies those rules makes the enactment intelligible, and especially if it carries out the obvious intention of the legislature as gathered from a general perusal of the whole statute, that grammatical construction ought not to be departed from.[4]

The test as to whether or not the meaning being applied is the ordinary meaning is the meaning which an ordinary person would place upon it: 'It is to my mind undesirable that the law should give a more limited meaning to a word than the ordinary man would do unless there is good ground for doing so.'[5]

If the meaning of the Act of Parliament is clear, the reader's opinion as to what Parliament's intention really was is not to be used to give the words of the

---

1   *Warburton v Loveland* (1831) 2 D & Cl 480 at 489; 6 ER 806, Tindal CJCP at 809; *Johnson v Moreton* [1980] AC 37, HL, Lord Salmon at 50.

2   *Attorney-General v Associated Newspapers Ltd* [1994] 2 AC 238, HL, Lord Lowry at 255.

3   *NWL Ltd v Woods* [1979] 1 WLR 1294, HL, Lord Scarman at 1314.

4   *R v Federal Steam Navigation Co Ltd* [1973] 1 WLR 1373, CA, unanimous decision at 1376–77; affd under the name of *Federal Steam Navigation Co Ltd v Department of Trade and Industry* [1974] 1 WLR 505, HL.

5   *British Eagle International Airlines Ltd v Compagnie Nationale Air France* [1975] 1 WLR 758, HL Lord Cross of Chelsea at 778.

Act a different meaning to agree with that supposed intention: 'The rule of construction that *prima facie* ordinary English words are to be understood in their ordinary sense is not lightly to be displaced.'[6]

This attention to the ordinary meaning of the words to be interpreted is important:

> If the Courts are unwilling to construe plain words in their natural and ordinary sense the prospect will be like one of those distressing scenes in a neurological ward: a patient has a 'crisis', which provokes some different idiosyncratic symptom in another patient, which in turn brings on fresh disorders in the first, and so on in a reciprocal and accumulating train of tribulation. So, if courts claim to discover tortuous and remote anomalies arising from the plain words of a statutory provision, and to modify those words accordingly, the draftsmen will reciprocate by attempting to meet such cases in a way which will throw up yet more labyrinthine anomalies. Forensic ingenuity will be matched by statutory anfractuosity; and the hapless citizen will be sucked down in a vortex of verbiage.[7]

The words of the Act are to be given their plain meaning even if doing so creates practical difficulties: these difficulties cannot displace the plain meaning of words. It is for Parliament and not for the courts to cure any injustice in what Parliament has enacted.

Hardship does not preclude the application of the plain meaning rule: 'Statutes have to be applied according to their terms where the terms are clear' even if hardship results to the private individual.[8]

The reader of an Act of Parliament may think that it is unjust, but that is no justification for giving it a meaning different to the plain meaning of its words:

> However ridiculous and unjust the results of the … Act may be, and this one produces peculiarly ridiculous and unjust results, it has been enacted by Parliament and it is our duty to enforce it.[9]

The literal and grammatical meaning of a section has been applied although the result is to 'produce unique, bizarre, inappropriate, absurd and unjust results which … Parliament can never have intended'.[10]

Even if giving the words their plain meaning has the result that the probable intention of Parliament is defeated, the plain meaning rule may still apply. Thus a case of actual hardship has been rejected because giving effect to it in the interpretation of the section would involve 'substantially rewriting the section on the supposition that the legislature, had it thought about the particular case, would have expressed itself in substantially different terms from those which it

---

6   *Haigh v Charles W. Ireland Ltd* [1974] 1 WLR 43, HL, Lord Diplock at 55.

7   *Lord Advocate v De Rosa* [1974] 1 WLR 946, HL, Lord Simon of Glaisdale at 961.

8   *Hare v Gocher* [1962] 2 QB 641, DC.

9   *Commissioner of Police of the Metropolis v Curran* [1976] 1 WLR 87, HL at 103–04; see also *Cox v Hakes* (1890) 15 App Cas 506, HL, Lord Herschell at 528.

10   *Commissioner of Police of the Metropolis v Curran* [1976] 1 WLR 87, HL, Lord Salmon at 102.

in fact chose to use'.[11] 'It is a strong thing to read into an Act of Parliament words which are not there, and in the absence of clear necessity it is a wrong thing to do.'[12] It is possible, however, in such circumstances that a court will be prepared to interpret the otherwise plain words in such a way as to give effect to what the court presumes to have been the Parliament's purpose in enacting the statute as a whole or the provision in which the words occur in particular. Thus the plain meaning rule has not been applied because the effect of applying it would 'not be consistent with the intention of Parliament ... inferred from a study of the statutory context'.[13] This purposive approach is considered in Chapter 25. The purposive approach is gaining increasing importance:

> If one looks back to the actual decisions of this House [of Lords] on questions of statutory construction over the past 30 years one cannot fail to be struck by the evidence of a trend away from the purely literal towards the purposive construction of statutory provisions.[14]

Nevertheless, the plain meaning rule must not be overlooked, for 'According to ordinary principles of construction, the literal interpretation of the enactment is to be accepted so long as it gives a reasonable meaning'.[15]

The importance of the plain meaning rule

The plain meaning rule is one of the basic rules for the reading of any Act of Parliament. Traditionally, if the meaning of the words is plain, the plain meaning rule is applied; and on that basis there is no room to use any other rule at all. 'The courts' first duty is to consider the meaning of the language used in the particular statute under consideration'.[16] Where the words of an Act of Parliament are clear, there is no room for applying any of the principles of interpretation, for they are merely presumptions applied in cases of ambiguity in the statute: 'If the words of the statute are in themselves precise and unambiguous, then no more can be necessary than to expound those words in their natural and ordinary sense.'[17]

The plain meaning rule is one of the most important rules for the reader of a statute to remember and apply. If he or she does not do so, subjective factors of hardship and unjust results may lead the reader into adopting a forced meaning that the Act does not bear and the plain meaning rule will not allow.

---

11 *Canterbury City Council v Colley* [1993] AC 401, HL, Lord Oliver of Aylmerton at 405–06.

12 *Thompson v Goold & Co* [1910] AC 409, HL, Lord Mersey at 420; approved in *Stock v Frank Jones (Tipton) Ltd* [1978] 1 WLR 231, HL, Viscount Dilhorne at 234–35.

13 *Howard v Borneman (No 2)* [1975] Ch 201, CA, Scarman LJ (later Lord Scarman) at 216; affd [1976] AC 301, HL.

14 *Carter v Bradbeer* [1975] 1 WLR 1204, HL, Lord Diplock at 1206–07.

15 *Sakhuja v Allen* [1973] AC 152, HL, Lord Pearson at 183.

16 *Dun v Dun* [1959] AC 272, PC, unanimous opinion at 288.

17 *Craies on Statute Law* (7th edn by Edgar, SGG, Sweet & Maxwell, London, 1971) 65.

The plain meaning rule cannot apply if the meaning is not plain

Although the plain meaning rule is a basic rule for the reading of any Act of Parliament, it can of course apply if, and only if, the meaning of the words is plain. If the statutory provision is ambiguous, the plain meaning rule cannot apply.

The effect of definitions on the plain meaning rule

A word or phrase used in a statute may seem to the ordinary person to bear its ordinary meaning. However, a definition in the statute itself or a definition in the Interpretation Act 1978 may specify a meaning which may differ substantially from what the ordinary person would regard as the ordinary meaning.

CHAPTER 23

MANIFEST ABSURDITY AND INJUSTICE ARE TO BE AVOIDED

The nature of the rule

There is a rule that, if there is ambiguity in an Act of Parliament, the plain meaning rule cannot apply and the Act should be read in such a way as to avoid a result of manifest absurdity or injustice.[1] The courts will conclude that the Parliament does not intend injustice or to authorise it.[2] As Lord Diplock said of an Act which the House of Lords had to interpret, 'The ordinary grammatical meaning of one or other of these provisions had to give way if justice and commonsense were not to be flouted'.[3] An absurd result is only to be accepted if there is no acceptable alternative available.[4]

> If the words of a statute are capable, without being distorted, of more than one meaning, the courts should prefer the meaning which leads to a sensible and just result complying with the statutory objective and reject the meaning which leads to absurdity or injustice and is repugnant to the statutory objective.[5]

It is a rule which could easily be carried too far, and it is a rule which must be applied very sparingly:

> It should only be exercised in cases that imperatively demand its application; for apart from the fact that its exercise comes perilously close to legislating that which seems absurd to one mind may not appear so to another.[6]

It must always be borne in mind that it is not for the person reading the Act of Parliament to substitute his or her own ideas of justice for Parliament's ideas of justice. The reader may not agree with the way in which Parliament has dealt with a matter in the Act of Parliament, but it is not open to agree or disagree on policy when seeking to find the meaning of the Act of Parliament:

> The duty of the court, and its only duty, is to expound the language of the Act in accordance with the settled rules of construction. It is ... as unwise as it is unprofitable to cavil at the policy of an Act of Parliament, or to pass a covert censure on the legislature.[7]

Even 'an extraordinary anomaly' may not justify departing from the plain meaning rule if that anomaly is the plain effect of the section.[8]

---

1   *Kelly v Pierhead Ltd* [1967] 1 WLR 65, CA, Salmon LJ (later Lord Salmon) at 70.

2   *Sakhuja v Allen* [1973] AC 152, HL, Lord Salmon at 198.

3   *W Devis & Sons Ltd v Atkins* [1977] AC 931, HL, Lord Diplock at 948.

4   *Gilbard v Amey Roadstone Corpn Ltd* (1974) 73 LGR 43, CA, Roskill LJ (later Lord Roskill) at 57.

5   *Johnson v Moreton* [1980] AC 37, HL, Lord Salmon at 50.

6   *Prince Ernest of Hanover v Attorney-General* [1956] Ch 188, CA, Romer LJ (later Lord Romer) at 218; affd [1957] AC 437, HL.

7   *Vacher & Sons Ltd v London Society of Compositors* [1913] AC 107, HL, Lord Macnaghten at 118; *NWL Ltd v Woods* [1979] 1 WLR 1294, HL, Lord Diplock at 1304; *Scher v Policyholders Protection Board (No 2)* [1993] 3 WLR 1030, HL, Lord Mustill at 1042.

8   *R v Bexley* [1993] 1 WLR 192, CA, unanimous decision at 201.

The fact that the application of the plain meaning rule 'may produce a crop of administrative difficulties' for the local council is not a ground for departing from the plain meaning of the words used in the statutory provision. In such a situation judges 'have simply to consider the Act'. As Mr Justice Donovan (later Lord Donovan) put it,

If the words were ambiguous, one would try to give them a construction which would avoid these difficulties, if a construction were reasonably open. But here the words are quite clear ... this court cannot modify the language simply to give the council administrative relief.[9]

Whilst the reader's own ideas of justice must not be substituted for those of Parliament, this does not mean that the reader's ideas of justice are always to be set aside. It is easy enough to say that an Act of Parliament must be read strictly as Parliament has written it if the meaning of the Act of Parliament itself is plain. If, however, a section has two or more possible meanings, the reader must choose between those meanings. In making that choice the Act should be so interpreted as 'to accord with the commonsense of a situation';[10] and, if one of those meanings gives an absurd or an unjust result, and the other does not, the reader should choose that meaning which avoids the absurdity or injustice:

where there are two meanings each adequately satisfying the language and great harshness is produced by one of them, that has legitimate influence in inclining the mind to the other ... It is more probable that the Legislature should have intended to use the word in that interpretation which least offends our sense of justice.[11]

Sometimes the giving of a literal meaning to the words in the Act can lead to so great an absurdity or so great an injustice that a court must give a more restricted meaning to it. Thus, as the Privy Council has pointed out,

the object of the construction of a statute being to ascertain the will of the legislature it may be presumed that neither injustice nor absurdity was intended. If therefore a literal interpretation would produce such a result and the language admits of an interpretation which would avoid it, then such an interpretation may be adopted.[12]

Paying regard to the intent of Parliament when enacting the ambiguous provision, or applying the purposive approach, may lead to rejection of the literal meaning of the statutory provision on the basis, as Lord Griffiths in the House of Lords put it, that 'I could not believe that Parliament intended ... a construction [that] ... will produce what I regard as such unfair and absurd results'.[13]

---

9 *Stepney Borough Council v Schneider* [1960] 58 LGR 202, DC at 205–06; see also *R v Havering Justices, ex p Smith* [1974] 3 All ER 484, DC, Bridge J (later Lord Bridge of Harwich) at 488.

10 *R v Reid (Philip)* [1973] 1 WLR 1283, CA, unanimous decision at 1289; see also *Groveside Properties Ltd v Westminster Medical School* (1983) 47 P & CR 507, CA, Fox LJ at 509; quoted with approval in *Graysim Holdings Ltd v P & O Property Holdings Ltd* [1994] 1 WLR 992, CA, Nourse LJ at 998.

11 *Simms v Registrar of Probates* [1900] AC 323, PC, Lord Hobhouse at 335.

12 *Mangin v Commissioner of Inland Revenue* [1971] AC 739, PC at 746; *Ishak v Thowfeek* [1968] 1 WLR 1718, PC at 1724–25.

13 *Pepper v Hart* [1993] AC 593, HL at 618.

In considering whether to accept an interpretation that does involve absurdity and injustice it may be important to bear in mind that words can have different meanings – even ordinary meanings. There can be the 'most usual meaning' and 'the less usual meaning', both of them falling within the concept of the ordinary meaning of a word. In those circumstances the court 'is entitled to ask whether giving the word its most usual meaning leads to an unreasonable result which would be avoided by taking the less usual meaning'.[14]

An interpretation to avoid injustice was adopted by Lord Simon of Glaisdale who said that 'The plain, primary and natural meaning of words used in a statute may be modified if that meaning produces injustice, to the extent necessary to obviate the injustice, provided that the words used are susceptible of such modification of meaning'.[15] Lord Wilberforce, also in the House of Lords, adopted an interpretation which he would otherwise have been 'very reluctant even to seek', doing so because the plain meaning of the words of the statute would have an effect which 'seems rather draconian'.[16] Lord Griffiths, whilst appreciating 'the strength of the linguistic argument' which would have applied the plain meaning rule, rejected it to avoid unfairness.[17]

The basis upon which the court acts is that

> The mere fact that the results of a statute may be unjust or absurd does not entitle this court to refuse to give it effect, but if there are two different interpretations of the words in an Act, the court will adopt that which is just, reasonable and sensible rather than that which is none of those things.[18]

and that arguments based upon uncertainty

> should only weigh with the court when there is patent ambiguity in the statutory provision which calls to be construed'.[19]

Moreover, a court has to be careful to ensure that the treatment it is giving to the particular provision is not such as to 'involve rewriting the Act ... not interpretation'.[20]

A warning about the rule

Although lawyers know this rule as the golden rule, in practice it has its dangers. The reader's own ideas of justice must not be substituted for the ideas upon which Parliament has acted. In fact, circumstances in which it can be said an Act is manifestly absurd or manifestly unjust (as distinct from operating

---

14 *Bristol-Myers Co v Beecham Group Ltd* [1974] AC 646, HL, Lord Reid at 665.

15 *W Devis & Sons Ltd v Atkins* [1977] AC 931, HL at 959.

16 *Walker v Leeds City Council* [1978] AC 403, HL at 417.

17 *Pepper v Hart* [1993] AC 593, HL, Lord Griffiths at 618.

18 *Holmes v Bradfield Rural District Council* [1949] 2 KB 1, DC, Finnemore J at 7.

19 *Plymouth Corpn v Secretary of State for the Environment* [1972] 1 WLR 1347, QBD, May J (later May LJ) at 1353.

20 *Bradford City Metropolitan Council v McMahon* [1994] 1 WLR 5, CA, Staughton LJ at 59.

harshly) rarely occur, although 'the greater the unfairness, the more it is to be expected that Parliament will make it clear if that is intended'.[21]

It must also be borne in mind that absurdity means something more than mere disagreement with what Parliament has done. Even if it can be shown that Parliament's policy is mistaken, nonetheless that policy must be enforced by the courts. For example, Parliament might adopt a policy of higher tariffs in defiance of the advice of economists, or a policy of rent control which harmed both landlords and tenants: this would not entitle a court to rewrite the Act. For a court to treat a provision as so absurd that the plain meaning rule has to be departed from it is not enough to point to absurdity in the colloquial sense: there must be 'absurdity or manifest injustice from an adherence to their literal meaning';[22] the 'court has nothing to do with the question whether the legislature has committed an absurdity'[23] and, if the only meaning the words have without rewriting the provision is 'peculiarly ridiculous and unjust', nevertheless 'it has been enacted by Parliament and it is our duty to enforce it'.[24]

21 *L'Office Cherifien des Phosphates v Yamashita-Shinnihon SS Co Ltd* [1994] 1 AC 486, Lord Mustill at 525 quoting and approving *Secretary of State for Social Services v Tunnicliffe* [1991] 2 All ER 712, CA, Staughton LJ at 724.

22 *Abley v Dale* (1851) 20 LJCP 233, Jarvis CJ at 235.

23 *R v Judge of City of London Court* [1892] 1 QB 273, Lord Esher MR at 290.

24 *Commissioner of Police of the Metropolis v Curran* [1976] 1 WLR 87, HL, Lord Salmon at 103–04.

CHAPTER 24

THE MISCHIEF RULE

The nature of the rule

For law students one of the best known rules to be used in reading an Act of Parliament is the mischief rule (or, as the law students know it, 'the rule in *Heydon's* Case'). This is a rule which is used to find the meaning of an Act when that meaning is obscure:

> It is very much part of the duty of the courts, in their task of statutory interpretation, to ascertain as best they can what was the mischief as conceived by Parliament for which a statutory remedy was being provided.[1]

What the reader of an Act of Parliament does in using the mischief rule is to consider how the law stood when the statute to be construed was passed, what the mischief was for which the old law did not provide, and the remedy provided by the statute to cure that mischief.[2]

To do this the reader must ask four questions:

1   What was the state of the law before the Act was passed?
2   What was the mischief or defect for which the law did not provide before the Act was passed?
3   What remedy has Parliament provided in the Act to cure the mischief or defect?
4   What is the true reason of the remedy?[3]

In applying the mischief rule to an ambiguous provision (and it can only be applied to an ambiguous provision) of an Act the court will do so to try to give such an interpretation to that ambiguous provision as will cure the mischief at which the Act is aimed: 'an Act must be construed ... so as to cure what mischief is being aimed at.'[4] The court will therefore try to find an interpretation that will prevent the mischief continuing but without exposing to criminal liability persons who do not fall within the mischief. Whether or not a court can achieve such a result will, of course, depend upon how intractable the ambiguous provision of the Act proves to be.

The state of the law before the Act was passed

In finding out what the state of the law was before the Act was passed the reader is not limited to the state of the Acts of Parliament as they then existed. Acts of Parliament are an important part of the law, but they are only part of it.

---

1   *Associated Newspapers Group Ltd v Fleming* [1973] AC 628, HL, Lord Simon of Glaisdale at 646.
2   *Re Mayfair Property Co* [1898] 2 Ch 28, CA, Lord Lindley MR at 35.
3   *Heydon's Case* (1584) 3 Co Rep 7; 76 ER 637. See also *Black-Clawson International Ltd v Papierwerke Waldhof-Aschaffenburg AG* [1975] AC 591, HL, Viscount Dilhorne at 621.
4   *C & J Clarke Ltd v Inland Revenue Commissioners* [1973] 1 WLR 905, Megary J (later Megarry V-C) at 912.

A great deal of the law is not to be found in Acts of Parliament at all. Much of it is to be found in what is known as subordinate legislation – the mass of statutory instruments, rules, regulations, bylaws, ordinances, proclamations and orders made not by Parliament itself but by somebody acting under the authority of an Act of Parliament. However, the greatest bulk of the law is to be found not in Acts of Parliament and not in subordinate legislation but in those fundamental principles of law which are known to the lawyers as the 'common law' and which are to be found in the judgments given by judges of superior courts[5] in deciding the cases before them. The person who seeks to use the mischief rule in reading an Act of Parliament must take the common law into account just as much as the statute law and the subordinate legislation.[6]

The mischief or defect

It sometimes happens that the Act of Parliament itself sets out the mischief or defect that it seeks to overcome. Frequently, however, the mischief or defect is not set out expressly in the Act and the reader has to spell out the mischief by seeking out the purpose of the statutory provision,[7] and this approach may be assisted by resort to extrinsic materials.[8]

Ascertaining the mischief or defect

If the statute does not set out the mischief or defect that it seeks to overcome, it is permissible *in order to find that mischief or defect* to look at contemporaneous circumstances:

> In interpreting an Act of Parliament you are entitled, and in many cases bound, to look to the state of the law at the date of the passing of the Act: not only the common law but the laws that then stood under previous statutes, in order to properly interpret the statute in question.[9]

It is also permissible to use such material as the report of a royal commission which led to the enactment of that statute:[10]

> It is legitimate to look at [such a] report ... so as to see what was the mischief at which the Act was directed. You can get the facts and surrounding circumstances from the report, so as to see the background against which the legislation was enacted. This is always a great help in interpreting it.[11]

Of course, at common law the report of the royal commission cannot be looked at to find *the meaning of the words* in the statute. It can be looked at

---

5   The superior courts are the High Court of Justice, the Court of Appeal, the House of Lords and the Privy Council.

6   *Craies on Statute Law* (7th edn by Edgar, SGG Sweet & Maxwell, London, 1971) 96.

7   See Chapter 25.

8   See Chapters 26 and 27.

9   *Macmillan v Dent* [1907] 1 Ch 107, CA, Fletcher Moulton LJ at 120.

10 *Black-Clawson International Ltd v Papierwerke Waldhof-Aschaffenburg AG* [1975] AC 591, HL, Lord Reid at 614–15.

11 *Letang v Cooper* [1965] 1 QB 232, CA, Lord Denning MR at 240; see also *Murray v Director of Public Prosecutions* [1994] 1 WLR 1, HL, Lord Slynn of Hadley at 10.

not to ascertain the intention of the words used in the subsequent Act but because ... no more accurate source of information as to what was the evil or defect which the Act of Parliament ... was intended to remedy could be imagined.[12]

Hansard, which is the official record of the proceedings in Parliament, can be used at common law to ascertain the mischief or defect but the use of *Hansard* deserves a chapter of its own and is considered in Chapter 26.

Whatever material is used to find the mischief at which the Act is aimed, even if the material does reveal the legislative purpose, there will continue to be boundaries beyond which the words used will not stretch even where it is known that they were intended to do so.

The remedy Parliament has appointed

The question as to what remedy Parliament has appointed is of course to be answered from the Act itself.

The reason for the remedy

In the first part of this chapter, four questions are set out as the questions that must be asked in order to apply the mischief rule. The answer to the fourth of those questions (what is the true reason of the remedy?) should become plain once answers to the first three questions have been found, but it must be remembered that in answering that question what has to be found is not the reader's view, and not the view of the court, as to what is the appropriate remedy:

In fact, Parliament may not have taken the same view of what is a mischief, may have decided as a matter of policy not to legislate for a legal remedy or may simply have failed to realise that the situation could ever arise.[13]

Applying the rule

In order to apply the mischief rule it is not enough merely to ask and to answer the four questions. Having found the reason of the remedy the reader of an Act should then be able to find that meaning which best cures the mischief and advances the remedy while at the same time not exposing to unnecessary liability persons not intended to be covered by the Act.

The mischief cannot limit the meaning of plain words

Like all the other rules considered in this book the mischief rule cannot be used to limit the meaning of words when that meaning is plain. If Parliament chooses to legislate more widely than the mischief requires, effect must be given to the statute unlimited by the mischief:

---

12 *Dullewe v Dullewe* [1969] AC 313, PC at 320.

13 *Carrington v Term-a-Stor* [1983] 1 WLR 138, CA, Sir John Donaldson MR (later Lord Donaldson of Lymington MR) at 142.

If the natural and ordinary meaning of the words is clear, I must give effect to them, even if I find their effect goes beyond what was needed to deal with the mischief.[14]

---

14 *Rance v Mid-Downs Health Authority* [1991] 1 QB 587, QBD, Brooke J at 617.

CHAPTER 25

THE PURPOSE OF THE ACT OF PARLIAMENT

A section specifying the purposes of the Act

Some recent Acts contain a section known as a statement of principle and which sets out the purpose or purposes of that legislation. Such a statement of principle section is considered in Chapter 11. The present chapter considers the method of interpretation by reference to the purpose of the Act whether or not there is a statement of principle section in the Act.

The Act is to be interpreted according to its object and intent

There is 'a growing tendency ... towards a purposive construction of statutes at all events if they do not deal with penal or revenue matters',[1] or vested rights.[2] The proper interpretation of an Act of Parliament is not a mere mechanical exercise. What the court is endeavouring to do in interpreting the statute is to give effect to the object and intent of Parliament in enacting that statute: 'It is the duty of a court so to interpret an Act of Parliament as to give effect to its intention.'[3] As Lord Widgery CJ delivering the unanimous reasons of the Court of Appeal said, 'We must make the statutory language work and make it sensible to fulfil what we believe to be the purpose of Parliament'.[4] As Lord Radcliffe has expressed it, 'every statute is to be expounded according to its manifest and express intention'.[5] The task

> is not to speculate on the actual states of mind of draftsmen or legislators: it is to interpret [the] section, so far as its language will permit, in a way which makes the best sense of what 'the judge [considers] to have been the purpose of ... the provisions'.[6]

The parliamentary intent should be effectuated, not defeated

Language, although the best available means of communicating an intention, has its difficulties because one word can have different meanings and different shades of meaning. In statutes there is often the added problem of complexity. Nevertheless, if the intention of the legislature can be discovered by the court

---

1   *R v Registrar-General, ex p Smith* [1991] 2 QB 393, CA, Staughton LJ at 404; see also *Carter v Bradbeer* [1975] 1 WLR 1204, HL, Lord Diplock at 1206–07.

2   *Chilton v Telford Development Corpn* [1987] 1 WLR 872, Purchas LJ at 878.

3   *Ealing London Borough Council v Race Relations Board* [1972] AC 342, HL, Lord Simon of Glaisdale at 360–61 and 367–68; *Tarr v Tarr* [1973] AC 254, HL at 268.

4   *R v Curran* [1975] 1 WLR 876, CA at 881; affd under the name of *Commissioner of Police for the Metropolis v Curran* [1976] 1 WLR 87, HL.

5   *Attorney General (Canada) v Hallet & Carey Ltd* [1952] AC 427, PC at 449.

6   *Smith v Schofield* [1990] 1 WLR 1447, Ch D at 1452.

from the words that have been used, it is the duty of the court to give effect to that intention and not to defeat it. Enunciating that principle Lord Justice Megaw said that 'An Act of Parliament ... must be construed so as to effectuate the intention of the makers of the Act and not to defeat it',[7] or as Megarry J (later Megarry V-C) put it, 'when an expression in a statute is fairly open to two constructions the court will adopt the construction which will effectuate the purpose of the Act and not the one which would stultify or lame it'.[8]

Thus an interpretation which would have the effect that the parliamentary purpose of attacking drug trafficking 'would be ... frustrated' was rejected because 'such a result cannot possibly have been intended'.[9]

The meaning of 'intention' in this context

What Parliament intended to achieve by enacting the particular statute may not necessarily be ascertainable from the words that Parliament has used. It is not unknown for people to say one thing and to mean another. The courts cannot ask Parliament what its intention was: they have to find that intention from the words that Parliament has employed, 'inferred from a study of the statutory context',[10] or from reports of commissions or other materials which Parliament has expressly authorised to be used or the common law as now understood allows to be employed.[11] As Lord Simon of Glaisdale has pointed out:

> in the construction of all written instruments including statutes, what the court is concerned to ascertain is, not what the promulgators of the instruments meant to say, but the meaning of what they have said. It is in this sense that 'intention' is used as a term of art in the construction of documents.[12]

In a later case that same distinguished judge said:

> The final task of construction is still, as always, to ascertain the meaning of what the draftsman has said, rather than to ascertain what the draftsman meant to say. But if the draftsmanship is correct these should coincide.[13]

It is to ascertain that intention that the various rules of statutory interpretation which are considered in this book have been evolved by the courts. If it were not for those rules, there could be confusion from finding a number of different or varying intentions held by a number of Members of Parliament all of whom voted in favour of the enactment of the statute – a matter well expressed by Lord Diplock when he said:

> Leaving aside the rare phenomenon in modern times of a genuine Private Member's Bill, what statutes are meant to give effect to is the intention of the

7   *Lucy v WT Henleys Telegraph Works Ltd* [1970] 1 QB 393, CA at 409.

8   *In re 'Fairview', Church Street, Bromyard* [1974] 1 WLR 579 at 582.

9   *R v Southwark Crown Court, ex p Customs and Excise Commissioners* [1990] 1 QB 650, DC unanimous decision at 662; see also *W Devis & Sons Ltd v Atkins* [1977] AC 931, HL, Viscount Dilhorne at 958.

10 *Howard v Borneman (No 2)* [1975] Ch 201, CA, Scarman LJ at 211; affd, [1976] AC 301, HL.

11 See Chapters 26 and 27.

12 *Farrell v Alexander* [1977] AC 59, HL at 81; see also *Black-Clawson International Ltd v Papierwerke Waldhof-Aschaffenburg AG* [1975] AC 591, HL, Lord Reid at 613.

13 *Stock v Frank Jones (Tipton) Ltd* [1978] 1 WLR 231, HL at 236.

government in power at the time that they are passed and as respects such matters of detail as are usually the subject of interstitial law making by the judges, the intention of the government department that was responsible for the promotion of the Bill. If the language to be construed is not clear and unambiguous one may be pretty sure that those members of the legislature who voted in favour of the Bill had no common intention one way or the other as to how the unperceived obscurity or ambiguity ought to be resolved.[14]

Interpretation by reference to the purpose of an Act is comparatively recent. It is still in the process of development. The judges themselves appear to be divided in opinion as to the basis of this purposive approach: Lord Reid took the view that the purposive approach is separate and distinct from the mischief rule[15] whilst Lord Roskill[16] and Lord Donaldson of Lymington MR[17] treated the purposive approach and the mischief rule as one and the same. The distinction is an important one: if Lord Roskill's view is the view that is ultimately accepted by the courts, royal commission reports[18] and other material outside the Act itself could be looked at to find the purpose as well as the mischief whereas on Lord Reid's view they could not.[19]

When the purposive approach is unavailable

There is a real risk that the reader of legislation may be led astray by the purposive approach. Whilst, as we have seen, 'Where there is an ambiguity ... the court will strive to give a purposive construction',[20] applying that approach to an unambiguous provision would be wrong. Lord Donaldson of Lymington MR has observed that 'If an Act of Parliament is unambiguous ... the policy underlying it may not be directly relevant'.[21] Lord Lowry has gone further and held that

> there is no room for a purposive construction if the words to be construed will not bear the interpretation sought to be put upon them and it must always be borne in mind that the art of statutory interpretation can be applied only when the provision to be interpreted is ambiguous.[22]

---

14 In an address in 1977 to the Fifth Commonwealth Law Conference, (1977) 26 *Town Planning and Local Government Guide*, p 572, para 2873.

15 *Black-Clawson International Ltd v Papierwerke Waldhof-Aschaffenburg AG* [1975] AC 591, HL at 613.

16 *Anderton v Ryan* [1985] 2 WLR 968, HL at 973.

17 *Attorney-General v Jones* [1990] 1 WLR 859, CA at 862.

18 Unless Lord Roskill's view is ultimately accepted the common law does not provide for the intention of Parliament to be sought by reference to committee reports or reports of royal commissions which preceded the passing of the Bill: *Black-Clawson International Ltd v Papierwerke Waldhof-Aschaffenburg AG* [1975] AC 591, HL.

19 *Hansard*, however, can now be used to ascertain the purpose of the legislation: *Pepper v Hart* [1993] AC 593, HL. See Chapter 26.

20 *Re Lonrho (No 2)* [1990] Ch 695, Ch D, Peter Gibson J at 706.

21 *Post Office v Union of Communication Workers* [1990] 1 WLR 981, CA, Lord Donaldson of Lymington MR at 989.

22 *R v Inland Revenue Commissioners, ex p Woolwich Equitable Building Society* [1990] 1 WLR 1400, HL at 1428.

and Sir Nicholas Browne-Wilkinson V-C (now Lord Browne-Wilkinson) held that

> however desirable it may be to construe the Act in a way calculated to carry out the parliamentary purpose, it is not legitimate to distort the meaning of the words Parliament has chosen to use in order to achieve that result. Only if the words used by Parliament are fairly capable of bearing more than one meaning is it legitimate to adopt the meaning which gives effect to, rather than frustrates, the statutory purpose.[23]

It

> is no function of a judge to add to the means which Parliament has enacted in derogation of rights which citizens previously enjoyed at common law, because he thinks that the particular case in which he has to apply the Act demonstrates that those means are not adequate to achieve what he conceives to be the policy of the Act.
>
> To do so is not to carry out the purpose of Parliament but to usurp its functions. The choice of means is itself part of the Parliamentary choice of policy. It represents the price, by way of deprivation of freedom to do or not to do as they wish, which Parliament is prepared to exact from individual citizens to promote those objects to which the Act is directed. To raise the price is to change the policy – not to give effect to it.
>
> If the policy is to be changed it is for Parliament not the courts to change it.[24]

Finding the intention by necessary implication

The very fact that the courts have had to evolve special rules for the interpretation of statutes shows that Parliament does not always use plain words to express its intention. When the words themselves fail to convey the intention it may be necessary for the court to ascertain that intention by necessary implication from the words that Parliament has used or from other material that Parliament has authorised to be used for that purpose. Understandably, the courts are reluctant to find an intention by mere implication. They will not normally make such an implication if it would result in a person being imprisoned or detained or being subjected to a fine or other penalty.[25]

> We are, as always trying to find the intention of the legislature. Where, taking into account the surrounding circumstances and the likely consequences of the various possible constructions, there can be any doubt at all about that intention, we must where penalties are involved, require that the intention shall clearly appear from the words of the enactment construed in light of those matters. But if we can say that those matters show that a particular result must certainly have been intended, we would, I think, be stultifying the underlying principle if we required more than that the statutory provisions are reasonably capable of an interpretation carrying out that intention.[26]

---

23 *Bristol Airport plc v Powdrill* [1990] 1 Ch 744, CA, Sir Nicholas Browne-Wilkinson V-C (later Lord Browne-Wilkinson) at 759.

24 *Director of Public Prosecutions v Bhagwan* [1972] AC 60, HL, Lord Diplock at 82.

25 *Kennedy v Spratt* [1972] AC 83, HL, Lord Reid at 89.

26 *Kennedy v Spratt* [1972] AC 83, HL, Lord Reid at 89.

That principle is not limited to the interpretation of penal provisions. Whatever category the legislation being interpreted falls into, 'If any clear indication of Parliament's intention is to be found, effect must be given to it'.[27]It should also be remembered that there are statutes the purpose of which cannot be ascertained by any judicial interpretation. As Sir Thomas Bingham MR said in the *Yamashita* case, 'I find none'.[28]

Caution must be exercised in interpreting by intention

People see the same thing in different ways, approaching it from a different basis. This is particularly so in seeking an intention. The answer to the question 'What was Parliament's intention?' can readily be influenced by political or other factors in the seeker's mind. If those factors were allowed to determine the meaning of the Act, two totally different results could be achieved depending upon whether the person interpreting the Act was a conservationist on the one hand or someone concerned with development on the other. It must therefore be remembered that 'The final task of construction is still, as always, to ascertain the meaning of what the draftsman has said, rather than to ascertain what the draftsman meant to say'[29] and that

> dislike of the effect of a statute has never been an accepted reason for departing from its plain language. Holt CJ said nearly three centuries ago '... an Act of Parliament can do no wrong, though it may do several things that look pretty odd'.[30] ... Accordingly, even if one regarded the policy implicit in [the Act] as open to criticism, [if] the statutory language is clear beyond doubt [it] must prevail.[31]

Intention is an unruly horse to ride

> The saying that it is the function of the courts to ascertain the will or intention of Parliament is often enough repeated, so often indeed as to have become an incantation. If too often or unreflectingly stated, it leads to neglect of the important element of judicial construction; an element not confined to a mechanical analysis of today's words, but, if this task is to be properly done, related to such matters as intelligibility to the citizen, constitutional propriety, considerations of history, comity of nations, reasonable and non-retroactive effect and, no doubt, in some contexts, to social needs.[32]

27 *L'Office Cherifien des Phosphates v Yamashita-Shinnihon SS Co Ltd* [1993] 3 WLR 266, CA, Sir Thomas Bingham MR at 275.

28 *L'Office Cherifien des Phosphates v Yamashita-Shinnihon SS Co Ltd* [1993] 3 WLR 266, CA, Sir Thomas Bingham MR at 275.

29 *Stock v Frank Jones (Tipton) Ltd* [1978] 1 WLR 231, HL, Lord Simon of Glaisdale at 236.

30 *City of London v Wood* (1701) 12 Mod Rep 669 at 687–688; 88 ER 1592, at 1602.

31 *Stock v Frank Jones (Tipton) Ltd* [1978] 1 WLR 231, HL, Lord Edmund-Davies at 238.

32 *Black-Clawson International v Papierwerke Waldhof-Aschaffenburg AG* [1975] AC 591, HL, Lord Wilberforce at 629–630.

CHAPTER 26

HANSARD

The nature of *Hansard*

What Members of Parliament say in the course of the proceedings in Parliament is recorded at the time and is printed as a permanent record. This record is known as *Hansard*. It takes its name from Mr Hansard, who was the compiler of this record in England for a long period of time.

The limited use of *Hansard* the common law previously allowed for in the interpretation of an Act of Parliament

The traditional view adopted by the courts was that the circumstances in which the common law would allow a judge to look at *Hansard* in the process of ascertaining the meaning of the Act of Parliament were limited. The second reading speech[1] of the minister who introduced the Bill into Parliament could be looked at, but only as evidence of the mischief aimed at by the Act.

Why the common law used to limit the use of *Hansard* to find the meaning of an Act of Parliament

It used to be a basic rule of the common law for the reading of an Act of Parliament that the reader must not turn to *Hansard* to find out directly what the Act means as distinct from finding out the mischief the Act was designed to cure.[2] The rule allowed the minister's speech in introducing the Bill for the Act to be used, and to be used only, to ascertain that mischief. It is easy to justify that very limited use of *Hansard*. Before it becomes an Act of Parliament every Bill must receive three readings in each House of Parliament.[3] That does not mean, however, that every Member of Parliament can state his or her views about the Bill. In fact, by far the majority of Members of Parliament would be unlikely to speak upon any particular Bill before Parliament. The views stated by those Members of Parliament who do speak upon the particular Bill might be quite different to the views of the other Members who vote in favour of the Bill. One could not say with any certainty that the views expressed by any particular Member of Parliament were the views of Parliament as a whole. It has been pointed out that 'the questions which give rise to debate are rarely those which

---

1   It is the Minister's speech on the second reading of the Bill in Parliament that is referred to (he or she makes no speech on the first and third readings: the debate takes place on the second reading).

2   As Phillips J has said, 'It is an error to suppose that ministerial intentions are the equivalent of enacted legislation': *Hereford and Worcester County Council v Craske* (1976) 75 LGR 174, at 177. The minister's speech reflects what the department intended the legislation to achieve, but what the legislation actually achieves depends upon the proper interpretation of the words of the Act as passed by Parliament. As to the mischief rule, see above, Chapter 24.

3   See Chapter 1.

later have to be decided by the courts'.[4] The courts have therefore repeatedly held that the reader of an Act of Parliament must not turn to *Hansard* to find out what the Act means.[5] However, the common law rule has been overturned by the House of Lords in a decision in which it allowed recourse to be made to *Hansard* not only for ascertaining the mischief at which the Act is aimed but for purposes of interpretation generally.[6]

The changed common law rule allowing the use of *Hansard* to interpret an Act

The judges comprising the House of Lords in its judicial capacity have reversed what was the common law rule in relation to *Hansard*. They have decided that *Hansard* can be looked at not only for ascertaining the mischief the legislation is intended to meet but also for the purpose of interpretation of an ambiguous provision in the statute to find out its meaning. Lord Browne-Wilkinson, in reasons for judgement with which three of the other Law Lords hearing the matter agreed, held that 'reference to parliamentary material should be permitted as an aid to the construction of legislation which is ambiguous or obscure or the literal meaning of which leads to an absurdity'. As to that, 'Even in such cases references in court to Parliamentary material should only be permitted where such material clearly discloses the mischief aimed at or the legislative intention lying behind the ambiguous or obscure words'.[7]

The decision to allow the use of *Hansard* as an aid to interpreting a statute was firm in relation to statements made by the relevant minister within the Parliament, but as to statements made by Members of Parliament other than the minister His Lordship's approach was tentative. He said that 'I cannot foresee that any statement other than the statement of the minister or other promoter of the Bill is likely to meet [the] criteria'.[8] His Lordship concluded that 'the exclusionary rule should be relaxed so as to permit reference to Parliamentary materials where (a) legislation is ambiguous or obscure, or leads to an absurdity; (b) the material relied upon consists of one or more statements by a minister or other promoter of the Bill together if necessary with such other Parliamentary material as is necessary to understand such statements and their effect; (c) the statements relied upon are clear'.[9] It is significant that the House of Lords has

---

4   *Black-Clawson International Ltd v Papierwerke Waldhof-Aschaffenburg AG* [1975] AC 591, HL, Lord Reid at 614.

5   *Millar v Taylor* (1769) 4 Burr 2303 at 2332; 98 ER 201 at 217; *South Eastern Rly Co v Rly Commissioners* (1881) 50 LJKB 201 at 203; *Lumsden v Inland Revenue Commissioners* [1914] AC 877, HL at 908; *Assam Rlys & Trading Co v Inland Revenue Commissioners* [1935] AC 455, HL at 438.

6   *Pepper v Hart* [1993] AC 593, HL, Lord Browne-Wilkinson at 634. See also *Melluish v BMI (No 3) Ltd* [1995] STC 964. It was decided in *Three Rivers District Council v Bank of England (No 2)*, (1995) Independent, 22 December, QBD that the court was entitled to admit in evidence Parliamentary materials such as speeches by ministers where the purpose or object of the statute as a whole was in issue.

7   *Pepper v Hart* [1993] AC 593, HL, Lord Browne-Wilkinson at 634.

8   *Pepper v Hart* [1993] AC 593, HL, Lord Browne-Wilkinson at 634.

9   *Pepper v Hart* [1993] AC 593, HL, Lord Browne-Wilkinson at 634.

contemplated the possibility of further relaxation of the old common law rule. Not only did Lord Browne-Wilkinson use the words 'as at present advised'[10] but in stating his criteria he concluded that 'further than this, I would not *at present go*'.[11]

In *Pepper v Hart* Lord Browne-Wilkinson contemplated that the speech of a proposer of a Bill could be used to interpret the resulting Act.[12] A year later the House of Lords did indeed consider the speech made by the proposer of the Bill and thereby had regard to committee recommendations referred to by the proposer as a guide to interpretation of the Act.[13] The House of Lords found Parliamentary material '[to be] decisive of a statutory ambiguity' and held the cases to which we have referred to be illustrating 'how useful the relaxation of the former exclusionary rule may be in avoiding unnecessary litigation'.[14]

The criterion established in *Pepper v Hart* that the minister's statement in Parliament could only be used if it was clear, is an important limitation that has resulted in the exclusion of a minister's speech from consideration because it lacked 'the clarity for which *Pepper v Hart* requires us to search'.[15]

We sound the warning that the mere fact that it is now possible to look at *Hansard* to find the meaning of words in the Act does not mean that *Hansard* will be of the slightest assistance in relation to the particular problem which the reader of a statute wishes to solve.[16] For example, the material in *Hansard* may not relate to the particular section at all, or may relate to an aspect of that section which is not the one being considered by the court in the particular case.

10 *Pepper v Hart* [1993] AC 593, HL, Lord Browne-Wilkinson at 634.
11 *Pepper v Hart* [1993] AC 593, HL, Lord Browne-Wilkinson at 634.
12 *Pepper v Hart* [1993] AC 593, HL at 634 and 640.
13 *Stubbings v Webb* [1993] AC 498, HL, unanimous decision at 507.
14 *Chief Adjudication Officer v Foster* [1993] AC 754, HL, unanimous decision at 772.
15 *Doncaster Borough Council v Secretary of State for the Environment* (1992) 91 LGR 459, CA, Simon Brown LJ at 478.
16 *Mendip District Council v Glastonbury Festivals Ltd* [1993] 91 LGR 447, DC at 456.

CHAPTER 27

USING OTHER MATERIAL FROM OUTSIDE AN ACT TO UNDERSTAND THE MEANING OF THAT ACT

Reports by law reform commissions

Law reform commission reports can lead to new legislation. They identify matters which the law needs to cover or which the existing law does not cover adequately, and they may make recommendations as to the form which new legislation should take. At common law, the courts are entitled to look at any relevant report of a law reform commission in order to discover the previous state of the law and the mischief requiring remedy as at the time when legislation consequent upon that report was enacted.[1] As we have seen,[2] the House of Lords has freed the use of *Hansard* from some at least of its traditional restrictions, and there are indications that the lifting of restrictions may apply in future to commissions' reports.[3]

Reports by royal commissions and boards or committees of inquiry

Royal commission and board or committee of inquiry reports can result in Parliament taking legislative action. Should this be so, the relevant report may be looked at by the judges in order to discover the mischief at which the subsequent legislation was aimed, and the House of Lords has now decided unanimously, that a committee report can be looked at if *Hansard* shows an 'express intention' to give effect to it.[4]

Explanations by government departments

When an Act has been passed by Parliament the government department which is responsible for enforcing the Act sometimes sends out a circular explaining what the department believes the Act to mean. The fact that the circular is issued by the department does not make it part of the Act itself. The basic rule is that what has to be found is the meaning of the Act itself, not what the department thinks the Act does mean or should mean. In finding the meaning of the Act, therefore, the courts did not look at the departmental circular:[5]

> the intention of the Home Office ... and the intention of Parliament are two different things. The latter, at any rate in the majority of cases, is to be ascertained only from the relevant legislation, be it statute or delegated

---

1 See, for example, *Murray v Director of Public Prosecutions* [1994] 1 WLR 1, HL, Lord Slynn of Hadley at 10.

2 See Chapter 26.

3 *Murray v Director of Public Prosecutions* [1994] 1 WLR 1, HL, Lord Mustill at 3.

4 *Stubbings v Webb* [1993] AC 498, HL, unanimous decision at 507.

5 *London County Council v Central Land Board* [1959] Ch 386, CA.

legislation. How the Home Office interpreted or sought to administer that legislation is irrelevant.'[6]

On the other hand, Lord Wilberforce, although accepting that 'as an interpretation of the Act ... under which it was issued, the [departmental] circular has no legal status' nevertheless held that 'it acquired vitality and strength when, through the years, it passed ... into planning practice and textbooks'.[7]

Planning policy guidelines

The Department of Environment issues planning policy guidelines (or, as they are commonly referred to, PPGs). It has been held of them that courts 'cannot allow our own view of the law to be affected by these notes of guidance'[8] and that the guidelines 'cannot affect us in our interpretation of powers'.[9]

Subordinate legislation

The use of subordinate legislation (that is, statutory instruments, bylaws, regulations, planning schemes and all other forms of legislation made by government, semi-government and local government bodies under a power conferred on them by Parliament) to assist in the interpretation of an Act of Parliament is considered in Chapter 43.

Treaties and conventions

The use which can be made of international treaties and conventions in interpreting Acts enacted to give effect to those treaties and conventions is considered in Chapter 44.

---

6   *Congreve v Home Office* [1976] QB 629, CA, Roskill LJ (later Lord Roskill) at 658.

7   *Coleshill and District Investment Co Ltd v Minister of Housing and Local Government* [1969] 1 WLR 746, HL at 765.

8   *Macree v Tower Hamlets London Borough Council* (1991) 90 LGR 137 at 143–44.

9   *Macree v Tower Hamlets London Borough Council* (1991) 90 LGR 137 at 143.

CHAPTER 28

THE ACT MUST BE READ AS A WHOLE

Words must be read in the light of the section as a whole

Words must be read in their context. In finding the right meaning to give to an Act of Parliament the reader must give close attention to the meaning of each word that is used. This will often involve turning to the judicial dictionaries or to the standard dictionaries such as the *Oxford English Dictionary* to find the meanings to be given to individual words in the section. This attention to individual words, necessary as it is, can cause the reader to lose sight of the fact that those words are only part of the whole. What is really sought is not the meaning of individual words but the meaning of the Act as a whole. It would be easy to assign a correct meaning to each word individually and yet have a meaning for the section as a whole that is not the true meaning of that section. The pianist who has to play a chord does not get the proper result by playing each of the notes in that chord separately – they must be played together. So, too, the reader of an Act of Parliament must consider all the words of the section together.

The true meaning of a word in a section can in fact only be found by considering that word in the context of the section in which it stands: 'words must ... be construed in the context of, rather than in isolation from, the words which follow in that subsection'.[1] The word 'forthwith' is a good example. There are some sections in which 'forthwith' must be read as meaning 'immediately'.[2] There are other sections in which 'forthwith' does not mean immediately but instead means only 'as soon as practicable'[3] having regard to the circumstances of the case and the subject matter.[4]

In some cases the reading of the word in the light of its context may give a wider meaning than it would have had if read on its own, and in other cases the meaning of the word when read in its context may be narrower than it would otherwise have been:

> Doubtless [a] word may be capable of slightly different meanings given the context in which it is used in any particular statute. In other words in interpreting the word, regard must be paid to the context in which it appears.[5]

---

1   *Sheffield Development Corpn v Glossop Sectional Buildings Ltd* [1994] 1 WLR 1676, CA, Rose LJ at 1683.

2   See, for example, *R v Berkshire Justices* (1879) 4 QBD 469.

3   *Saneen v Abeyewickrema* [1963] 2 WLR 1120, PC.

4   *Re Southam, ex p Lamb* (1881) 19 Ch D 169, CA.

5   *Wychavon District Council v National Rivers Authority* [1993] 1 WLR 125, DC, Watkins LJ at 133.

A section must be read in the light of the Act as a whole

If it is necessary to read words in the light of the section as a whole, it is equally necessary to read the section in the light of the Act as a whole. 'It is a commonplace that the meaning of the provision is to be gathered from the statute as a whole'.[6] As Lord Lowry has held, 'an expression which is *prima facie* neutral must be looked at in both its immediate and its more remote context'.[7] When it is said that words must be read in their context, that context is not limited to the particular section or subsection but extends to the whole of the Act:

> To arrive at the true meaning of any particular phrase in a statute, that particular phrase is not to be viewed, detached from its context in the statute, it is to be viewed in connection with its whole context.[8]

In the complex task of wresting the true construction of an Act it cannot be compartmentalised and scrutinised molecularly: 'The office of a good compositor of an Act of Parliament is to make construction of all the parts together and not of one part only by itself.'[9]

If a section is capable of two meanings, a consideration of that section in the context of the Act in which it appears may show which of the two meanings is to be given to that section. As has been held by the Court of Appeal,

> If the words of one section are ambiguous and one construction would make the provisions of great importance, whereas another would reduce them to triviality, I consider it legitimate to look at other sections or subsections as throwing light on how much importance Parliament attached to the matter.[10]

If the Act is one which is divided into parts, the context to be looked at is not just the part in which the particular section appears: it is the Act as a whole. An example is afforded by the judicial consideration of s 3(1) Health and Safety at Work etc Act 1974 (United Kingdom), the Court of Appeal holding that

> It is ... that the broad purpose of this part of the legislation was preventive. Section 3 must, therefore, not be read in isolation. The powers set out in sections 20, 21 and 22 are an important contextual aid to the construction of section 3(1).[11]

An expression wherever used in a statute should be accorded a consistent meaning unless the context clearly indicates a contrary intention. The basic approach in this regard is that 'where the draftsman uses the same word or phrase in similar contexts, he must be presumed to intend it in each case to bear the same meaning'.[12] However, 'The same words used in different sections or

---

6   *Daymond v South West Water Authority* [1976] AC 609, HL, Lord Kilbrandon at 651.

7   *Hampson v Department of Education & Science* [1991] 1 AC 171, HL at 181.

8   *Brett v Brett* (1826) 3 Add 210; 162 ER 456; affd (1872) 3 Russ 437 (note).

9   *Lincoln College's case* (1595) 3 Co Rep 58b; 76 ER 764; *Mills v Funnell* (1824) 2 B & C 988; 107 ER 616; *R v North Metropolitan Rly Co* (1856) 27 LTOS 156.

10 *Milford Haven Conservancy Board v Inland Revenue Commissioners* [1976] 1 WLR 817, CA, Cairns LJ at 825.

11 *R v Board of Trustees of the Science Museum* [1993] 1 WLR 1171, CA, unanimous decision at 1177.

12 *Farrell v Alexander* [1977] AC 59, HL, Lord Simon of Glaisdale at 85.

subsections of the same Act may in some cases have different meanings'.[13] However, in the absence of the context precluding it

'It is no doubt correct that if you find the same word appearing in two places in a statute or in several statutes covering the same subject matter, it ought in the absence of a controlling context to be given the same meaning.'[14]

Limits to the use of this rule

The rule that an Act of Parliament is to be read as a whole must not be used to destroy the clear meaning of a part of the Act that is being read:

No rule of construction can require that when the words of one part of a statute convey a clear meaning it shall be necessary to introduce another part of a statute for the purpose of controlling or diminishing the efficacy of the first part.[15]

The principle that is the basis of this rule is clear. That principle is that

Every clause of a statute should be construed with reference to the context and other clauses in the Act, so as, as far as possible, to make a consistent enactment of the whole statute or series of statutes relating to the subject matter.[16]

Care must, however, be taken in using this rule. As Salmon LJ (later Lord Salmon) has pointed out, 'It is not ... an invariable practice that the Courts must give it the same meaning'.[17] Care is particularly necessary when reading an Act which is a consolidating Act consolidating an earlier Act with a large number of Acts amending that earlier Act. In the case of an Act of Parliament of that nature, the drafting is far less likely to be consistent, and a search for consistency could lead the reader away from the real meaning of the section:

It is no doubt true that every Act should be read as a whole but that is, I think, because one assumes that in drafting one clause of a Bill the draftsman had in mind the language and substance of other clauses, and attributes to the Parliament a comprehension of the whole Act. But where ... quite incongruous provisions are lumped together and it is impossible to suppose that anyone, draftsman or Parliament, ever considered one of these sections in light of another, I think that it would be just as misleading to base conclusions on the different language of disparate sections as it is to base conclusions on the different language of sections in different Acts.[18]

---

13 *Director of Public Prosecutions v Turner* [1974] AC 357, HL, Lord Reid at 365. See also *Martin v Lowry* [1926] 1 KB 550 where Atkin LJ (later Lord Atkin) at 561 held that 'if one could adopt as a rigid canon of construction an assumption that in any statute the same word is always used for the same meaning, one's task would perhaps be easier: but it is plain that the assumption is ill-founded ... we must have regard to the context'.

14 *Lee-Verhulst (Investments) Ltd v Harwood Trust* [1973] 1 QB 204, CA, Stamp LJ at 218.

15 *Warburton v Loveland* (1831) 2 D & Cl 489, at 500; 6 ER 809 at 813.

16 *Canada Sugar Refining Co v The Queen* [1898] AC 735, PC, Lord Davey at 741. As to the interpretation when drafting precludes the giving of a consistent meaning see Chapter 36.

17 *Stott v West Yorkshire Road Car Co Ltd* [1971] 2 QB 651, CA at 658.

18 *Inland Revenue Commissioners v Hinchy* [1960] AC 748, HL, Lord Reid at 766.

This follows from the fact that a consolidating Act takes provisions drafted at different times and appearing in different Acts and places them together in the one statute. Those who drafted those provisions of course attempted to achieve consistency, but it is all too easy in drafting amendments and new sections to overlook other sections of the Act which bear upon the same or a similar subject matter. Similarly, when an Act has been amended so that provisions in a schedule have been inserted at different times, were perhaps prepared by different drafters, and dealt with different legislative provisions, they will not necessarily be read together.

CHAPTER 29

EFFECT MUST BE GIVEN TO THE WHOLE ACT

Words should not be discarded

Parliament's intention is not to be found by substituting the reader's presumption as to that intention in place of the clear meaning of the words used. Similarly, it is not for the reader to assume that Parliament has used words idly. Except when it is impossible to do so effect must be given to every word in the Act. The reader must bear in mind that 'a statute is never supposed to use words without a meaning.'[1] The rule is that if it can be prevented, no clause, sentence, or word shall be superfluous, void, or insignificant,[2] and that accordingly the reader should 'give proper weight if possible to every word used'.[3]

Sense should be made of a provision if possible

Since Parliament must be assumed not to have used words idly, it must also be assumed that Parliament intended the words to make sense. It meant the Act of Parliament to be effective. Therefore, if two meanings could be given to the words used in the Act of Parliament, what the reader should do is 'to adopt that construction which will give some effect to the words rather than that which will give none'.[4] This rule is a basic one, and 'nothing short of impossibility should allow a judge to declare a statute unworkable'.[5] Thus, quoting Lord Denning (later Lord Denning MR),

> When a statute has some meaning, even though it is obscure, or several meanings, even though there is little to choose between them, the courts have to say what meanings the statute is to bear, rather than to reject it as a nullity.[6]

Repetition and surplusage

Although the reader of an Act of Parliament must try to give a sensible meaning to all the words of the Act, there are cases in which one is forced to find that Parliament has repeated itself or that surplus words have been included in the Act. This is a reading of the Act which should only be used as a last resort.[7] Applying that principle, Megaw LJ said that 'Presumably the three words "of a kind" have not been introduced merely for elegance of prosody or to provide

---

1 *Auchterarder Presbytery v Lord Kinnoull* (1839), 6 Cl & F 646 at 686, 7 ER 841, Lord Brougham at 856.
2 *Whitney v Inland Revenue Commissioners* [1926] AC 37, HL, Lord Dunedin at 42.
3 *Cartwright v MacCormack* [1963] 1 WLR 18, CA, Harman LJ at 21.
4 *Cargo ex 'Argos'* (1873) LR 5 PC 134, at 153.
5 *Murray v Inland Revenue Commissioners* [1918] AC 541, HL at 553.
6 *Fawcett Properties Ltd v Buckingham County Council* [1961] AC 636, HL, Lord Denning at 676.
7 *R v St John Westgage Burial Board* (1862) 2 B & S 703, at 706; 121 ER 1232, Erle CJ at 1234.

meaningless padding. They have been introduced in order to affect the meaning'.[8]

Thus, a court will interpret a word in an Act in such a way as to avoid it being synonymous with another word in the same provision. Nevertheless, there have been cases in which the courts have been forced to treat words in an Act of Parliament as repetition or as surplus words.[9] As one of the greatest of the judges has admitted, 'It may not always be possible to give a meaning to every word used in an Act of Parliament'.[10] Nevertheless, it is a bold step to treat words as if they were not in the Act, and it is a step that should only be taken in a case of necessity.[11]

---

8   *Customs and Excise Commissioners v Mechanical Services (Trailer Engineers) Ltd* [1979] 1 WLR 305, CA at 316.

9   *Income Tax Commissioners v Pemsel* [1891] AC 532, HL, Lord Macnaghten at 589.

10   *Yorkshire Insurance Co v Clayton* (1881) QBD 421, CA, Jessel MR at 424.

11   *Cowper-Essex v Acton Local Board* (1889) 14 App Cas 153, HL, Lord Bramwell at 169.

CHAPTER 30

OMISSIONS FROM THE ACT

The rule as to things left out of the Act

All the rules for reading an Act of Parliament are rules that have been laid down by the courts to enable the reader to find out what Parliament meant by the words that it in fact used in the Act. It must always be borne in mind that what the reader must try to do is to find the meaning of the words in fact used, not the meaning of the words he or she thinks should have been used.

No matter how carefully an Act of Parliament may be drafted, and no matter how carefully it may be considered by Parliament, there is always the chance that something will be overlooked or forgotten. There have been various Acts of Parliament which have failed to deal with matters that they could reasonably have been expected to deal with. When that happens it is certainly not for the reader to deal with the matter personally: the Act of Parliament must be read as it stands, and must be read as failing to deal with that matter. This is a rule that has been laid down time and time again by the courts.[1] Rejecting an argument that such an approach would create a defect in the Act it was held that 'If there is such a defect, it is not for us sitting judicially to remedy it by legislating to put into s 30 words which Parliament could, if it had wished, have inserted'.[2] 'The courts have no power to fill in a gap in a statute, even if satisfied that it had been overlooked by the legislature and that, if the legislature had been aware of the gap, the legislature would have filled it in'.[3]

> In *Thompson v Goold & Co* [1910] AC 409 at 420 Lord Mersey said: 'It is a strong thing to read into an Act of Parliament words which are not there, and in the absence of clear necessity it is a wrong thing to do.' This proposition has never been doubted and has frequently been endorsed.[4]

There are many cases in which the courts have drawn Parliament's attention to the need to amend an Act to deal with something that has been overlooked in the Act, but this is as far as the courts can normally go.

Of course, if Parliament itself has legislated to overcome the gap, the courts can take Parliament's intention into account in interpreting the later Act by which Parliament has tried to cover the gap:

> In interpreting [the section] it is essential to bear the statutory objective in mind. This was to make good the lacuna to which attention has been drawn in [a

---

1   See, for example, *Mersey Docks v Henderson* (1888), 13 App Cas 595, Lord Halsbury, at 603; *Crawford v Spooner* (1846), 6 Moore PC 1, at 8–9; 13 ER 582, at 585; *Western Bank Ltd v Schindler* [1977] Ch 1; [1976] 3 WLR 341, CA, Scarman LJ (later Lord Scarman) at 355; *Craies on Statute Law* (7th edn by Edgar, SGG Sweet & Maxwell, London, 1971) p 70.

2   *Daymond v South West Water Authority* [1976] AC 609, HL, Viscount Dilhorne at 645. See also *Western Bank Ltd v Schindler* [1977] Ch 1; [1976] 3 WLR 341, CA, Scarman LJ (later Lord Scarman) at 355.

3   *Johnson v Moreton* [1980] AC 37, HL, Lord Salmon at 50.

4   *Grunwick Processing Laboratories Ltd v Advisory Conciliation and Arbitration Service* [1978] AC 655, HL, Lord Salmon at 699.

previous judicial decision]. If the words ... can extend to cover [the gap in the legislation] they should therefore be so construed.[5]

Implied terms

A distinction has been drawn between filling a gap which Parliament itself has failed to fill (which is something that is not permissible in the interpretation of a statute) on the one hand and supplying a missing word or words on the other. In the latter case there are very limited circumstances in which it may be possible for the court to supply the missing words. Words can only be implied into a statute if it is clearly necessary to do so.[6] Before this can be done three conditions must be fulfilled:

> it must be possible to determine from a consideration of the provisions of the Act read as a whole precisely what the mischief was that it was the purpose of the Act to remedy; [it must be] apparent that the draftsman and Parliament had by inadvertence overlooked, and so omitted to deal with, an eventuality that required to be dealt with if the purpose of the Act was to be achieved; [it must be] possible to state with certainty what were the additional words that would have been inserted by the draftsman and approved by Parliament had their attention been drawn to the omission before the Bill passed into law.[7]

Today the courts are readier than in the past to try to meet the problem of omissions from the Act, and it has been said that they 'should now be very reluctant to hold that Parliament has achieved nothing by the language it used, when it is tolerably plain what Parliament wished to achieve.'[8]

Of course, a term cannot be implied into a statute if the court is unable to determine what words have been omitted by Parliament. Furthermore, the courts are reluctant to imply terms into a penal statute:

> The law is supposed to be certain: the subject is entitled, and presumptively bound, to know what laws, particularly what criminal laws, apply to him. To say that a law which fails to satisfy these demands is void for uncertainty, is certainly a last resort, but if that conclusion is to be avoided, some intelligible meaning must be found by supplying or substituting, words within the limits of what courts may legitimately do.[9]

The courts are also reluctant to imply terms into a rating Act.[10]

---

5   *Director of Public Prosecutions of Jamaica v White* [1978] AC 426, PC at 433–34.

6   The House of Lords has applied this stringent test of 'clear necessity' (*Thompson v Goold & Co* [1910] AC 409, Lord Mersey at 420; *Northman v Barnet London Borough Council* [1979] 1 WLR 67, Lord Salmon at 72) and so has the Privy Council (*BP Refinery (Westernport) Pty Ltd v Shire of Hastings* (1977) 52 ALJR 20 at 25).

7   *Jones v Wrotham Park Settled Estates* [1980] AC 74, HL, Lord Diplock at 105.

8   *BBC Enterprises Ltd v Hi-Tech Xtravision Ltd* [1990] Ch 609, CA, Staughton LJ at 615; affd [1991] 2 AC 327, HL.

9   *Federal Steam Navigation Co Ltd v Department of Trade and Industry* [1974] 1 WLR 505, HL, Lord Wilberforce at 520.

10 *BP Refinery (Westernport) Pty Ltd v Shire of Hastings* (1977) 52 ALJR 20, PC.

CHAPTER 31

MISTAKES IN AN ACT OF PARLIAMENT

Common causes of mistakes in Acts of Parliament

The mass of legislation which has to be drafted and printed today is so great that it is not surprising that some mistakes do occur in it. Mistakes can be made by the drafter, by Parliament itself, and by the printer who is responsible for printing the Act after Parliament has passed it. Mistakes by the drafter or by Parliament itself can arise either through ignorance of the true position or by oversight.

The effect of a mistake as to the facts

It has been said that Parliament can do anything except make a man a woman. Obviously, if an Act of Parliament stated that a person named in that Act was a woman whereas in fact he was a man, the wrong statement in the Act of Parliament could not make him a woman in fact. The facts would remain unchanged notwithstanding the Act of Parliament. Similarly, if an Act of Parliament wrongly stated that a road was in a certain township whereas in fact it was not, the statement in the Act of Parliament could not have the effect of putting that road into that township. As a result, a court which was called upon to find the meaning of that Act of Parliament would have to consider that Act in the light of the true fact that the road was not in the township.[1]

If the Act of Parliament says that something is so when in fact it is not so, the person reading that Act of Parliament may read it in the light of the true facts. Quite a different case arises, however, when Parliament has passed the whole Act of Parliament under a mistake as to what the real facts are. The judge who is called upon to say what an Act of Parliament means cannot take into account the fact that the whole Act of Parliament being considered was passed by Parliament by mistake. If, for example, Parliament thought that somebody who had entered into a contract with the government had made an exorbitant profit out of that contract and it therefore passed an Act of Parliament reducing the total contract price by £100,000, the courts would have no power to set aside the Act of Parliament even if it was fully proved that the contractor, instead of making an exorbitant profit, had in fact made a loss; and the question as to whether the contractor had made a profit or loss could not be brought up in court in considering the true meaning of the Act.

This principle applies even if the Act has been obtained by fraudulently misleading Parliament into a particular belief.[2] As Lord Reid, upholding that basic principle, said:

---

1   *R v Houghton (Inhabitants)* (1853) 1 E&B 501; 118 ER 523.
2   *British Rlys Board v Pickin* [1974] AC 765, HL, Lord Reid at 787–88.

The function of the court is to construe and apply the enactments of Parliament. The Court has no concern with the manner in which Parliament or its officers carrying out its Standing Orders perform these functions.[3]

The effect of a mistake as to the law

It has been pointed out that 'it is, of course, true that Parliament may misconceive the existing law'.[4] If an Act of Parliament is prepared upon a mistake as to the legal position, the result is just the same as if the Act had been prepared upon a mistake as to the facts. If Parliament, in making a new Act, includes a statement that the existing law before the passing of that Act had a certain effect whereas actually it did not have that effect, the wrong statement in the Act of Parliament does not ordinarily alter the law: 'if the view be truly erroneous the section has misfired.'[5] This was put forcefully by the Court of Appeal in unanimous reasons for judgment, saying that 'There is high authority for the proposition that the "beliefs or assumptions of those who frame Acts of Parliament cannot make the law"'.[6] In such a case the law must be applied correctly, and not according to the erroneous statement of it in the new statute.[7]

When an Act has been drafted upon a wrong basis so far as the law is concerned, it may be difficult to give a meaning to the Act. The reader of the Act must, however, try to do so:

It is ... a very serious matter to hold, that where the main object of a statute is clear, it shall be reduced to a nullity by the draftsman's unskilfulness or ignorance of law. It may be necessary for a court of justice to come to that conclusion, but ... nothing can justify it except necessity, or the absolute intractability of the language used.[8]

However, in an extreme case the mistake made by Parliament may be so fundamental to the operation of the new Act as to change the previous law by implication, in which case 'the burden of proving that the legislature has fallen into a mistake is cast upon those who say so'.[9]

The effect of a mistake as to policy

It is for Parliament, not the courts, to decide on the policy underlying an Act of Parliament. Even if the judge is sure that Parliament's policy is misguided, he or she must nevertheless accept the Act as it stands. There is no right of appeal from Parliament to the courts.

---

3   *British Rlys Board v Pickin* [1974] AC 765, HL at 787.

4   *First National Securities Ltd v Chiltern District Council* [1975] 1 WLR 1075, Ch D at 1082.

5   *Re County of London Housing Order* [1956] 1 WLR 499, Ch D, Upjohn J (later Lord Upjohn) at 503.

6   *Re Walker dec'd (in bankruptcy)* [1974] Ch 193, CA, unanimous decision at 207. The court was there quoting from *Inland Revenue Commissioners v Dowdall O'Mahoney & Co Ltd* [1952] AC 401, HL, Lord Radcliffe at 407.

7   *West Midland Baptist (Trust) Association Inc v Birmingham Corpn* [1970] AC 874, HL, Lord Reid at 898. See, for example, *Norton v Spooner* (1854) 9 Moore PC 103; 14 ER 237.

8   *Salmon v Duncombe* (1886) 11 App Cas 627 at 634.

9   *R v Treasury* [1851] 20 LJQB 305, Lord Campbell at 311.

Some people may think the policy of the Act unwise and even dangerous to the community. Some may think it at variance with principles which have long been held sacred. But a judicial tribunal has nothing to do with the policy of any Act which it may be called upon to interpret ... The duty of the court, and its only duty, is to expound the language of the Act in accordance with the settled rules of construction. It is, I apprehend, as unwise as it is unprofitable to cavil at the policy of an Act of Parliament, or to pass a covert censure on the legislature.[10]

As Megaw LJ has rightly put it, 'If Parliament has made a mistake, it has full sovereign power to correct the mistake'.[11]

The effect of a drafter's oversight

Working against time as he or she does, the drafter of Acts of Parliament can be led into error by oversight. No matter how careful the drafter may be, mistakes can and do happen. An interesting example is provided by a section of an Act[12] which provided that the loans dealt with in that Act must be secured by a mortgage 'in the form set forth in the third schedule hereto'. The Act did not in fact have a third schedule, and no forms were set out in the Act. Some four years later Parliament passed another Act[13] which stated that the words referring to the third schedule had been 'inserted by mistake' and that the Act of 1875 had to be read as if the words in that section 'had not been inserted therein'.

Misprints

It is a well known fact that, no matter how careful the printer, and no matter how carefully the proofs are checked before the document is finally printed, misprints do occur. Many of the misprints that occur in newspapers have their humorous side, one of the milder examples being the statement that 'the dogs, patrolling day and night, kept an area of more than 5,000 acres free of rates'.[14] Misprints in statutes, however, are seldom of a humorous nature. Parliament is not under any duty to correct a misprint; but, if its attention is drawn to the misprint by the courts, it is likely to do so – usually some years after the enactment of the statute. Misprints are inevitable, and from time to time Parliament does pass further Acts to correct the misprints. No doubt the remarkable thing is that the number of misprints is so small.

The real problem of course arises if an Act has to be considered by the courts at a time when it contains a misprint and that misprint has not been corrected by Parliament. The rule is that, if the misprint is plain, the Act of Parliament is to be read as if the misprint had not been made. In England more than a century ago an Act of Parliament repealed several earlier Acts. Owing to a misprint one

---

10 *Vacher & Sons Ltd v London Society of Compositors* [1913] AC 107, HL, Lord Macnaghten at 118.
11 *Wilson v Dagnall* [1972] 1 QB 509, CA, Megaw LJ at 519.
12 Section 22(3) Artisans and Labourers' Dwellings Act 1875.
13 43 Vict c 8.
14 *The Liverpool Echo*, quoted in 5 *Town Planning and Local Government Guide* para 685.

of the Acts to be repealed was referred to as '13 Geo 3 c 56' but it should have been referred to as '17 Geo 3 c 56'. Lord Chief Justice Denman said:

> A mistake has been committed by the legislature; but having regard to the subject matter, and looking at the mere contents of the Act itself we cannot doubt that the intention was to repeal the Act of 17 Geo 3,[15]

and the Act was accordingly held to repeal the Act to which it should in fact have referred, namely 17 Geo 3 c 56.

The extent to which the courts will correct mistakes in Acts of Parliament

When it is called upon to find the meaning of an Act of Parliament a court is bound to proceed upon the assumption that the legislature is an ideal person that does not make mistakes.[16] However, there are circumstances in which despite that principle it must be recognised that a mistake has been made. The extent to which the courts will go in cases in which there has been a mistake as to the facts or as to the law has been considered earlier in this chapter. So far as mistakes in words, or misprints, are concerned, the courts are limited to the correction of obvious slips.[17] The courts have no power to treat an Act of Parliament as being altered in such a way as to agree with the judge's idea of what is right or reasonable.[18] It is not the court's function to repair the blunders that are to be found in legislation. They must be corrected by the legislature: 'A court is not at liberty to make laws, however strongly it may feel that Parliament has overlooked some necessary provision or has even been overreached by the promoters of a private Bill.'[19]

In the ordinary course, even if Parliament has used a word ungrammatically, the court is bound to read it as Parliament has enacted it. However, a simple grammatical mistake may be corrected and the words treated as if they were in their correct form when failing to do so would lead to an absurdity.

---

15 *R v Wilcock* (1845) 7 QB 317, at 338; 115 ER 509 at 518.

16 *Income Tax Commissioners v Pemsel* [1891] AC 531, HL, Lord Halsbury LC at 549.

17 *Salmon v Duncombe* (1886) 11 App Cas 627 at 634.

18 *Abel v Lee* (1871) LR 6 CP 365 at 371.

19 *Cape Brandy Syndicate v Inland Revenue Commissioners* [1921] 2 KB 403, CA, Lord Sterndale MR at 414.

CHAPTER 32

THE CLASS RULE

The nature of the class rule

Where there are two or more specific words forming a class followed by general words the courts may limit the scope of the general words to the scope of the class constituted by the specific words.[1] This rule of interpretation is known as the class rule.

The class rule is a rule that is used to find the meaning of a broad general word when that word follows after a group of specific words. Typically, the class rule applies where there is a group of specific words followed by the words 'or other' and then general words. Note, however, that the use of the words 'or other' is not a condition precedent to the applicability of the class rule.[2]

The word 'building' is a typical word to which the class rule could be applied. The difficulty of finding the meaning of the word 'building' has already been referred to earlier in this book.[3] The word 'building' is a word the meaning of which can vary a great deal depending on the context in which it is used. If a section of an Act states that it applies to

any building

and there are no words to limit the meaning of 'building', that word would be given a broad general meaning. It would include houses, and it would also include, for example, shops, factories, office blocks and hotels. If, on the other hand, the words used in the section were

any house, flat, cottage or other building

the class rule could be used to find the meaning of the word 'building', and the use of the class rule would show that the word 'building' is limited in that context to things of the same class as the class which precedes it – things of the same class as any 'house', 'flat' or 'cottage', that is, residential buildings.

A very good example of the way in which the class rule operates is to be found in a decision in a case in which the court had to determine the meaning of the words 'and other provisions' in the phrase 'meat, fish, poultry, vegetables, fruit and other provisions'. Mr Justice Buckley (later Lord Justice Buckley) said:

This is a case in which the ... rule must certainly apply for I think that the composite expression 'for the sale of meat, fish, poultry, vegetables, fruit and other provisions' is just such an expression as to be appropriate for the application of the doctrine. The problem is to decide what is the true nature of the [class] to which 'other provisions' is to be confined. [Counsel] has suggested that the common characteristic of meat, fish, poultry, vegetables and fruit is that they are all solids used for human consumption. That is quite true. But I think the

---

1   *Thames & Mersey Marine Insurance Co Ltd v Hamilton, Fraser & Co* (1887) 12 App Cas 484 at 490.

2   *Brownsea Haven Properties Ltd v Poole Corpn* [1958] Ch 574, CA at 598.

3   See Chapter 16.

class is more restrictive than that, for they seem to be all solids fit for human consumption which are natural products. They have not been subjected to a manufacturing process. They are what one might describe as the raw materials of the kitchen, and not finished articles which would be put on the table ... I think that applying the ... rule here 'other provisions' must be confined to other natural products of a kind which go to fill the larder and not extend it to anything like bread or confectionery which is the product of a baker's activities, converting natural flour into a finished article.[4]

There must be a general word

The class rule only applies to the case of a word which is a general one and which therefore has a somewhat indefinite meaning. It cannot be used to find the meaning of a word which is of a specific nature.

The general word must follow after a class of specific words

The class rule can of course only be used if there is a class of words in the section.[5] 'Unless you can find a category there is no room for the application of the *ejusdem generis* doctrine.'[6] In the example already given ('any house, flat, cottage or other building') the class is to be found in the words

any house, flat, cottage.

Those words form a common class which might be said to be the class of buildings used for residential purposes, and therefore the class rule applies:

You have to see whether you can constitute a genus of the particular words, and if you can, then unless there is some indication to the contrary, you must construe the general words as having relation to that genus.[7]

It can happen that a general word in an Act of Parliament follows a number of specific words but those specific words do not form a class. Again using the word 'building' as the general word, the lack of a class can be shown in the following example:

'any house, flat, factory, bridge, jetty, aviary, kennel or other building'.

In that example the words 'any house, flat, factory, bridge, jetty, aviary, kennel' do not form a class at all. They are all specific words, but they cannot be made to form a class. In fact in the example given there are two words which are of the one class ('house, flat') but the other words do not fall into that class. Therefore, even although some of the words can form a class the whole of the specific words cannot and accordingly there is nothing on which to base a use of the class rule. In other words, all the specific words that come before the general word must be of the one class.[8]

---

4   *Hy Whittle Ltd v Stalybridge Corpn* (1967) 65 LGR 344, at 353–354.

5   *Re Herbert Berry Associates Ltd (in liquidation)* [1977] 1 WLR 617, CA at 622; affd [1977] 1 WLR 1437, HL.

6   *Tilmans & Co v SS Knutsford Ltd* [1908] 2 KB 395, CA, Farwell LJ at 403.

7   *Mudie & Co v Strick* (1909) 100 LT 701, Pickford J (later Lord Sterndale) at 703.

8   *United Towns Electric Co Ltd v Attorney-General for Newfoundland* [1939] 1 All ER 423, PC at 428.

Another example of the principle that the class rule cannot be applied if the specific words do not form a class is to be found in a case in which the words which the court had to consider were

> loss of time from deficiency of men, or owner's stores, breakdown of machinery, or damage to hull or other accident preventing the work of the steamer.

The court had to find the meaning of the words 'or other accident'. It held that the words 'loss of time from deficiency of men, or owner's stores, breakdown of machinery, or damage to hull' did not form a class and that therefore the class rule could not be used to find the meaning of the words 'or other accident'.[9]

There must be two or more specific words before the general word

Since the class rule can only apply if there is a class of specific words before the general word, it cannot be used in the case in which there is only one specific word before the general word. Furthermore, if you cannot construe the general words as forming a class 'you must read all the particular words separately, and take the general words separately also'.[10] If the phrase used in the Act of Parliament is

> any house or other building,

the word 'building' is a general word and the word 'house' is a specific word, but the word 'house' has no other specific word with it and it therefore cannot form a class. The class rule therefore does not apply to the phrase 'house or other building'.

This aspect of the class rule arose in a case in which the words which the court had to consider were

> theatres and other places of public entertainment.

The court of course held that the class rule could not be used to find the meaning of the phrase 'other places of public entertainment' because the one word 'theatres' could not form a class.[11] In another example the words the court had to consider were 'landlord or other person' and, holding the class rule to be inapplicable, it was said that

> There is here no series of words from which one can discover any genus to which the words 'other person' could be construed as *ejusdem generis*; and I do not see any reason for thinking that the words 'or other person' ought to be limited in any way.[12]

---

9 *SS Magnhild v McIntyre Bros & Co* [1920] 3 KB 321.

10 *Mudie & Co v Strick* (1909) 100 LT 701, Pickford J (later Lord Sterndale) at 703.

11 *Allen v Emmerson* [1944] 1 KB 262.

12 *Re Herbert Berry Associates Ltd (in liquidation)* [1977] 1 WLR 617, CA, Buckley LJ at 620; affd [1977] 1 WLR 1437, HL. See also *Quasi v Quasi* [1980] AC 744, HL, Lord Diplock at 807–08.

The name lawyers give to the class rule

The class rule is known to lawyers as the *ejusdem generis* rule – *ejusdem generis* being two Latin words meaning 'of the same class'.

A court will not necessarily apply the class rule

If the specific words form two distinct classes instead of one, the class rule is inapplicable: all the specific words must fall within a single class for the rule to operate. Moreover, even if there is only one class comprised by the specific words the boundaries of the class may be difficult to determine with accuracy and the choice between different limits for the class constituted by the specific words may be fraught with such difficulty as to render the use of the class rule unwise. The purposive approach (Chapter 25), mischief rule (Chapter 24) or golden rule (Chapter 23) may be of assistance in deciding whether to apply the class rule and, if so, which formulation of the class to adopt.[13]

Excluding the class rule

The insertion of the words 'or things of whatever description' excludes the class rule.[14]

The class rule does not give guidance on the meaning of specific words within the class

The class rule is a rule for the finding of the scope to be given to the general words. It is not a rule to be used to find the meaning of any of the specific words.[15] Indeed, if the meaning of the specific words is ambiguous it may well be impossible to find a class.

---

13   *Nutton v Wilson* (1889) 22 QBD 744, CA, Lindley MR at 748.
14   *Attorney-General v Leicester Corpn* [1910] 2 Ch 359 at 369.
15   In such a case the rule 'words of similar meaning' may be of use – see Chapter 33.

CHAPTER 33

WORDS OF SIMILAR MEANING

The nature of the rule

This is a rule that is somewhat like the class rule.[1] It is known to lawyers as the *noscitur a sociis* rule, and is a rule for finding the meaning of a word which could have one of several meanings, and it is a rule which finds that meaning by considering the meaning of other words with which that word is associated in the section. Unlike the class rule, however, this rule does not depend upon having a broad general word following after two or more specific words: the question resolved by this rule is likely to be a question as to the width or scope to be given to a specific word within a group of specific words.

The meaning of similar words when they are associated with each other

When words of similar meaning are set out together in one section of an Act, and they are words which could bear several meanings, the meaning of any of them could be found by considering the general nature of the others.

A good example of the use of this rule occurs in a case in which the court had to find the meaning of the word 'footways'. The section in which that word occurred used the words

> roads, highways, footways, commons, streets, lanes, alleys, passages, and public places.

The question which the court had to decide was whether the word 'footways' was wide enough in its meaning to include a path available to the public but running through a private field. The court held that it was not wide enough to include that path. It made that decision because it found that the word 'footways' must be taken to have a meaning similar to that of the other words with which it was associated in the section: 'Construing the word "footway" from the company in which it is found ... the legislature appears to have meant those paved footways in large towns.'[2]

The basis of the rule is that the coupling together of words which are similar in their nature shows that Parliament means them to be read in the same sense.

1　Most textbook writers treat the rule about words of similar meaning and the class rule as being the same. *Maxwell, The Interpretation of Statutes* (12th edn, NM Tripathi Private Ltd, 1969) pp 320, 326, however, treats them as being different rules; and it seems better to treat them as separate rules.

2　*Scales v Pickering* (1828) 4 Bing 448 at 452, 453; 130 ER 840, Best CJ at 841 and Park J at 842.

CHAPTER 34

EXPRESS INCLUSIONS AND IMPLIED EXCLUSIONS

The effect of the rule

There is a rule that, if a section of an Act of Parliament sets out certain specific things as being within its scope, it impliedly excludes all others from its operation.[1] Thus, for example, a section which stated that it applied to

every factory, shop, office and workroom

would not apply to a hotel: the express statement of 'every factory, shop, office and workroom' would impliedly exclude the hotel from the operation of the section.[2]

The rule of course can only operate if Parliament in the particular section is giving a complete list of what it intends to refer to. If Parliament, rather than giving a complete list, is giving examples, the rule cannot apply. Thus when an Act referred to 'housing, town planning, etc'[3] those words could not be used to restrict the operation of the Act to housing and town planning.

The use of the rule in relation to definitions

It is important to note how the rule operates when what is to be interpreted is a definition. In Chapter 16 attention was drawn to the fact that definitions in Acts of Parliament sometimes use the words 'means', sometimes use 'includes', and sometimes use 'means and includes'. If the definition uses the word 'means' (without 'includes'), the rule as to express inclusions and implied exclusions applies because the definition is giving the complete list. If, however, the definition uses the word 'includes', Parliament is merely giving examples and the rule cannot operate. There can be no implied exclusion when Parliament intends to include more things than are specifically stated in the definition.

The rule must be applied with caution

The rule that the express inclusion of certain matters in a section operates to impliedly exclude all others is a useful one but like most generalisations has its dangers. It has been described as a valuable servant, but a dangerous master. It is 'not to be applied, when its application ... leads to absurdity or injustice'[4] or where the alleged limiting words are intended to be illustrative only. Describing the rule as 'a well known technique adopted by lawyers' and as 'a very good maxim' Lord Justice Diplock (later Lord Diplock) added the cautionary words – 'except when you apply it to words which are intended to be illustrative and

1   *London & Harrogate Securities Ltd v Pitts* [1976] 1 WLR 1063, CA.
2   *Whiteman v Sadler* [1910] AC 514, HL, Lord Dunedin at 527.
3   Housing, Town Planning, etc, Act 1909 (United Kingdom).
4   *Colquhoun v Brooks* (1888) 21 QBD 52, CA, Lopes LJ (later Lord Ludlow) at 65.

nothing more, and incorporate expressions like "such as" and "*et cetera*".'[5] The reason why it can be a 'dangerous master' is that Acts of Parliament are not always drafted as precisely as would be desirable. Because of the rush in which Acts of Parliament have often been written, it is not possible to produce the careful wording to which this rule could be applied with confidence: 'The *exclusio* is often the result of inadvertence or accident.'[6]

The dangers of the rule, however, do not preclude its use when it does afford guidance in interpreting an Act. The rule must be applied with caution, but it often affords assistance in matters of construction, and has been applied to 'all kinds of charges' including dock dues, railway and canal charges, rating, and stamp duty.[7]

The rule is one of increasing importance because of the growth of both environmental and town planning controls. The legal document which is part of environmental controls or town planning controls is often drafted upon the basis of setting out expressly those uses which are permitted or setting out expressly those uses which are prohibited. When such documents drafted in that way have to be considered by the courts the rule considered in this chapter will be likely to be used.

The name lawyers give the rule

Lawyers know this rule by the Latin words *expressio unius exclusio alterius est* – to express the one is to exclude all others.

---

5   *C Maurice & Co Ltd v Ministry of Labour* [1968] 1 WLR 1337, CA at 1345; affd under the name of *Secretary of State for Employment and Productivity v C Maurice & Co Ltd* [1969] 2 AC 346, HL.

6   *Colquhoun v Brooks* (1888) 21 QBD 52, CA, Lopes LJ (later Lord Ludlow) at 65.

7   *Craies on Statute Law* (7th edn by Edgar, SGG, Sweet & Maxwell, London, 1971) at p 116.

CHAPTER 35

INTERPRETING AN ACT IN THE LIGHT OF OTHER ACTS

Acts which are related to the Act being considered

From time to time it becomes necessary for Parliament to pass a series of Acts on the one topic, or to pass a series of Acts that are so far related to each other as to form a system of legislation. Such Acts are referred to by lawyers as Acts *in pari materia*. The proper way to read Acts of that kind is to read them together. They 'are to be taken together as forming one system, and as interpreting and enforcing each other',[1] and words which appear in both should be given the same meaning:

> It seems to me entirely logical and normal drafting that when a new Act is to be read as one with an earlier, it should use ... words in the same sense as they are used in the earlier.[2]

Expressing the same view, Lord Justice Stamp said that 'It is no doubt correct that if you find the same word appearing ... in several statutes covering the same subject matter, it ought in the absence of a controlling context to be given the same meaning'.[3]

All Acts of Parliament that relate to the same person are treated as related for the purpose of this rule. So also are all Acts which relate to the same class of persons.[4] Acts of Parliament relating to the same subject matter are, of course, related to each other for the purposes of this rule, and various Acts of Parliament relating to pilotage have therefore been read together.[5]

Acts of Parliament upon the same branch of the law are of course to be read together.[6]

Whilst related Acts are to be read together in this way, it must be remembered that the basic rules still apply: if an Act has a plain meaning it is to be given that plain meaning. Therefore, if any section of one of the related Acts has a plain meaning it should be given that plain meaning without reference to any other of the related Acts at all.[7]

The fact that related Acts are to be read together to cure any uncertainty about the meaning to be given to any of the sections does not mean that they are to be treated in the same way as they would be treated if they were just one single Act of Parliament. For example, if one of the related Acts contains a

---

1   *Palmer's case* (1784) 1 Leach CC (4th edn) 355, quoted in *Craies on Statute Law* (7th edn by Edgar, SGG, Sweet & Maxwell, London, 1971) p 134.

2   *Northern Ireland Trailers Ltd v Preston Corpn* [1972] 1 WLR 203, DC, Lord Widgery CJ at 208.

3   *Lee-Verhulst (Investments) Ltd v Harwood Trust* [1973] 1 QB 204, CA at 218.

4   See, for example, *R v Loxdale* (1758) 1 Burr 445; 97 ER 394; *Davis v Edmondson* (1803) 3 B & P 382; 127 ER 209.

5   *Redpath v Allan* (1872) LR 4 CP 518.

6   *Ex p Copland* (1852) 22 LJ Bank 17, Knight-Bruce LJ at 21.

7   *R v Titterton* [1895] 2 QB 61, DC, Lord Russell of Killowen CJ at 67.

particular provision and another does not, that particular provision cannot be read into the Act that lacks it: the Act that does not have that provision must be read without that provision, however unfortunate that may be from the viewpoint of enforcing the Act.[8]

The fact that related Acts are to be read together in this way does not mean that guidance about the meaning of the earlier Acts can be obtained by reading the later Acts: 'it would be quite wrong to construe an earlier statute in the light of a later one'.[9] However, this preclusion has not been so expressed as to prevent guidance about the meaning of the later Acts being obtained by reading the earlier Acts.

Although Lord Mansfield had said that

> Where there are different statutes in pari materia, although made at different times, or even expired and not referring to one another, they shall be taken together and construed together, as one system, and as explanatory of each other,[10]

that statement appears to us to be too wide and Lord Justice Harman has held that it must be taken 'with a pinch of salt when a long series of Acts is being dealt with'.[11]

Incorporating one Act into another

Parliament may provide that an earlier Act is to be read as one with a later Act on the same topic, or it may provide that the later Act is to be read as incorporated in the earlier one. In either case the effect is the same, namely 'Prima facie the same words and phrases should be construed in the same sense in the two Acts'.[12]

The effect of Acts which are not related to the Act under consideration

Even if some section of an Act of Parliament is one which is capable of having two or more meanings, no help can be gained by comparing that section with sections in other Acts of Parliament that are not related to the Act in which that section appears:[13] 'It is trite law that it is not permissible to construe the

---

8 *Casanova v The Queen* (1866) LR 1 PC 268, PC. Notwithstanding that the decision in *Casanova* is a decision of the Privy Council the Court of Appeal has subsequently decided the opposite, importing into one of the related Acts a definition not contained in it but contained in another of them: *R v Herrod, ex p Leeds City District Council* [1976] QB 540; on appeal under the name of *Walker v Leeds City Council* [1978] AC 403, HL; *R v Wheatley* [1979] 1 WLR 144 at 147.

9 *National Rivers Authority v Yorkshire Water Services Ltd* [1994] 3 WLR 1202, HL, Lord Mackay of Clashfern LC at 1209.

10 *R v Loxdale* (1758) 1 Burr 445 at 447; 97 ER 394 at 395.

11 *Littlewoods Mail Order Stores v Inland Revenue Commissioners* [1961] Ch 597 at 633.

12 *Crowe v Lloyds British Testing Co Ltd* [1960] 1 QB 592, CA, Willmer LJ at 619.

13 *Knowles & Sons v Lancashire & Yorkshire Rly Co* (1889) 14 App Cas 248, HL, Lord Halsbury at 253.

language of one statute by reference to the language of another.'[14] The reason is that 'the same expression, of course, may well be used in different Acts with significantly different meanings'.[15]

The effect of an Act repealing and replacing an earlier Act

When words in the replacement Act are 'virtually identical with the words used in [the comparable section] in the repealed Act that cannot be an accident. Parliament must have used the same phrase in order that it shall have the same meaning.'[16]

---

14 *Ministry of Housing and Local Government v Sharp* [1970] 2 QB 223, CA, Salmon LJ (later Lord Salmon) at 272. See also *Lake v Bennett* [1970] 1 QB 663, CA, Salmon LJ (later Lord Salmon) at 672.

15 *Re 'Fairview', Church Street, Bromyard* [1974] 1 WLR 579, Megarry J (later Megarry V-C) at 582.

16 *Lincoln Corpn v Parker* [1974] 1 WLR 713, DC, Lord Widgery CJ at 718. See also **Re-enactment after an Act has been interpreted by the courts** in Chapter 42.

CHAPTER 36

ACTS INCONSISTENT WITH EACH OTHER

Conflicts between different Acts of Parliament

As is only to be expected, Parliament is continuing to make new Acts of Parliament every year. Some of the new Acts replace older ones, but most of the new Acts are in addition to the Acts of Parliament already in existence. Year by year, therefore, the total number of Acts of Parliament continues to increase. Even if a Parliament were to carry out a thorough spring-cleaning of its statute books, its statutes would fill a very large number of pages.

When the Acts of Parliament are so numerous and increase at such a rate, it is not surprising that some of them are in conflict with each other; and, with the number of amending Acts conflicting provisions within the same Act are common. It would be an almost impossible task to ensure that no conflict at all arose. The courts have developed rules for the reading of Acts of Parliament whose provisions are in conflict, and those rules are considered in this chapter.

Conflict between a general and a specific Act

In Chapter 12 the rule for interpreting a conflict between a general provision and a specific provision in the same Act is set out. The same rule applies when the general provisions and the specific provisions are contained in different Acts of Parliament:

> When there are general words in a later Act capable of reasonable and sensible application without extending them to subjects specially dealt with by earlier legislation, you are not to hold that earlier and special legislation indirectly repealed, altered, or derogated from merely by force of such general words, without any indication of a particular intention to do so.[1]

Other conflicts between Acts of Parliament

A conflict may of course occur between Acts of Parliament when the Acts concerned do not fall into the classes of a general Act on the one hand and a specific Act on the other hand. In such a case, if it is impossible to read the two Acts together without conflict, it has been held that the later Act prevails over the earlier one.[2]

---

1 *Seward v Vera Cruz* (1884) 10 App Cas 59, HL, Lord Selborne LC at 68. See also *Associated Minerals Consolidated Ltd v Wyong Shire Council* [1975] AC 538, PC, unanimous advice at 553–54.

2 *Argyll (Duke) v Inland Revenue Commissioners* (1913) 109 LT 893, Scrutton J (later Scrutton LJ) at 895; *Kariapper v Wijesinha* [1968] AC 716. However, without referring to those decisions the Court of Appeal refused to apply what it described as the 'so called' rule to a conflict between provisions in the same Act: *Re Marr* [1990] Ch 773. The fact that the decision in *Kariapper v Wijesinha* is a decision of the Privy Council might well dissuade the Court of Appeal from refusing to apply the rule to a conflict between two statutes.

Implied repeal

The conflict between one Act and another may lead to the conclusion that the later Act impliedly repeals the earlier to the extent of the conflict: 'if two Acts are inconsistent or repugnant, the later will be read as having impliedly repealed the earlier'.[3] However, 'the court leans against implying such a repeal: unless the two Acts are so plainly repugnant to each other that effect cannot be given to both at the same time, a repeal will not be implied'.[4]

As a result of the strong judicial preference for avoiding an implied repeal the law is that a later affirmative enactment does not repeal an earlier affirmative enactment unless the words of the later enactment are 'such as by their necessity to import a contradiction'.[5] Because of that strong preference against an implied repeal a party to litigation who contends that there has been an implied repeal must discharge the heavy onus which is always borne by a litigant who asserts an implied repeal.

---

3   *Herbert Berry Associates Ltd v Inland Revenue Commissioners* [1977] 1 WLR 1437, HL, Lord Simon of Glaisdale at 1443.

4   *Herbert Berry Associates Ltd v Inland Revenue Commissioners* [1977] 1 WLR 1437, HL, Lord Simon of Glaisdale at 1443.

5   *Garnett v Bradley* (1978) 3 App Cas 944, Lord Blackburn at 966.

CHAPTER 37

NINE CLASSES OF ACTS OF PARLIAMENT

Amending Acts

An Act of Parliament may of course be amended by any other Act of Parliament. The amending Act will not necessarily have the same sort of short title as the Act which it amends. For example, an Act of Parliament dealing with hotels may alter the Act of Parliament dealing with local government so as to permit local government authorities to conduct community hotels.

The Act which is amended by the later Act is generally referred to as the 'principal Act'.

Parliament of course has power to pass an amending Act even although that Act has the effect of amending a statute that has been enacted but has not yet come into force.

Codes

Unlike a consolidating Act (which is basically a putting together of an original Act and all the amendments to it) a code is an attempt by Parliament to enact legislation to set out the whole of the law to cover a particular subject matter or field of law, and in doing so to cover not only any existing statutory provisions but also the common law. The courts therefore take the basic approach to a code that it is to be interpreted in the light of its own language without resort to the previously existing law whether statutory or common law. To adopt any other approach

> would imply a highly unusual limitation imposed by the legislature upon one of its own Acts; it is hard to see what purpose could be served by a code which did not supercede but merely competed with an uncodified system operating in an identical field.[1]

However, if a provision in the code is ambiguous or uncertain of meaning, the courts may still have to take the pre-existing law, and particularly the pre-existing common law, into consideration.

Consolidating Acts

When an Act of Parliament has been amended by a number of later Acts, it becomes awkward to use. The reader either has to paste the amendments into the principal Act, or else has to chase from one Act to another while reading the principal Act. There is also the risk that the reader may miss some amendment and thereby be misled:

---

1   *Farquharson v R* [1973] AC 786, PC, unanimous advice at 795. See also *Bank of England v Vagliano Bros* [1891] AC 107, HL, Lord Herschell at 144.

The modern practice of parliamentary draftsmen in preparing for adoption by Parliament legislation to affect a change in the existing law, particularly when the subject matter of the law is one, such as taxation, in which legislative changes are frequent, is to express the changes to be effected in the form of amendments to the language of particular provisions in earlier statutes dealing with the same subject matter. This method of drafting becomes progressively more cryptic as amendments to previous amendments follow one another in successive statutes. The need to refer to and fro and back and forth between ever increasing numbers of different statutes in order to discover what a particular provision of any of those statutes means reaches a point at which the difficulty of finding out what the law is may have the practical consequence of depriving the citizen of his right to know, in advance of a decision of your Lordships' House which must needs be *ex post facto*, what the legal consequences will be of a course of conduct which he contemplates adopting.[2]

There are two ways of meeting this difficulty. One way is for Parliament to authorise the Queen's Printer to print the principal Act with all the amendments actually worked into it. The other way is for Parliament itself to pass a new Act of Parliament consolidating into one Act the original Act and the various amendments to it:

> The purpose of a consolidation Act is to remove this difficulty by bringing together in a single statute all the existing statute law dealing with the same subject matter which forms the general context in which the particular provisions of the Act fall to be construed, so that it will be no longer necessary to seek that context in a whole series of amended and re-amended provisions appearing piecemeal in earlier statutes.[3]

The object of a consolidating Act is 'to consolidate and reproduce the law as it stood before the passing of that Act':[4]

> This is the only purpose of a consolidation Act: this is the only 'mischief' it is designed to cure. It is true that a consolidation Act is not intended to alter the law as it existed immediately before the Act was passed.[5]

The rule for reading a consolidating Act is to start on the basis that the consolidating Act is merely intended to bring together into one Act the principal Act and its various amending Acts and that the consolidating Act is not intended to make any alterations to the law: 'One must presume that such an Act makes no substantial change in the previous law unless forced by the words of the Act to a contrary conclusion.'[6] This rule is applied so that the consolidating Act is treated as not being intended to alter the law, even if there is a change of wording from the preceding legislation.[7]

---

2   *Inland Revenue Commissioners v Joiner* [1975] 1 WLR 1701, HL, Lord Diplock at 1710–11.

3   *Inland Revenue Commissioners v Joiner* [1975] 1 WLR 1701, HL, Lord Diplock at 1710–11.

4   *Gilbert v Gilbert and Boucher* [1928] P 1, CA at 7.

5   *Inland Revenue Commissioners v Joiner* [1975] 1 WLR 1701, HL, Lord Diplock at 1710–11.

6   *Inland Revenue Commissioners v Hinchy* [1960] AC 748, HL, Lord Reid at 768. See also *R v Crown Court at Leeds, ex p City of Bradford Chief Constable* [1975] QB 314, DC.

7   *Re Rolls-Royce Co Ltd* [1974] 1 WLR 1584 at 1590–91.

Even although an Act is described by Parliament as a consolidating Act there is nothing to prevent Parliament from including in that consolidating Act provisions which do make changes – and even major changes – in the law.

> The presumption that a consolidation Act was not intended to alter the previous statute law which it repeals and replaces is a legitimate aid to its interpretation where its language is fairly and equally capable of bearing more than one meaning; but one of the purposes of a consolidation Act is to resolve possible ambiguities in the language of the statutes which it repeals – not to perpetuate them or to add to the obscurity of the law.[8]

If a consolidating Act contains a section the words of which are plain and which, if given their plain meaning, would make a change in the law, the plain meaning rule must be applied to give the words their plain meaning: 'the presumption is that such an Act is not intended to alter the law, but this *prima facie* view must yield to plain words to the contrary.'[9]

Lord Diplock said of this principle that

> if you find ... that the actual words are clear and unambiguous in their meaning it is not permissible to have recourse to the corresponding provisions in the earlier statute repealed by the consolidation Act and to treat any difference in their wording as capable of casting doubt upon what is clear and unambiguous language in the consolidation Act itself.[10]

In the same case Lord Hailsham of St. Marylebone held that

> In construing a consolidation Act which itself is unambiguous, we are, of course, bound to consider its terms rather than the terms of any antecedent statutes. If this were not so, the whole benefit of consolidation might be lost.[11]

The fact that 'the layout of the provisions of [a section in the consolidating Act] differs significantly from the layout of the corresponding provisions in the [earlier Act]' does not cause the court 'to depart from the well known principle that consolidating Acts presumably are not intended to change the law'.[12]

The fact that a consolidating Act can alter the law may prove to be a trap for the unwary. An amendment placed in a consolidating Act would be placed in a statute where the public and the profession would not be in the least degree on their guard to look for it. Evershed MR (later Lord Evershed MR) has warned that 'one does not look for substantial changes in the law ... in a consolidating Act'[13] and Lord Justice Romer observed that 'It is a consolidation Act ... it is, therefore, extremely unlikely, to say the least of it, that it effected any substantial change in the pre-existing law'.[14] Extremely unlikely though it be, it has in fact happened that a consolidating Act contains an amendment or

---

8   *Commissioner of Police of the Metropolis v Curran* [1976] 1 WLR 87, HL, Lord Diplock at 94.

9   *Beswick v Beswick* [1968] AC 58, HL, Lord Guest at 84.

10 *Commissioner of Police of the Metropolis v Curran* [1976] 1 WLR 87, HL at 90–91.

11 *Commissioner of Police of the Metropolis v Curran* [1976] 1 WLR 87, HL at 94.

12 *Zimmerman v Grossman* [1972] 1 QB 167, CA, Lord Justice Widgery (later Lord Widgery CJ) at 180.

13 *R v Brixton Prison Governor, ex p De Demko* [1959] 1 QB 268; affd under the name of *De Demko v Home Secretary* [1959] AC 654, HL.

14 *Re Turner's Will Trusts* [1937] Ch 15.

amendments of the pre-existing statute. A well-respected, and indeed major work, *Halsbury's Laws of England*,[15] states that 'statutes to consolidate the law with amendments are occasionally found' and gives as an example the Supreme Court Act 1981.

The consolidating Act will of course repeal all the Acts which it is consolidating. They go out of force and the consolidating Act comes into force at one and the same time. There is therefore no break in the law: its effect continues unchanged and it is merely the place where it is to be found that is altered. There is no moment of time at which the law as formerly set out in the principal Act and its amendments and as now set out in the consolidating Act ceases to have effect. As Lord Simon of Glaisdale said:

> All consolidation Acts are designed to bring together in a more convenient, lucid and economical form a number of enactments related in subject matter (and often by cross-reference) previously scattered over the statute book. All such previous enactments are repealed in the repeal schedule of the consolidation Act. It follows that, once a consolidation Act has been passed which is relevant to a factual situation before a court, the 'intention' of Parliament as to the legal consequences of that factual situation is to be collected from the consolidation Act and not from the repealed enactments. It is the relevant provision of the consolidation Act, and not the corresponding provision of the repealed Act, which falls for interpretation. It is not legitimate to construe the provision of the consolidation Act as if it were still contained in the repealed Act – first, because Parliament has provided for the latter's abrogation; and secondly, because so to do would nullify much of the purpose of passing a consolidation Act.[16]

Declaratory Acts

If doubts arise as to the state of the law, Parliament may decide to pass a declaratory Act setting out what the law is. Parliament can do so, and it is not limited to setting out what the state of the law as written in Acts of Parliament is: it can also set out the state of the common law. A declaratory Act usually sets out that the law is and always has been what it is said to be in the declaratory Act itself. A typical example is the Act which says: 'Whereas the rightful jurisdiction of Her Majesty, her heirs and successors, extends and has always extended ...'[17] The very nature of a declaratory Act is such that it will usually be found to operate from a date before the date on which it is passed by Parliament.[18]

Enabling Acts

An enabling Act is an Act passed to empower the doing of something which would not otherwise be lawful. For example, Parliament may enact legislation empowering a company to lay a pipeline through private property for the very

---

15 4th edn (Butterworths, London, 1983) vol 44, para 809.

16 *Farrell v Alexander* [1977] AC 59, HL at 82.

17 Territorial Waters Jurisdiction Act 1878 (UK), quoted in *Craies on Statute Law* (7th edn by Edgar, SGG, Sweet & Maxwell, London, 1971) p 59.

18 *Attorney-General v Theobold* (1890) 24 QBD 556. See also Chapter 39.

long distance from its oil refinery to a major distribution point, or from a gas field to a large city. Ordinarily, powers conferred by such an Act will be interpreted strictly. However, there is a different class of enabling Act which is one conferring jurisdiction upon a court or other body, and in respect of this type of legislation the jurisdiction conferred is construed liberally.

The enactment of an enabling Act carries with it the ability to imply necessary subsidiary powers. As *Craies* puts it,

> one of the first principles of law with regard to the effect of an enabling Act is that if the legislature enables something to be done, it gives power at the same time, by necessary implication, to do everything which is indispensable for the purpose of carrying out the purpose in view.[19]

Again,

> If a statute is passed for the purpose of enabling something to be done, but omits to mention in terms some detail which is of great importance (if not actually essential) to the proper and effectual performance of the work which the statute has in contemplation, the courts are at liberty to infer that the statute by implication empowers that detail to be carried out.[20]

Explanatory Acts

Sometimes Parliament passes an Act to explain the meaning of an earlier Act of Parliament. When that happens, the earlier Act is to be read in the light of the explanatory Act, and it is to be read as if that explanation in the explanatory Act had been available to the reader at the time when the original Act was passed.[21]

If a law case has already been decided on the basis of the earlier Act before the explanatory Act is passed, the passing of the explanatory Act does not alter the decision in that law case unless Parliament expressly says so in the explanatory Act. The explanatory Act does, however, affect any law cases which were started before the explanatory Act came into force but which had not been completed at that time, for the law cases must then proceed upon the basis of the original Act as read in the light of the explanatory Act.[22] It would seem that, if a case had been decided on the basis of the earlier Act before the explanatory Act is passed but was the subject of an appeal which had not been decided before the coming into force of the explanatory Act, the appeal court would have to apply the law as set out in the explanatory Act unless the explanatory Act contains a transitional provision to cover such a case.

Remedial Acts

What is known as a remedial Act is an Act introduced by Parliament to remedy what Parliament perceives to be an existing problem. Such an Act should so far

---

19 *Craies on Statute Law* (7th edn by Edgar, SGG, Sweet & Maxwell, London, 1971) p 258.

20 *Craies on Statute Law* (7th edn by Edgar, SGG, Sweet & Maxwell, London, 1971) p 111.

21 *R v Dursley (Inhabitants)* (1832) 3 B & Ad 465; 110 ER 168.

22 *Re Westby's Settlement* [1950] Ch 296, CA at 303.

as reasonably possible be given a wide construction and application.[23] It should be construed so as to give the fullest relief which the fair meaning of its language will allow. Applying this principle it has been held that

> There may, perhaps, be some obscurity in the words of the statute, but there is none in the title, and this being a remedial statute, we should construe it so as to give full effect to the intention of the legislature.[24]

However, the application of this principle does not authorise a court to push the meaning of a remedial statute beyond its literal interpretation where it can be seen that the extended meaning does not accord with the manifest intention of the legislature. The court's authority to extend the meaning and application of a remedial statute beyond the strict literalism of the words in which the remedial purpose is enacted does not permit a court to extend the remedial purpose itself.[25]

The remedy provided by the remedial Act is *prima facie* to be regarded as the exclusive remedy[26] but only if the right and the remedy are created in the same remedial Act.

Repealing Acts

Parliament has prescribed the effect of a repealing Act. It has required that 'the repeal does not revive any enactment previously repealed unless words are added reviving it'.[27]

Parliament has also prescribed what is to happen when a repealing Act repeals a previous enactment but substitutes its own provisions for those in the enactment that has been repealed. It requires that 'the repealed enactment remains in force until the substituted provisions come into force'.[28]

What happens when some other statute refers by name to one which has been repealed by a repealing Act? That question, too, has been considered by Parliament. Instead of the situation in which a repealing Act re-enacts the pre-existing law with or without modification it has decided that the reference in that other Act to the repealed Act shall be interpreted as if it were referring not to the repealed Act but to the re-enacted one.[29]

Validating Acts

If something has been done invalidly, Parliament has the power to pass an Act of Parliament saying that it is to be treated as if it had been done validly.

---

23 *Moseley v Stonehouse* (1806) 7 East 174; 103 ER 67.

24 *Ex p Steavenson* (1823) 2 B & C 34 at 37.

25 *Jortin v South Eastern Railway Co* (1855) 6 De GM & G 270; 43 ER 1237.

26 *Doe dem Bishop Rochester v Bridges* (1831) 1 B & Ad 859; 109 ER 1001, Lord Tenterden CJKB at 1005; *Pasmore v Oswaldtwistle Urban District Council* [1898] AC 387, HL at 394 and 397.

27 Section 15 Interpretation Act 1978.

28 Section 17(1) Interpretation Act 1978.

29 Section 17(2)(a) Interpretation Act 1978.

A validating Act may be passed because someone has discovered the invalidity although the matter has not been taken to court, or it may be passed because some court has held that the particular thing has been done invalidly.

A validating Act must by its very nature be treated as coming into force on a day before the date on which it was actually passed.[30]

---

30 For a further example of a validating Act see **The power of Parliament to make Acts that apply from a date before the date on which they were passed** in Chapter 39.

CHAPTER 38

ACTS WHICH ARE READ NARROWLY

The kinds of Acts that are read narrowly

There are some kinds of Acts to which the courts may give a narrow meaning rather than a wide meaning if the words used by Parliament are capable of either meaning. The major kinds of these Acts[1] are:

(a) Acts which impose a penalty;

(b) Acts which empower arrest or detention;

(c) Acts which impose a tax, a rate or charge;

(d) Acts which take away vested rights; and

(e) Acts affecting a fundamental principle of the common law.

The way in which to read Acts of these kinds is to give the words a narrow meaning rather than a wide one; but, of course, that can only be done if the words used in the Act are words that are capable of having the narrow meaning. If the words which Parliament has used are plain, they must be given that plain meaning even although they do impose a tax or a penalty or take away existing vested rights.

The giving of a narrow meaning to Acts of this kind is a rule which the courts once applied far more strongly than they do today. The position today is that the rule still applies, and that the Act is therefore to be read in favour of the individual rather than of the state, but that the rule only applies in that way if the words used by Parliament are clearly words of doubtful meaning. Acts of this kind must never be read narrowly so as to limit their plain meaning or so as to thwart Parliament's intention.

Acts which impose a penalty

What the rule really amounts to is that, if an Act imposes a penalty for a criminal offence, a person who is charged with that offence is entitled to the benefit of any doubt as to the meaning of the Act:

> Where there is an enactment which may entail penal consequences, you ought not to do violence to the language in order to bring people within it, but ought rather to take care that no one is brought within it who is not brought within it by express language.[2]

This applies particularly in the case of creation by Parliament of a new offence:

---

1   Reference should also be made to retrospective Acts (considered in Chapter 39) and extraterritorial Acts (considered in Chapter 40).

2   *Rumbolt v Schmidt* (1882) 8 QBD 603, Huddleston B at 608.

If Parliament seeks to create a new offence, it must do so in plain words. All the more so if it creates an absolute offence – of which a person may be found guilty, even though he had no guilty knowledge or intent and took all reasonable care.[3]

This well known 'rule of construction' that 'penal provisions should be construed narrowly'[4] carries with it the principle that 'if the language of a penal statute is capable of two interpretations, then that most favourable to the subject is to be applied'.[5] In construing a statute which creates a criminal offence 'each word must be given its ordinary or natural meaning'.[6] Because it is a penal enactment the court interpreting it 'should resist the temptation to make good any shortcomings of ... language in order to effect the supposed policy of the legislation'. Instead, the courts should 'adopt the narrow construction'.[7]

In relation to an ambiguous penal provision the court stands as a guardian of liberty:

> The court must not strain to bring within the offence ... conduct which does not fall within the well-established bounds of the offence. On the contrary, the court must safeguard against extension of those bounds save by the authority of Parliament.[8]

Of course, although ambiguity in an Act imposing a penalty is to be resolved in favour of the individual by giving a strict interpretation to the Act, nevertheless this rule of interpretation must not be used to defeat the apparent intention of Parliament. It is not for the court to find or make doubt or ambiguity in a penal Act if the words are such that, if they had been used in an Act that does not impose a penalty, no doubt or ambiguity would be found to exist. As Lord Reid said:

> As the section creates a criminal offence it must not be loosely construed. Each word must be given its ordinary or natural meaning. It may be permissible, where necessary, to give some word a secondary meaning of which it is reasonably capable in ordinary speech. But we must not substitute for any word some other word or phrase or write in anything which is not there.[9]

The protection of the individual by reading a penal provision narrowly may, however, have to give way to avoiding the provision being treated as surplusage:

> The law is supposed to be certain: the subject is entitled, and presumptively bound, to know what laws, particularly what criminal laws, apply to him. To say that a law which fails to satisfy these demands is void for uncertainty, is certainly a last resort, but if that conclusion is to be avoided, some intelligible meaning

---

3   *Re F (orse A) (a minor) (publication of information)* [1976] 3 WLR 813, CA, Lord Denning MR at 821.

4   *Zimmerman v Grossman* [1972] 1 QB 167, CA, Widgery LJ (later Lord Widgery CJ) at 176. For an example, see *R v Callender* [1993] QB 303, CA, unanimous decision at 307.

5   *Alphacell Ltd v Woodward* [1972] AC 824, HL, Viscount Dilhorne at 841.

6   *Director of Public Prosecutions v Turner* [1974] AC 357, HL, Lord Reid at 364.

7   *McDonald v Howard Cook Advertising Ltd* [1972] 1 WLR 90, DC, unanimous decision at 94.

8   *R v Mohan* [1976] QB 1, CA, unanimous decision at 11. See also *Fawcett Properties Ltd v Buckingham County Council* [1961] AC 636, HL, Lord Keith of Avonholm at 671.

9   *Director of Public Prosecutions v Turner* [1974] AC 357, HL at 364.

must be found by supplying or substituting, words within the limits of what courts may legitimately do.[10]

Another factor to bear in mind in interpreting a penal provision is that 'where strict construction of a penal statutory provision does become called for, the strictness of the construction will vary directly with the heinousness of the crime and the severity of the penalty'.[11]

One question remains to complete this consideration of the proper interpretation of penal provisions. What is penal? A reader unfamiliar with the legal meaning of 'penal' might be misled into treating it as something that carries imprisonment as the penalty. However, even if a statutory provision is such as 'to invoke the possibility of a fine' it 'has to be considered as a penal section'.[12]

Acts which empower arrest or detention

Allied with the principle that Acts which impose a penalty should be interpreted, in case of ambiguity, in such a way as to give the individual the benefit of the doubt created by that ambiguity is the principle that ambiguity in an Act should be resolved against implying a power to arrest or to detain: 'a section which interferes with the liberty of the subject ... should clearly be construed as strictly as possible and so as to give no wider effect than the words strictly require.'[13] The protection of personal liberty may even extend as far as to accept an interpretation which would otherwise be rejected as absurd where the alternative is an interpretation which interferes with personal liberty.[14]

Acts which create a tax, a rate or a charge

Acts of Parliament which impose a tax or charge are also read narrowly if they are in words which could bear both a wide and a narrow meaning. Certainly 'the subject is not to be taxed unless the language of the statute clearly imposes the obligation'.[15] Whether the Act be one which imposes a tax, a rate or a charge 'it is, as always, the task of the [bodies contending that the tax, rate or charge applies] to bring each case fairly within the taxing words'.[16] A tax or charge is not to be read into an Act – it must appear from the express words used in the Act itself.

> In a taxing Act one has to look merely at what is clearly said. There is no room for any intendment. There is no equity about a tax. There is no presumption as to

10 *Federal Steam Navigation Co Ltd v Department of Trade and Industry* [1974] 1 WLR 505, HL, Lord Wilberforce at 520.

11 *Farrell v Alexander* [1977] AC 59, HL, Lord Simon of Glaisdale at 89.

12 *R v Newham East Justices, ex p Hunt* [1976] 1 WLR 420, DC at 422.

13 *Whitehead v Haines* [1965] 1 QB 200, DC, Phillimore J at 213.

14 *Spicer v Holt* [1977] AC 987, HL, Lord Fraser of Tullybelton at 1013.

15 *Hull Dock Co v Browne* (1831) 2 B & Ad 43; 109 ER 1059; see also *D'Avigdor-Goldsmid v Inland Revenue Commissioners* [1953] AC 347, HL.

16 *Reed International Ltd v Inland Revenue Commissioners* [1976] AC 336, HL, Lord Wilberforce at 359.

a tax. Nothing is to be read in, nothing is to be implied. One can only look fairly at the language used.[17]

As Lord Wilberforce has put it,

A subject is only to be taxed on clear words, not on 'intendment' or on the 'equity' of an Act. Any taxing Act of Parliament is to be construed in accordance with this principle. What are 'clear words' is to be ascertained on normal principles; these do not confine the courts to literal interpretation. There may, indeed should, be considered the context and scheme of the relevant Act as a whole, and its purpose may, indeed should, be regarded.[18]

'It is well-established', Lord Edmund-Davies held, 'that all charges upon the subject must be imposed by clear and unambiguous language'.[19]

However, the principle that, if there is a real doubt as to the meaning of the words of the section, the meaning which is more favourable to the taxpayer should be adopted[20] cannot mean that taxpayers and ratepayers are to be allowed to avoid their clear obligations! Orr LJ made that plain when he said that 'I agree that taxing Acts are to be construed strictly. I do not agree with the addition of the words "against the Crown", which suggests that words are to be unduly restricted against the Crown'.[21]

Parliament has power to legislate in such a way as to make a tax, rate or charge retrospective. However, 'the court, in construing a taxing statute, will be very reluctant to construe it as having a retrospective effect and will construe it as not having such effect if the words used allow such construction'.[22]

A court is less likely to read a taxing, rating or charging provision narrowly if the case before it involves a tax evasion scheme.

Acts which affect vested rights

The rule is that, if the Act is one which could take away vested rights, its words should only be given that effect if they clearly require it: 'Statutes should be interpreted, if possible, so as to respect vested rights.'[23] Indeed, 'If a vested right is to be defeated, the section must plainly say so'.[24] This rule has been stated by the courts over and over again. As one of many possible examples, Lord Justice Russell has said that

I am impressed by this, that if I am asked to construe a provision of a statute which limits the ordinary freedom of the subject to conduct his affairs as he will,

---

17 *Cape Brandy Syndicate v Inland Revenue Commissioners* [1921] 1 KB 64, CA, Rowlatt J at 71.

18 *W T Ramsay v Inland Revenue Commissioners* [1982] AC 300, HL at 323.

19 *Daymond v South West Water Authority* [1976] AC 609, HL at 657.

20 *C & J Clark Ltd v Inland Revenue Commissioners* [1975] 1 WLR 413, CA, Scarman LJ (later Lord Scarman) at 419.

21 *Delbourgo v Field* [1978] 2 All ER 193, CA at 196.

22 *James v Inland Revenue Commissioners* [1977] 1 WLR 835, DC, Slade J (later Slade LJ) at 838.

23 *Hough v Windus* (1884) 12 QBD 224, at 237.

24 *Engineering Industry Training Board v Samuel Talbot (Engineers) Ltd* [1969] 2 QB 270, CA at 275.

then I have a preference for finding a clear definition of the circumstances in which he is limited in his freedom of action.[25]

The rule protecting vested rights has been applied to enforcement notices under the town planning legislation.[26]

Nevertheless, of course, the words can be so plain and so strong that they have to be given their effect of taking away vested rights.[27] Such a provision is to be strictly construed and applied, 'the right ... cannot be taken away by a mere implication, which is not necessary for the reasonable construction of the statute'.[28]

However, the latter half of the twentieth century in particular has seen Parliament often making inroads into individual rights, claiming to do so in the interests of the wider community. Drawing attention to that circumstance it was held that 'In a modern civilized society, there must always be a delicate balance between the right of the individual and the need of the community at large'.[29] Another possible limitation on the rule protecting vested rights is what has been described as 'the possible practical advantages of a liberal interpretation'.[30]

The rights to be protected must be vested rights

The rule that, when choosing between different meanings of a section, that meaning is to be chosen which will not take away existing vested rights is limited to those rights which have actually vested when the Act of Parliament has come into force. There is

> a manifest distinction between an investigation in respect of a right and an investigation which has to decide whether some rights should or should not be given. Upon a repeal the former is preserved. The latter is not.[31]

The rule deals only with vested rights. It does not deal with existing rights that have not vested at the date when the Act comes into force. Thus, when a statute providing for the granting of a permit or certificate is repealed a permit or certificate under it continues as a vested right, but a promise to issue such a permit or certificate does not confer any rights that could be said to be vested at the time of the repeal.[32] A moment's thought shows that this must necessarily

---

25 *Sudders v Barking London Borough Council* [1974] 72 LGR 430, CA at 433.

26 *East Riding County Council v Park Estate (Bridlington) Ltd* [1957] AC 223, HL, Viscount Simonds at 233.

27 *Canterbury City Council v Colley* [1993] AC 401, HL, Lord Oliver of Aylmerton at 405–06; *Brightman & Co Ltd v Tate* [1919] 35 TLR 209, KBD; *Attorney-General for Canada v Hallett & Carey Ltd* [1952] AC 427, PC.

28 *R v Wimbledon Local Board* [1882] 8 QBD 459, CA, Brett LJ (later Lord Esher MR) at 464.

29 *Pattinson v Finningley Internal Drainage Board* [1970] 2 QB 33, Bean J at 39.

30 *Tarr v Tarr* [1973] AC 254, HL, Lord Pearson at 264.

31 *Director of Public Works v Ho Po Sang* [1961] AC 901, PC, unanimous advice at 922.

32 *Director of Public Works v Ho Po Sang* [1961] AC 901, PC, unanimous advice at 922.

be so, for 'most Acts of Parliament in fact do interfere with existing rights',[33] and in fact they must do so.

Taking property compulsorily

The rule that, in case of doubt, Acts which could have the effect of taking away vested rights must be given a narrow meaning in favour of the person who is entitled to those rights is a rule that applies with particular force in the case of an Act of Parliament that could have the effect of taking property compulsorily.[34] 'Any court will be reluctant to infer that Parliament intended a situation which might lead to a loss of private rights without compensation.'[35] In interpreting legislation conferring powers of compulsory purchase a court has 'to bear in mind that it is a statute which is depriving the citizen of his rights in property and his title, and the right to enjoy occupation of his lands, or perhaps somebody else's lands'.[36]

A statute should not be held to take away private rights of property without compensation unless the intention to do so is expressed in unambiguous terms.[37]

That is a statement that has been reaffirmed repeatedly. For example, Lord Reid has said 'I entirely accept the principle'.[38] In the Privy Council in a unanimous holding it was said that

Their Lordships would add, in view of the difficulty of reaching a certain conclusion on the legislative formula, that they consider that such obscurity as there is ought to be resolved in favour of the person whose property is taken away, all the more so since the effect of the Third proviso may, in such cases as the present, be of a confiscatory nature.[39]

In another affirming of the principle it was said that

'I agree ... that in an Act ... which, although it is not a confiscatory Act, it is certainly a dispropietary Act, if there is any doubt as to the way in which language should be construed, it should be construed in favour of the party who is to be dispropriated rather than otherwise'.[40]

---

33 *West v Gwynne*, [1911] 2 Ch 1, CA, Buckley LJ (later Baron Wrenbury) at 12.

34 *Westminster Bank Ltd v Minister of Housing and Local Government* [1971] AC 508, HL, Lord Warrington of Clyffe at 529.

35 *Ministry of Housing and Local Government v Sharp* [1970] 2 QB 223, Fisher J at 240.

36 *Chilton v Telford Development Corpn* [1987] 1 WLR 872, CA, Purchas LJ at 878.

37 *Colonial Sugar Refining Co Ltd v Melbourne Harbour Trust Commissioners*, [1927] AC 343, PC, Lord Warrington of Clyffe at 359. See also *Hartnell v Minister of Housing and Local Government* [1963] 1 WLR 1141 at 1147; affd [1965] AC 1134, HL.

38 *Westminster Bank Ltd v Minister of Housing and Local Government* [1971] AC 508, HL at 529.

39 *Robinson & Co Ltd v Collector of Land Revenue, Singapore* [1980] 1 WLR 1614, PC, unanimous advice at 1621.

40 *Methuen-Campbell v Walters* [1979] QB 525, CA, Buckley LJ at 542.

If legislation does not provide for compensation

The general legal approach unquestionably is that the absence of compensation clauses from an Act conferring powers affords an important indication that the Act was not intended to authorise interference with private rights ... But the indication is not conclusive.[41]

Legal rules as to court procedure or as to law costs do not create 'vested rights'

The rule for reading an Act of Parliament in such a way as to protect vested rights does not apply to an Act which lays down a new court procedure[42] or which makes a new provision about law costs. What is protected is the right in respect of which the court proceedings are taken, not the way in which those court proceedings are to be conducted: 'alterations in the form of procedure are always retrospective, unless there is some good reason or other why they should not be.'[43] The distinction between vested rights on the one hand and questions of court procedure on the other hand is best understood by bearing in mind that an Act which affects vested rights alters those rights themselves or the entitlement to them, whereas an Act which affects procedure does not assume to alter any rights, it merely invests the court with a measure of jurisdiction to ascertain and compel the observance of rights.

An Act which affects vested rights, cannot properly be described as 'procedural' even when 'it extinguishes conditions which previously had to be fulfilled as a prerequisite to the emergence of a right to compensation'.[44] It has been held in respect of an Act affecting vested rights that

it is wrong to treat the ... Act as a procedural Act. Where vested rights are affected, *prima facie* it is not a question of procedure ... as a general rule when one speaks of an Act as being a procedural Act, one means it is an Act relating to proceedings in litigation.[45]

Acts affecting a fundamental principle of the common law

Clear words are necessary for an Act to be interpreted as setting aside a fundamental principle of the common law. 'It is a well-established principle of construction that a statute is not to be taken as effecting a fundamental alteration in the general law unless it uses words that point unmistakably to that conclusion.'[46] The principle requires a court 'to construe a statute in

---

41 *Allen v Gulf Oil Refining Ltd* [1981] AC 1001, HL, Lord Edmund-Davies at 1016.

42 An act affecting the admissibility of evidence in court proceedings is an Act governing court procedure and not one relating to 'vested rights': *Selangor United Rubber Estates Ltd v Craddock (No 2)* [1968] 1 WLR 319, ChD.

43 *Gardner v Lucas* [1878] 3 App Cas 582, Lord Blackburn at 603.

44 *Re 14 Grafton Street London W1* [1971] 2 All ER 1, ChD, Brightman J (later Lord Brightman) at 9–10.

45 *National Real Estate and Finance Co Ltd v Hassan* [1939] 2 KB 61, CA, Scott LJ at 74.

46 *National Assistance Board v Wilkinson* [1952] 2 QB 648, DC, Devlin J (later Lord Devlin) at 661.

conformity with the common law rather than against it, except where and so far as the statute is plainly intended to alter the course of the common law'.[47] One example is the common law right to privacy in a person's own home:

> The present appeal is concerned exclusively with the subject's right to the privacy of his home ... The appeal turns on the respect which Parliament must be understood, even in its desire to stamp out drunken driving, to pay to the fundamental right of privacy in one's own home, which has for centuries been recognised by the common law.[48]

Another example is the right to silence – the right of a person not to answer questions if that person might be incriminated by the replies. This privilege against self-incrimination can only be abrogated by the manifestation of a clear legislative intention, express or implied. However, if the language of the Act is plain, Parliament clearly can abrogate even such a fundamental principle of the common law for, 'if there be a clash, the statute prevails as the legislative will of Parliament'.[49] Similarly a court will interpret laws in the light of a presumption that the Parliament does not intend to abrogate human rights and fundamental freedoms.

Acts that apply from before the date on which they were passed

The proper interpretation of Acts that apply from before the date on which they were passed is considered in Chapter 39.

---

47 *R v Morris* [1867] LR 1 CCR 90, Byles J at 95.

48 *Morris v Beardmore* [1981] AC 446, HL, Lord Scarman at 465.

49 *Bromley London Borough Council v Greater London Council* [1983] 1 AC 768, HL, Lord Scarman at 838.

CHAPTER 39

ACTS THAT APPLY FROM BEFORE THE DATE ON WHICH THEY WERE PASSED

The power of Parliament to make Acts that apply from a date before the date on which they were passed.

Parliament has power to make an Act apply from a date earlier than the date on which the Act itself was passed by Parliament. An Act of this kind is known as a retrospective Act. Parliaments have from time to time exercised the power to make an Act of this kind.

The commonest cause of the making of an Act of Parliament of this kind is the desire to treat something as having been done properly when actually it had not been done properly. An Act having that effect is known as a validating Act.

The meaning of 'retrospective'

A leading textbook on statutory interpretation has stated that a statute is retrospective 'which takes away or impairs any vested right acquired under existing laws, or creates a new obligation, or imposes a new duty, or attaches a new disability in respect to transactions or considerations already passed'.[1]

It has been held that

there is nothing retrospective in an enactment providing that a right which existed when it was passed shall on its passing cease to exist. That does not have any effect on anything which happened or was done before it was passed: it only affects the future after it was passed.[2]

Taking away existing rights

Unfortunately, Parliament's power to pass retrospective Acts is not limited to cases in which no one will be harmed. Parliament has power not only to make an Act operate from any date that it chooses, even from a date earlier than the date on which the Act first came before Parliament as a Bill, but it has power to take away existing rights. It can even set aside the result of litigation, so that someone who has been successful in litigation can have the benefit of the court order taken away from him or her and the court order itself set aside by the statute. Plain words would of course be necessary in order to achieve such an effect. However, the rule against retrospective destruction of existing substantive rights should be applied only with caution and subject to Parliament's intention.

---

1   *Craies on Statute Law* (7th edn by Edgar, SGG, Sweet & Maxwell, London, 1971) p 387.
2   *Commissioners of Customs and Excise v Gallaher Ltd* [1971] AC 43, HL, Lord Reid at 59.

Providing penalties for things done before the coming into force of the Act

Parliament has power not only to make an Act take effect from a date before the Act itself was passed, but it also has power to use that Act to make something a criminal offence even although it was not a criminal offence at the time it was done. It would take clear words to have that effect, for as Lord Reid has said 'there has for a very long time been a strong feeling against making legislation, and particularly criminal legislation, retrospective'.[3]

> The presumption against retrospection applies in general to legislation of a penal character, and it is to be presumed that a statute creating a new offence, or extending an existing one, is not intended to render criminal an Act which was innocent when it was committed and that a statute increasing the penalties for existing offences is not intended to apply in relation to an offence committed before its commencement.[4]

Therefore it is unusual to give a penal statute any retrospective operation except for the benefit of an accused or convicted person. Unless a penal Act expressly states that it is retrospective it should not be so interpreted as to make something an offence which was not an offence at the time that it was done. There have, however, been Acts of Parliament that have been specifically passed to make something an offence even although it was done before the Act itself was passed. An example is to be found in an Act passed by the English Parliament in 1531 to make the penalty for poisoning death by being boiled alive. It was expressly retrospective.[5]

Another example is that of the retrospective tax imposed by the British Parliament which increased the amount to be paid on a previous year's income even although the taxpayer had already paid everything he owed. The courts do not like this kind of Act, but when the words are clear the judges have no choice but to enforce them. Mr. Justice Slade[6] said:

> I am bound to say that I have a measure of sympathy with this submission, since section 8 of the Act of 1974 does appear to me to represent retrospective legislation of a fairly extreme kind. As the taxpayer said, if Parliament was content in the Act of 1974 retrospectively to increase surtax liabilities laid down by the Act of 1973 for the fiscal year 1972–1973, there seems in principle no reason why it should not hereafter increase surtax laid down by earlier Finance Acts, for even more distantly past fiscal years. It is obvious that retrospective legislation of this kind can operate harshly in individual cases, particularly, as the taxpayer pointed out, in a case where, at the time when the new legislation is introduced, the taxpayer has actually discharged the whole of his liability for the relevant fiscal year on the basis of the previously existing law; that being so, he may naturally have regarded his liability for that year as finally settled once and for all and may have arranged his affairs on that basis.

---

3   *Waddington v Miah alias Ullah* [1974] 1 WLR 683, HL at 694.

4   *Halsbury's Laws of England* (4th edn, Butterworths, London, 1983) vol 44, para 923. This quotation does not appear in the 1995 reissue of vol 44 (1), *Statutes*, para 1286, but this does not affect the quotation's validity.

5   The Act is referred to in more detail in Chapter 1 of this book under the heading **How an Act of Parliament begins**.

6   Later Slade LJ.

No doubt with considerations such as this in mind, the court, in construing a taxing statute, will be very reluctant to construe it as having a retrospective effect and will construe it as not having such effect if the words used allow such construction. As Lord Atkinson said in *Ingle v Farrand* [1927] AC 417 at 428: 'Your Lordships were referred to several authorities laying down the principle upon which the question should be determined whether a statute acts retrospectively or not. Amongst those authorities the case of *Smith v Callender* [1901] AC 297 and Lindley LJ's[7] judgment in *Lauri v Renad* [1892] 3 Ch 402 at 421 were included. The rule which according to those authorities is to be applied is thus stated in *Maxwell on Statutes* p 382: "It is a fundamental rule of English law that no statute shall be construed so as to have a retrospective operation unless such a construction appears very clearly in the terms of the Act, or arises by necessary and distinct implication."

This, however, marks the limit of the court's powers to refuse to give effect to retrospective legislation. As Lord Atkinson went on to say in *Ingle v Farrand*: 'If a clause in a statute says in so many plain words that the statute shall have retrospective operation, then it must not be construed so as to defeat those express words.'

Thus, in answer to submissions to the contrary made by the taxpayer, it is in my judgement clear that, as the constitutional law of England stands today, Parliament has the power to enact by statute any fiscal law, whether of a prospective or retrospective nature and whether or not it may be thought by some persons to cause injustice to individual citizens. If the wording of that legislation is clear, the court must give effect to it, even though it may have, or will have, a retrospective effect.[8]

The power to make an Act operate from a date earlier than the date on which the Act itself was passed by Parliament of course extends to anything that Parliament thinks fit to include in the Act. There are various cases, for example, in which the courts have held to be valid provisions which increase the penalties for things done before the coming into force of the provisions that increased those penalties.[9]

Clear words are needed to make an Act operate from before the date on which it was passed

It is a very far-reaching step to make an Act of Parliament operate from a date prior to the day on which it was passed by Parliament. Clear words are therefore necessary before an Act can be read as having that effect:

Unless there is some declared intention of the legislature – clear and unequivocal – or unless there are some circumstances rendering it inevitable that we should take the other view, we are to presume that an Act is prospective and not retrospective,[10]

---

7   Later Lord Lindley MR.

8   *James v Inland Revenue Commissioners* [1977] 1 WLR 835, DC at 838.

9   *Director of Public Prosecutions v Lamb* [1941] 2 KB 89, DC; *Buckman v Button* [1943] KB 405; *Mischeff v Springett* [1942] 2 KB 331; *R v Oliver* [1944] KB 68, CCA.

10 *Gardner v Lucas* (1878) 3 App Cas 582, HL, Lord O'Hagan at 601. See also *Carson v Carson* [1964] 1 All ER 681, PDA, Scarman J (later Lord Scarman) at 687.

and substantive statutory provisions are not to be treated as retrospective unless that effect cannot be avoided without doing violence to their language.[11] That is an approach which

> ensures that the courts are constantly on the alert for the kind of unfairness which is found in, for example, the characterisation as criminal of past conduct which was lawful when it took place, or in alterations to the antecedent natural, civil or familial status of individuals.[12]

There is a growing practice today for statutes to be expressed to be retrospective to the date on which the Cabinet, or the relevant Minister, announced an intention to bring in legislation to change the law on a particular matter. That practice does not destroy the basic presumption against retrospectivity in cases in which there is no expressed dating back:

> The very nature and purpose of enacted law give rise to an inference or presumption that unless the language of a statute clearly indicates to the contrary, any changes that it makes in the law as it existed previously, were not intended to have retrospective effect upon transactions that were carried out before the new law came into effect. The growing practice of backdating the effect of statutes to the date of the first minatory announcement by the executive government of its intention to promote legislation to change the law does not weaken the presumption against retroactivity where there is no express provision in a statute to that effect. Rather, it serves to confirm that the reason for the presumption is that in a civilized society which acknowledges the rule of law individual members of that society are entitled to know when they embark upon a course of conduct what the legal consequences of their doing so will be, so that they may regulate their conduct accordingly.[13]

If, therefore, the Act is in words which could fairly be read either as operating from before the passing of the Act or as operating only from the passing of the Act, it should be read as applying only from the date of the passing of the Act:[14] 'If the meaning of words in an enactment is clear, there is no presumption against them having a retrospective effect if that is indeed the result they produce'.[15]

The need for clear words does not, however, mean that the word 'retrospective' has to be used or that the Act has to say expressly that it operates from some date prior to the date of its passing: its necessary intendment may show that it is to be retrospective,[16] or circumstances relevant to its interpretation may be 'sufficiently strong to displace' the presumption.[17]

The strength of the presumption against retrospectivity in any particular case must depend on the nature and degree of the injustice which would result from giving a statute a retrospective operation. The task of interpretation

---

11 *Madden v Madden* [1974] 1 WLR 247, FD, Stirling J at 249.

12 *L'Office Cherifien des Phosphates v Yamashita Shinnihon SS Co Ltd* [1994] 1 AC 486, HL, Lord Mustill at 524.

13 *Inland Revenue Commissioners v Joiner* [1975] 1 WLR 1701, HL, Lord Diplock at 1714.

14 *Main v Stark* (1890) 15 App Cas 384, PC, Lord Selborne at 387.

15 *Customs and Excise Commissioners v Thorn Electrical Industries Ltd* [1975] 1 WLR 437, DC at 446.

16 *Zainal bin Hashim v Malaysia (Government)* [1980] AC 734, PC at 742.

17 *Sunshine Porcelain Potteries Pty Ltd v Nash* [1961] AC 927, PC, unanimous decision at 937 and 938.

Is not simply a question of classifying an enactment as retrospective or not retrospective. Rather, it may well be a matter of degree – the greater the unfairness, the more it is to be expected that Parliament will make it clear if that is intended.[18]

The weight to be given to injustice done to one party may be reduced if the same interpretation is clearly required to rectify a manifest injustice to others.

Even if an Act is retrospective to some extent the court will not give retrospective effect further than is necessary to comply with the plain meaning of the statute:

> The general rule is that all statutes, other than those which are merely declaratory, or which relate only to matters of procedure or of evidence, are *prima facie* prospective, and retrospective effect is not to be given to them unless, by express words or necessary implication, it appears that this was the intention of the legislature.[19]

Acts declaring the existing law are retrospective

Parliament may be concerned to make clear what the existing law is:

> where there are ambiguities in the existing statute law it is a legitimate purpose of legislative action by Parliament to clarify the law by indicating in which of the two alternative meanings the ambiguous language of the earlier statute is to be understood.[20]

The need for it to do so may arise because a court decision has shown it to be unclear or because there is a dispute amongst people who have to use the Act as to what its meaning is. In such a case Parliament can resolve the difficulty by passing a declaratory Act which says that the law is and always has been what that Act declares it to be.

> Where it does so, this will have retrospective effect upon transactions undertaken before the clarifying statute by persons whose guess as to the meaning of the earlier statute differed from the meaning subsequently attributed to it by Parliament.[21]

Acts relating to procedure or evidence are usually retrospective

The person who finds that his or her rights in litigation are changed because Parliament has passed an Act changing the procedure may well consider that Act to be unfair, but the courts treat a procedural Act as *prima facie* intended to be retrospective.[22]

---

18 *Secretary of State for Social Services v Tunnicliffe* [1991] 2 All ER 712, CA, Staughton LJ at 724; approved *L'Office Cherifien des Phosphates v Yamashita-Shinnihon SS Co Ltd* [1994] 1 AC 486, HL, Lord Mustill at 525.

19 *Waddington v Miah alias Ullah* [1974] 1 WLR 683, CA, unanimous decision at 690–91; affd [1974] 1 WLR 683, HL.

20 *Inland Revenue Commissioners v Joiner* [1975] 1 WLR 1701, HL, Lord Diplock at 1715.

21 *Inland Revenue Commissioners v Joiner* [1975] 1 WLR 1701, HL, Lord Diplock at 1715.

22 *Grimes v London Borough of Sutton* [1973] 2 All ER 448, NIRC at 452.

Surprisingly, and with 'very much doubt, it has been held that legislation affecting awards of costs in litigation is to be treated as procedural and therefore as retrospective'.[23]

This is also true of Acts relating to the rules of evidence – Acts which make something admissible in evidence that would not otherwise be admissible, or which give an effect to evidence which it would not otherwise have:

> The rule that an Act of Parliament is not to be given retrospective effect only applies to statutes which affect vested rights. It does not apply to statutes which only alter the form of procedure, or the admissibility of evidence, or the effect which the courts give to evidence.[24]

The attempt to give justice by distinguishing between 'accrued substantive and procedural rights' can raise problems of its own. The distinction 'leaves out of the account the fact that some procedural rights are more valuable than some substantive rights' and in some instances, it may be impossible 'to assign rights ... unequivocally to one category rather than another'. To overcome that difficulty the court may 'look to the practical value and nature of the rights involved as a step towards an assessment of the unfairness of taking them away after the event'.[25]

---

23 *R v Dunwoodie* [1978] 1 All ER 923, QBD, Slynn J (later Lord Slynn of Hadley) at 928–29.

24 *Blyth v Blyth (No 2)* [1966] AC 643, HL, Lord Denning (later Lord Denning MR) at 666.

25 *L'Office Cherifien des Phosphates v Yamashita-Shinnihon SS Co Ltd* [1994] 1 AC 486, HL, Lord Mustill at 527–28.

CHAPTER 40

THE AREA IN WHICH AN ACT OF PARLIAMENT OPERATES

A British Act operates within the territories the people of which are subject to the British Parliament

For most practical purposes, and unless the Act provides otherwise, a British statute operates within the territories the people of which are subject to the British Parliament:[1] 'there is an established presumption that in the absence of clear and specific words to the contrary, a statute does not make conduct outside the jurisdiction a criminal offence'.[2]

> The general principle is that legislation applies only to British subjects or foreigners who come to England. The general principle is subject to any express enactment to the contrary or to any plain implication to the contrary.[3]

> Lord Diplock expressed this principle by saying:

> Because sovereignty is territorial, there is a presumption based on international comity that Parliament, when enacting a penal statute, unless it uses plain words to the contrary, does not intend to make it an offence in English law to do acts in places outside the territorial jurisdiction of the English courts – at any rate unless the act is one which necessarily has its harmful consequences in England.[4]

It must, however, be borne in mind that this principle is a principle of interpretation and not a restriction upon the power of Parliament to make laws. Parliament can, if it chooses, express a statute to operate beyond the territorial limits of the area which it governs; and, in such a case, the courts would have to give that statute the full operation it is expressed to have.

Foreigners within the United Kingdom are required to comply with British legislation. This principle applies not only to tourists moving from country to country but to people who happen to be in a country, or a local government area, other than that in which they ordinarily reside. For example, if a person living in London goes to the City of Glasgow that person is required to obey the laws of Scotland and of the City of Glasgow, and the same approach would apply to a Russian visiting an English city.

Applying the principle to bodies under Parliament

A very similar principle is applied to laws made by bodies acting under parliamentary authority. Parliament has delegated the power to make law to a large and growing number of statutory bodies such as government departments, commissions, boards and local government authorities. Those

---

1   *Attorney-General (Alberta) v Huggard Assets Ltd* [1953] AC 420, PC at 441.

2   *Re adoption application (non-patrial: breach of procedures)* [1993] Fam 125, FD, Douglas Brown J at 132.

3   *Re Seagull Manufacturing Co Ltd (No 2)* [1994] 2 Ch 91, Mary Arden QC sitting as a Deputy High Court Judge at 98. See also *Cooke v Charles A Vogeler Co* [1901] AC 102, HL at 107.

4   *Lawson v Fox* [1974] AC 803, HL at 808.

bodies make law in a wide variety of forms such as statutory instruments, proclamations, and planning, environmental and heritage controls. A body making law in that way is presumed to be empowered to make laws that operate only within its own territorial boundaries unless Parliament has expressly given it a wider law-making power.

A local authority cannot validly make extraterritorial legislation without specific parliamentary authorisation, whereas Parliament can do it but is presumed not to have done so unless the Act makes that intention plain.

Defining the territories of Parliament

It is clear enough that, if two countries have a common boundary, the territorial area of each ends at that common boundary. Where, however, is the boundary line to be drawn when the country extends to the sea? It is difficult to give any firm answer to that question. Some countries retain the old concept of a 3 mile limit beyond low water mark. Other countries have adopted different tests. So far as the validity of an Act of Parliament is concerned, it would seem that its control can now extend as far to seaward as is necessary for purposes such as defence, fisheries and commerce in its various forms. The principle applied by the courts today is that

> the area to which an Act of Parliament ... applies may vary ... as the Crown, in the exercise of its prerogative, extends its claim to areas ... in which it did not previously assert its sovereignty.[5]

Statutes of the British Parliament ordinarily operate throughout the United Kingdom – England, Scotland, Wales and Northern Ireland – but they can be expressed to be limited to part only of the United Kingdom. An example of this restriction is afforded by the Statute Law Revision (Northern Ireland) Act 1980, s 22 of which states that 'this Act extends to Northern Ireland only'.

Parliament can make the Act operate beyond its territories

Basically, there is nothing to prevent a Parliament expressing a law to operate beyond its territorial boundaries. It can, for example, make a law controlling the activities of its own citizens irrespective of where they happen to be living. Thus the British Parliament could validly make a law controlling the activities of British citizens even though they happen to be living, for example, in Fiji – provided, of course, that they have retained British nationality.

Whether or not any particular statute does bind those nationals even although they are living outside the territorial boundaries can only be decided by a proper interpretation of the Act itself. Some kinds of Acts are more likely than other kinds to be held to apply to nationals living in another country. For example, a statute controlling marriages and prohibiting persons of close relationship marrying each other may apply to those nationals irrespective of where they live,[6] but a statute that prescribes the particular weights and

---

5   *Post Office v Estuary Radio Ltd* [1968] 2 QB 740, HL, Diplock LJ (later Lord Diplock) at 764.

6   *Brook v Brook* (1861) 9 HLC 193 at 210; 11 ER 703 at 710.

measures to be used when measuring goods for the purpose of sale will not operate outside the territories of the Parliament.[7]

If the Act of Parliament being interpreted creates an offence, there is 'a presumption that an offence-creating section was not intended by Parliament to cover conduct outside the territorial jurisdiction of the Crown'.[8] However, this is not a rigid rule. For instance, the English Court of Appeal held it to be an offence to supply advertising material to be broadcast from outside the jurisdiction by a pirate radio station.[9]

Applying the Act to foreigners beyond the territories

The general rule is that a statute does not apply to things done by foreigners outside the territories governed by the British Parliament:

> Parliament has no proper authority to legislate for foreigners outside its jurisdiction, ... no statute ought therefore to be held to apply to foreigners with respect to transactions out of British jurisdiction, unless the words of the statute are perfectly clear.[10]

However, if the foreigners living outside the territorial bounds have some sufficient connection within them, they can take advantage of a statute made by Parliament.[11]

Actions outside the territorial bounds affecting persons inside them

Even although a person is living outside the territorial bounds of the British Parliament and is not a British national, Parliament may still have power to govern his or her actions to some extent,[12] particularly if the actions have harmful consequences in the United Kingdom.

The international drug trade, and international terrorism, are fields in which British legislation may operate outside the territorial bounds.

---

7   *Rosseter v Cahlmann* (1853) 8 Ex 361; 155 ER 1586.

8   *Air-India v Wiggins* [1980] 1 WLR 815, HL, Lord Scarman at 820. See also *Cox v Army Council* [1963] AC 48 at 68 and 72–73.

9   *R v Murray (Nicholas)* [1990] 1 WLR 1360, CA at 1368–69.

10 *The Amalia* (1863), 1 Moore PC (NS) 471, at 474; 15 ER 778, PC at 779; *Air-India v Wiggins* [1980] 1 WLR 815, HL, Lord Scarman at 820.

11 *Davidson v Hill* [1901] 2 KB 606; *Re Seale's Marriage Settlement,* [1961] Ch 574, DC.

12 *Lawson v Fox* [1974] AC 803, HL, Lord Diplock at 808.

CHAPTER 41

HOW ACTS OF PARLIAMENT AFFECT THE CROWN

The meaning of 'the Crown'

In this chapter the phrase 'the Crown' is used as meaning what the ordinary person in the street would probably call 'the government'. 'The Crown' is a phrase meaning the State as a body, by whatever name it is known in the particular country concerned. It does not mean the king or queen personally.

When an Act of Parliament binds the Crown

An Act of Parliament is made by the Crown in Parliament. The rule therefore is that the Act of Parliament does not bind the Crown unless the Act expressly says it does. In the absence of express terms the Crown is not bound,[1] or unless the necessary implication from the words used in the Act is that the Crown is to be bound.[2] The fact that an Act expresses certain of its provisions as not binding on the Crown does not give rise to a presumption of the Crown being bound by the other provisions of the Act.[3]

The rule of non-application of an Act to the Crown does not depend upon an implication that the Act was passed for the public benefit.[4] Further, a statute must 'bind the Crown either generally or not at all'. An Act cannot be held to bind the Crown when the Crown is acting without any right to do so but not when the Crown does have such rights.[5]

Even although the Crown is not bound by the particular Act it can still take advantage of it. Indeed, it 'can take the benefit of any statute although not specifically named in it'.[6]

The extent of 'the Crown'

It is not difficult to apply this rule when the question as to the meaning of the Act arises with respect to land owned and occupied[7] by the State itself. Difficulty does arise, however, in deciding whether the rule applies to some statutory authority that has been set up by Parliament. The present position is

---

1   *Theberge v Laudry* (1876) 2 App Cas 102, HL; *Cushing v Lupuy* (1880) 5 App Cas 409, PC at 419.

2   *Bombay Province v Bombay Municipal Corpn* [1947] AC 58, PC; *Lord Advocate v Dumbarton District Council* [1990] 2 AC 580, HL, Lord Keith of Kinkel at 597–98.

3   *Bombay Province v Bombay Municipal Corpn* [1947] AC 58, PC, unanimous advice at 65.

4   *Lord Advocate v Dumbarton District Council* [1990] 2 AC 580, HL, Lord Keith of Kinkel at 598.

5   *Lord Advocate v Dumbarton District Council* [1990] 2 AC 580, HL, Lord Keith of Kinkel at 599 and 603–04.

6   *Town Investments Ltd v Department of the Environment* [1976] 1 WLR 1126, CA, Lawton LJ at 1142.

7   This means that the protection accorded to the government does not apply to tenants of Crown land.

that there is a strong tendency to regard a statutory corporation formed to carry on public functions as distinct from the Crown unless Parliament has by express provision given it the character of a servant of the Crown.[8]

A warning as to whether the Crown is bound

It is all very well to say that the Crown is bound by an Act that expressly states that that is so, but the reader might reasonably expect to find that statement at the outset of that Act. Readers more familiar with the customary location of definitions in an English Act might expect to find the provision about the Crown at the end of the sections of the Act or at the beginning of an Appendix. Unfortunately, that is by no means always the case. The very important s 21(2) Interpretation Act 1978 (an Act of 27 sections) springs the trap:

Supplementary

21 – (1) In this Act 'Act' includes a local and personal or private Act; and 'subordinate legislation' means Orders in Council, Orders, rules, regulations, schemes, warrants, byelaws and other instruments made or to be made under any Act.   Interpretation etc

(2) This Act binds the Crown.

Set in a section which contains two definitions which ought to have been with the other definitions in the schedule to the Act and which make no reference to the Crown, under a heading which makes no reference to the Crown and with a marginal note that makes no reference to the Crown the subsection may readily be overlooked.

---

8   See for example, *Tamlin v Hannaford* [1950] 1 KB 18, CA. The question as to when statutory bodies are to be treated as part of the 'Crown' for the purpose of gaining exemption from the provisions of an Act of Parliament is a complicated question that is beyond the scope of the present book.

CHAPTER 42

HOW JUDICIAL DECISIONS AFFECT THE READING OF AN ACT

Prior judicial decisions can be taken into consideration

It is not all judicial decisions that can be looked at for assistance in understanding an Act of Parliament. To be usable for this purpose the decision must be a decision of the High Court of Justice or a higher court.

Judicial decisions on principles of the common law

The most important judicial decisions for use in understanding an Act of Parliament are those which expound or develop the principles of the common law. For example, the rules of natural justice (which require the giving of a fair hearing without bias on the part of the person conducting the hearing) have long been established as an important part of the common law, but the expounding of those rules by the courts has led to the establishment of a principle applicable to understanding Acts of Parliament for the courts have held that the rules of natural justice apply unless the particular Act of Parliament excludes them.[1]

Judicial decisions on the meaning of particular words and phrases

It is not surprising that over the years a great body of judicial decisions has been built up on the meaning of particular words and phrases. These decisions are to be found in various judicial dictionaries. Care has to be taken in using them because a word or phrase may derive its meaning from the context in which it occurs but, subject to that qualification, resort to a judicial dictionary can assist the reader to understand the meaning of a word or phrase which would otherwise be ambiguous.

Re-enactment after an Act has been interpreted by the courts

If, after a provision in an Act of Parliament has been interpreted by a superior court, Parliament enacts legislation which includes that same provision, there is a presumption that Parliament knew of the decision and intended the new legislation to have the meaning the courts had already placed upon that provision. It has been accepted 'without question' that

---

1   *R v Secretary of State for the Environment, ex p Hammersmith and Fulham London Borough Council* [1991] 1 AC 521, HL, unanimous decision at 598.

Where once certain words in an Act of Parliament have received a judicial construction in one of the superior courts, and the legislature has repeated them without alteration in a subsequent statute, ... the legislature must be taken to have used them according to the meaning which a court of competent jurisdiction has given to them.[2]

Repeating that principle in a later decision, and in stronger terms, it was held that

If it can be inferred from the terms in which subsequent legislation has been passed that Parliament itself has approved of particular judicial interpretation of words in an earlier statute, this would be decisive in ... adhering to it.[3]

It is important to note that in the application of the presumption 'it is only the actual decisions of courts on such matters which should be regarded as having been endorsed by the legislature, and not all the views expressed by the judges concerned in making them'.[4]

Even if Parliament has adopted a judicial decision that is erroneous, Parliament's endorsement of it by legislating on that basis nevertheless attracts the presumption.[5]

Of course, the situation may also occur in reverse: Parliament may deliberately legislate to change what the courts have decided was the effect of the existing law.[6] In that case the judicial decision may assist in understanding the change that Parliament has made.

The presumption is limited to decisions upon the meaning of a word in a statute and does not extend to the meaning of a word in subordinate legislation:

It is not to be presumed that Parliament in any subsequent Act of Parliament dealing with a related but not identical subject matter has taken account of and adopted as correct all judicial pronouncements as to the meaning of ordinary English words appearing in statutory instruments, notwithstanding that they might otherwise be overruled by a higher court.[7]

The presumption that Parliament endorses a prior judicial decision by its subsequent legislation does not apply to a consolidating Act because the parliamentary procedures in relation to a consolidating Act 'afforded no opportunity to Parliament of reconsidering the previous Acts which were consolidated. It left the existing law ... unchanged'.[8]

---

2   *Dun v Dun* [1959] AC 272, PC, unanimous advice at 292.

3   *Geelong Harbour Trust Commissioners v Gibbs Bright & Co (a firm)* [1974] AC 810, PC, unanimous advice at 820.

4   *The Eschersheim; Erkowit (owners) v Salus (owners)* [1975] 1 WLR 83, QBD, Brandon J at 89.

5   *Herbert Berry Associates Ltd v Inland Revenue Commissioners* [1977] 1 WLR 1437, HL, Lord Russell of Killowen at 1448.

6   *Simmons v Pizzey* [1979] AC 37, HL, Lord Hailsham of St Marylebone at 60.

7   *Haigh v Charles W Ireland Ltd* [1974] 1 WLR 43, HL, Lord Diplock at 57.

8   *Haigh v Charles W Ireland Ltd* [1974] 1 WLR 43, HL, Lord Diplock at 57.

Technical legal terms

There are many terms which have their own special meaning in law. Sometimes the meaning may be wider and sometimes it may be narrower than the ordinary meaning of the word. When Parliament uses a word with a well known legal meaning the presumption is that it intended to use the word in its strict legal sense 'unless a contrary intention appears'.[9]

---

9   *Commissioners of the Income Tax v Pemsel* [1891] AC 531, HL, Lord Macnaghten at 580.

CHAPTER 43

SUBORDINATE LEGISLATION

Subordinate legislation

Parliament delegates to Ministers, government departments, semi-government authorities and local authorities (amongst others) the power to make law. The law-making power so delegated by Parliament covers many fields of which environmental, planning, resources and heritage controls are increasingly common. Just as the subjects delegated by Parliament are many and various, so too are the forms which the subordinate legislation may take. It is defined authoritatively as meaning 'Orders in Council, orders, rules, regulations, schemes, warrants, byelaws and other instruments made or to be made under any Act'[1] – a definition which curiously fails to make reference to the term statutory instruments which is certainly a very common and well known type of document today. Traditionally, subordinate legislation cannot be used to interpret a statute: 'It is legitimate to use the Act as an aid to the construction of the regulations. To do the converse is to put the cart before the horse.'[2] As Viscount Dilhorne has said, 'I have no hesitation in rejecting the contention that rules made in the exercise of a statutory power can be relied on as an aid to the construction of a statute.'[3] A distinction has to be drawn, however, between subordinate legislation of the ordinary type and subordinate legislation expressly authorised by Parliament to amend the Act. In the latter case reference may be made to the subordinate legislation to interpret the Act in case of ambiguity. Lord Lowry has expressed the position in six propositions:

(1) Subordinate legislation may be used in order to construe the parent Act, but only where power is given to amend the Act by regulations or where the meaning of the Act is ambiguous.

(2) Regulations made under the Act provide a parliamentary or administrative [contemporaneous exposition] of the Act but do not decide or control its meaning: to allow this would be to substitute the rule-making authority for the judges as interpreter and would disregard the possibility that the regulation relied on was misconceived or [invalid].

(3) Regulations which are consistent with a certain interpretation of the Act tend to confirm that interpretation.

(4) Where the Act provides a framework built on by contemporaneously prepared regulations, the latter may be a reliable guide to the meaning of the former.

(5) The regulations are a clear guide, and may be decisive, when they are made in pursuance of a power to modify the Act, particularly if they come into operation on the same day as the Act which they modify.

(6) Clear guidance may also be obtained from regulations which are to have effect as if enacted in the parent Act.[4]

---

1 Section 21(1) Interpretation Act 1978.

2 *Lawson v Fox*, [1974] AC 803, HL, Lord Diplock at 809.

3 *Jackson v Hall* [1980] AC 854, HL at 884.

4 *Hanlon v Law Society* [1981] AC 124, HL at 193–94.

Section 11 Interpretation Act 1978 states that

Construction
of subordinate
legislation
11 Where an Act confers power to make subordinate legislation, expressions used in that legislation have, unless the contrary intention appears, the meaning which they bear in the Act.

Subordinate legislation needs authorisation to be retrospective

Subordinate legislation even if stated to be retrospective will not have that effect unless the statute under which it is made authorises retrospectivity.[5]

---

5   *Customs & Excise Commissioners v Thorn Electrical Industries Ltd* [1975] 1 WLR 1661, HL; see also *R v Oliver* [1944] KB 68.

CHAPTER 44

INTERNATIONAL TREATIES AND CONVENTIONS

An Act giving effect to a treaty or convention is presumed to intend to fulfil Britain's obligations

If an Act is passed to give effect to an international convention, the courts will presume that Parliament intended to fulfil its international obligations rather than to depart from them: 'the court should so construe the statute as to give effect, so far as possible, to the presumption that Parliament intended to fulfil, rather than to break, its international obligations'.[1] As Lord Denning MR has expressed it,

> The position ... is that if there is any ambiguity in our statutes or uncertainty in our law, then these courts can look to the convention as an aid to clear up the ambiguity and uncertainty, seeking always to bring them into harmony with it.[2]

The treaty or convention can be examined to resolve ambiguity in the British Act

If the words of the Act are ambiguous, the words of the convention itself may be examined in order to find out which of the alternative meanings is to be preferred in construing the Act:[3]

> Where the meaning of an English statute intended to give effect to an international convention to which the UK is a signatory is not clear, the court can and should look at the terms of the convention to assist it in construing the statute.[4]

Words in the treaty or convention are to be given their ordinary meanings

In using the treaty or convention to ascertain the meaning of the Act to give effect to the treaty or convention

> the words [of the treaty or convention] are to be understood in their natural meanings, if this differs from some technical meaning which has been ascribed to similar words in an English statute dealing with an analogous subject matter.[5]

---

1   *Medway Drydock & Engineering Co Ltd v MV Andrea Ursula* [1973] 1 QB 265, PD, Brandon J (later Lord Brandon of Oakbrook) at 271.

2   *R v Chief Immigration Officer Heathrow Airport, ex p Salamat Bibi* [1976] 3 All ER 843, CA at 847.

3   *The Eschersheim; Erkowit (owners) v Salus (owners)* [1975] 1 WLR 83, QBD at 89.

4   *Medway Drydock & Engineering Co Ltd v MV Andrea Ursula* [1973] 1 QB 265, PD, Brandon J (later Lord Brandon of Oakbrook) at 270–71.

5   *Beese v Ashford Remand Centre (Governor)* [1973] 1 WLR 1426, HL at 1429.

The purposive approach is to be applied

The words of the treaty or convention

> should be given a purposive rather than a narrow literalistic construction, particularly wherever the adoption of a literalistic construction would enable the stated purpose of the international convention ... to be evaded by the use of colourable devices that, not being expressly referred to ... , are not specifically prohibited.[6]

The purpose being sought for interpretative purposes is the purpose of 'those who made' the treaty or convention.[7] In seeking that purpose the court 'should interpret [the treaty or convention] in the same spirit and by the same methods as the judges of the other countries do', and this is so even although those methods differ from or conflict with the methods traditionally applied in the common law courts in interpreting legislation.[8]

This is so to try to gain uniformity in the interpretation of the treaty or convention:

> as it is an international convention, we must do our best to interpret it, so far as we can, with a view to promoting the objective of uniformity in its interpretation and application in the Courts of the states which are parties to the convention.[9]

Using a treaty or convention in two or more languages

It is not unusual for an international treaty or convention to be written in two or more languages. In resolving ambiguities it is permissible to look at one of the foreign language texts of the treaty or convention even although that treaty or convention is embodied in the English Act.[10]

In using a foreign language text of an international treaty or convention it is permissible to use a dictionary which is in the language of that text.[11] However, the primary approach is to use the English text:

> the correct approach is to interpret the English text which after all is likely to be used by many others than British businessmen, in a normal manner, appropriate for the interpretation of an international convention, unconstrained by technical rules of English law or by English legal precedent but on broad principles of general acceptation.[12]

---

6   *The Hollandia* [1983] 1 AC 565, HL, Lord Diplock at 572–73.

7   *James Buchanan & Co Ltd v Babco Forwarding & Shipping (UK) Ltd* [1978] AC 141, HL, Viscount Dilhorne at 157.

8   *James Buchanan & Co Ltd v Babco Forwarding & Shipping (UK) Ltd* [1977] 2 WLR 107, CA at 112; affd [1978] AC 141, HL.

9   *Ulster-Swift Ltd v Taunton Meat Haulage Ltd* [1977] 1 WLR 625, CA at 628.

10 *James Buchanan & Co Ltd v Babco Forwarding & Shipping (UK) Ltd* [1977] 2 WLR 107, CA at 118 and 121; affd [1978] AC 141, HL.

11 *Fothergill v Monarch Airlines Ltd* [1978] QB 108, Kerr J (later Kerr LJ) at 115; restored after intermediate reversal [1981] AC 251, HL.

12 *James Buchanan & Co Ltd v Babco Forwarding & Shipping (UK) Ltd* [1978] AC 141, HL, Lord Wilberforce at 152.

Extrinsic evidence may be used to determine whether an international treaty or convention is relevant

In order to bring into operation the principles enunciated in this chapter it is not necessary for the Act being interpreted to have an express reference to the international treaty or convention:

> If from extrinsic evidence it is plain that the enactment was intended to fulfil Her Majesty's Government's obligations under a particular convention, it matters not that there is no express reference to the convention in the statute. One must not presume that Parliament intended to break an international convention merely because it does not say expressly that it is intending to observe it.[13]

However, the extrinsic evidence must be 'cogent' – 'the court must not merely guess that the statute was intended to give effect to a particular international convention'.[14]

The effect of conventions being more loosely worded than Acts

The procedures for producing a treaty or convention acceptable to two or more countries are different to those involved in the drafting and acceptance of an Act of Parliament. This is an aspect of which the courts must take cognizance when interpreting a treaty or convention:

> In construing the terms of a convention it is proper and indeed right ... to have regard to the fact that conventions are apt to be more loosely worded than Acts of Parliament. To construe a convention as strictly as an Act may indeed lead to a wrong interpretation being given to it.[15]

The presumptions do not apply if the words being interpreted are unambiguous

Where the words of an English statute are plain and unambiguous it is not open to the courts of this country to look to the convention for assistance in their interpretation.[16]

---

13 *Salomon v Commissioners of Customs and Excise* [1967] 2 QB 116, CA, Diplock LJ (later Lord Diplock) at 144.

14 *Salomon v Commissioners of Customs and Excise* [1967] 2 QB 116, CA, Diplock LJ (later Lord Diplock) at 144.

15 *James Buchanan & Co Ltd v Babco Forwarding & Shipping (UK) Ltd* [1978] AC 141, HL, Viscount Dilhorne at 157.

16 *R v Secretary of State for the Home Department, ex p K* [1991] 1 QB 270, CA at 280.

The special rules for interpreting the European Community's Access Act and Directives

Britain's entry into the European Community has produced a rapidly expanding number of decisions of the European Court binding on Britain. Those decisions are based on the principles of European Law.

In many respects the principles of interpretation adopted by the European Court are different from, or even directly opposed to, the English principles of interpretation. They are set out in Chapters 45–48.

Of course, the European Court can only apply the European Community principles of interpretation if the document to be interpreted is such as to be subject wholly or in part to the Community system. In all the other instances the basic principles of the English system continue to be applied.

CHAPTER 45

THE EUROPEAN LAW APPROACH

Introduction

By contrast with ordinary international treaties, the EC Treaty has created its own legal system which, on the entry into force of the Treaty, became an integral part of the legal systems of the Member States.[1]

The European Court of Justice has established the principle that the European Community is a community based on the rule of law, in as much as neither its Member States nor its institutions can avoid a review of whether the measures adopted by them are in conformity with the basic constitutional charter namely the EC Treaty.[2]

The EC Treaty established the European Court of Justice as the judicial body responsible for ensuring that both the Member States and the Community institutions comply with the law.

In that Community subject to the rule of law relations between the Member States and the Community institutions are governed, according to Article 5 of the EC Treaty, by a principle of sincere co-operation. That principle firstly requires that Member States take all the measures necessary to guarantee the application and effectiveness of Community law[3] and secondly imposes on Member States and the Community institutions mutual duties of sincere co-operation.[4]

It is incumbent upon every Community institution to give its active assistance to national courts in national legal proceedings by producing documents to the national court and authorising its officials to give evidence in the national proceedings.[5]

In this chapter we highlight some of the differences in approach to interpretation between European Community Law and English law.

Community treaties

By virtue of Article 31 of the ECSC Treaty, Article 164 of the EC Treaty and Article 136 of the EURATOM Treaty the Court of Justice must in construing a provision of Community law give to it its full effect interpreting it in the light of Community law as a whole so that Community law is observed. Article 164, for example, says that the Court of Justice shall ensure that in the interpretation and application of the EC Treaty the law is observed. The Court of Justice must interpret Community law not only in a way which is consistent with other

---

1   Case 6/64 *Costa v Enel* [1964] ECR 585.

2   Case 294/83 *Les Verts v Parliament* [1986] ECR 1357, para 23.

3   Case 68/88 *Commission v Greece* [1989] ECR 2965, para 23.

4   Case 230/81 *Luxembourg v Puliat* [1983] ECR 255, para 37.

5   Case 2/88 *Criminal Proceedings v J J Zwartveld and Others* [1990] ECR 1-3365, para 22.

provisions of Community law but also with the so-called 'spirit' of Community law and its unwritten principles.

The rules of construction are different from those appertaining to each of the Member States. Legal terms used in Community law do not necessarily have the same meaning as in a national law.

The Community has also developed its own terminology.

The general principle of construction is, however, that the European Court of Justice must place a provision in context,[6] have regard to the general scheme relating to the provision,[7] have regard to the general provisions of Community law[8] and have regard to the objectives of Community law.[9] Thus, the Court will look at the founding Treaties and the instrument creating the provision[10] and interpret that in the light of the general principles behind the framing of the instrument in question.[11]

The purpose of a legislative instrument can usually be gathered from reviewing the recitals and documents mentioned in the recitals. From a close study of these documents it is possible to determine whether a broad or narrow construction should be given to a provision.[12]

It may also be necessary in the case of some measures to look at the surrounding circumstances[13] and possibly at general social developments which relate closely to measures dealing with the human environment.[14]

It should be noted that Denmark, Germany, Greece, Italy, the Netherlands, Spain and the UK are parties (together with over 50 other countries) to the Vienna Convention on the Law of Treaties[15] which establishes rules governing the conclusion, application, interpretation, modification, termination, suspension and validity of treaties.

---

6   See for example Case 9/70 *Grad v Finanzamt Traunstein* [1970] ECR 825 at 839 and Case 67/79 *Fellinger v Bundesanstalt für Arbeit Nuremberg* [1980] ECR 535.

7   See for example Case 89/81 *Staatssecretaris van Financien v Hong Kong Trade Development Council* [1982] ECR 1277 at 1285.

8   See for example Case 152/73 *Sotgiu v Deutsche Bundespost* [1974] ECR 153 at 165, Case 7/82 *GBL v Commission* [1983] ECR 483 at 502, and Case 375/85 *Campana v Bundesanstalt für Arbeit* [1987] ECR 2387.

9   See Case 283/81 *CILFIT Srl v Ministry of Health* [1982] ECR 3415 at 3430.

10 There are numerous cases but see for example Case 19/81 *Burton v British Railways Board* [1982] ECR 555 at 575; Case 84/81 *Staple Dairy Products Ltd v Intervention Board for Agricultural Produce* [1982] ECR 1763 at 1778; Case 232/82 *Baccini v The Office National de l'Emploi* [1983] ECR 583 at 595 and 596 and Case 254/85 *Irish Grain Board v Minister for Agriculture* [1986] ECR 3309 at para 10.

11 See for example Case 6/72 *Europemballage Corporation and Continental Can Co Inc v Commission* [1973] ECR 215 at 243–45.

12 See for example Case 320/85 *Ministère Public v. Maniglier* [1986] ECR 2917 at para 9; Case 13/84 *Control Data v Commission* [1987] ECR 275 at para 16; Case 29/69 *Stauder v Ulm* [1969] ECR 419 at 425, and Case 232/86 *Nicolet Instrument v Hauptzollamt Berlin-Packhof* [1987] ECR 5025 at para 11.

13 See Case 215/85 *BALM v Raiffeisen Hauptgenossenschaft* [1987] ECR 1279 at paras 18 and 19.

14 See Case 59/85 *Netherlands v Reed* [1986] ECR 1283, para 15.

15 UKTS 58 (1980), Cmnd 7964, entered into force on 27 January 1980.

International treaties

Following EC Council Accession Decisions of 22 January 1972 the Treaty of Accession was ratified by Denmark, Ireland and the United Kingdom in accordance with their respective Constitutions.[16] These three countries acceded by the Act of Accession (1972) to the Decisions and Agreements adopted by the European Council of Ministers and to certain Conventions provided for by Article 220 of the EC Treaty as well as the Protocols on the interpretation of those Conventions[17] and to Declarations and Resolutions made by the Council.

Under Community law Member States become bound by the Agreements or Conventions entered into by any of the three Communities with third countries, international organisations or nationals of third countries. There is a tendency in drafting modern Community Regulations for Regulations to make binding on Member States the provisions of certain named Conventions.[18]

A Directive or Decision, although addressed to sovereign Member States is to be regarded as an internal Community instrument and cannot be regarded as an international agreement.[19] Each of the European Communities has the capacity to establish relations with international organisations and to conclude international agreements, subject to certain qualifications. One has to look at the specific Articles of each of the Treaties for the powers.

The problem which arises is whether the Community competence to enter into treaties is an exclusive competence, a concurrent competence or a joint competence. The general principle is that the Member States remain free to act as sovereign states until the Community has claimed its exclusive competence by using it.[20]

The Court of Justice has jurisdiction over Community actions with regard to treaties. It can decide whether or not a proposed international agreement is compatible with the enabling treaty. Whilst the Court can address itself to questions relevant to the validity of a proposed treaty and its impact upon Community law, it is not open to the Court in such a procedure to give a final judgement on the interpretations of texts referred to it for its Opinion.[21]

The treaties having been duly concluded by the English Crown were converted by Parliament into domestic law by virtue of the European Communities Act 1972.

---

16 Treaty of Accession (1972) (TS16) (1979); Cmnd 7461.

17 Article 3(2) Act of Accession (1972).

18 See for example Article 32 of EEC Regulation 259/93 which requires compliance with ADR, COTIF, RID, SOLAS, CHICAGO, MARPOL and ADNR; see also Article 3 of EC Directive 95/21 which requires compliance with applicable provisions of the International Convention on Load Lines, SOLAS, MARPOL, STEW, COLREG, the International Convention on Tonnage Measurement of Ships and the Merchant Shipping (Minimum Standards) Convention.

19 Case 38/69 *Commission v Italy* [1970] ECR 47, [1970] CMLR77; Case 91/79 *Commission v Italy* [1980] ECR 1099 at 1105; Case 92/79 *Commission v Italy* [1980] ECR 1115 at 1121.

20 Joined Cases 3, 4 and 6/76 *Officier van Justitie v Kramer* [1976] ECR 1279.

21 See Opinion 1/76 [1977] ECR 741 at 961.

How a Directive comes into force

A Directive, once adopted, is deemed to be perpetual unless and until it is repealed by some later Directive. It comes into force on the date stated conventionally towards the end of the Directive. However, if it is defective it can be annulled by the European Court of Justice. In the case of *Commission v Council*[22] Directive 89/428 on Waste from the Titanium Dioxide Industry was held to be void on the grounds that it used an inappropriate legal base. It was accordingly replaced by Directive 92/112 using a different legal base. In *Re Trade in Animal Glands: Commission v Council*[23] the Court declared void Council Directive 87/64 because it fell within the field of application of Article 43 of the EC Treaty and in consequence the Council was not justified in adopting it on the basis of Articles 100 and 113.

Where the validity of a Community Regulation is the subject of a reference to the European Court of Justice for a preliminary ruling, the Court of the Member State can grant interim relief to settle disputed legal positions or relationships arising from national administrative measures adopted on the basis of the Regulation.[24]

The elements of a Directive

The following are the more important elements which may be found in a Directive:

Official Journal reference,

number of the Directive and Community concerned (EC, ECSC, Euratom),

date of Directive,

title of Directive,

legislating body (EP and Council, Council or Commission),

Treaty Article relied upon as legal basis,

recitals of:
Proposal,
Ecosoc Opinion,
EP Opinion,
procedure used,
history,
purposes,
objectives,

Articles,

Parts,

paragraphs,

---

22 Case C-300/89, 11 June 1991, Transcript.

23 Case 131/87, 16 November 1989, [1991] 1 CMLR 780.

24 Case C-465/93 *Atlanta Fruchthandelsgesellshaft mbH and Others v Bundesamt für Ernährung und Forstwirtschaft* (1995) Times, 29 November.

sub-paragraphs,

definitions,

main objectives,

date for compliance,

repeals,

reports,

entry into force,

Member States addressed,

date,

signature,

Annexes.

The nature of the preamble

A Regulation, Directive or Decision may well contain a number of recitals which usually set out the reasons for making the legislative instrument and its scope. A Directive normally contains a recital of the proposal for the Directive. Care should be exercised here because the Commission's document setting out its adopted proposal as promulgated normally contains an explanatory memorandum at the beginning. The explanatory memorandum is not reproduced in the Official Journal, presumably to save the additional costs of printing. Parliamentary and Ecosoc Opinions normally contain a useful commentary on the reasons for making a legislative instrument and are useful aids towards interpretation. Thus, the European Court of Justice uses the preamble to try and ascertain the meaning of the legislative instrument and generally its scope and purpose.

A Community instrument does not have a long or a short title. It has a reasonably short title but it is customary to give Directives nicknames for the purposes of easy identification but which have no effect on construction whatsoever. Thus, Council Directive 92/43/EEC of 21 May 1992 on the conservation of natural habitats and of wild fauna and flora is usually called the Habitats Directive and Council Directive 79/409/EEC of 2 April 1979 on the Conservation of Wild Birds is generally known as the Birds Directive.

European legislation does not use enacting words. In the numbering of Regulations the year is put after the oblique line, such as 1/95 whereas in the case of Directives or Decisions the year is put first, such as 95/1.

Drafting procedure

There is no European legislation by reference. This is perhaps due to the fact that most texts are drafted in the French language by Commission employees where French is the usual language of the Commission and translated into Community languages after adoption but prior to publication. Thus the date shown on a Directive, for example, is the date of signature but a Directive does not come into force until it is published in the Official Journal in all its various

Community languages. It may, of course, come into force later than the date of publication in the Official Journal. The matter is normally dealt with by an express provision appearing towards the end of the Directive.

Every part of a published Directive is treated legally as part of the legislative act. A European Directive, therefore, includes, as part of the legal text, footnotes, headings, marginal headings, the title, the annexes and the signature.

Whilst in English law there is an understandable reluctance to refer to the preamble as an aid to interpretation of an Act if the provision in the Act that is being considered is one with plain meaning,[25] in Community law the judges of the European Court of Justice will look at the preamble for confirmation of a plain meaning interpretation.[26] So, whilst marginal notes or side notes are not part of an Act of Parliament, they are part of a European Community instrument. The European Court of Justice can use marginal notes as a means of finding the true meaning of an Article when the meaning of that Article is in doubt.

Commission and Parliamentary Reports

What the Commission intended a Regulation, Decision or Directive to do and what the European Parliament opines about that in a written Opinion and what the Economic and Social Committee think about a Commission proposal can all be referred to in the process of ascertaining the meaning of a Community instrument, unlike the case in English law where references to *Hansard* are of a somewhat restricted nature.[27] In English law reference to Parliamentary materials is permitted as an aid to the construction of legislation which is ambiguous or obscure or where its literal meaning leads to an absurdity.[28] The European Court of Justice may look at materials recited in the preamble to a Community instrument for a number of purposes including confirmation of an initial construction. Such materials include Commission communications or reports, policy guidelines, treaties and conventions, other legislation and publications.

Incorporated and conflicting terms

Of more recent times English subordinate legislation has incorporated Community definitions and terms. A good example is the Waste Management Licensing Regulations 1994 which incorporate the concept of 'Directive waste'. It is a moot point whether waste in this sense has to be construed in accordance with the Community rules of construction or the English rules of construction. Under the treaties a Regulation is directly applicable throughout the Community. Its terms are not nationally re-enacted. Section 2(4) European Communities Act 1972 requires future enactments to be construed and to have

---

25 *Powell v Kempton Park Racecourse Co* [1899] AC 143, HL, Lord Halsbury at 157.

26 See below Chapter 48.

27 See above Chapter 26.

28 *Pepper v Hart* [1993] AC 593, Lord Browne-Wilkinson at 634.

effect subject, among other things, to s 2(1). Section 3(1) requires United Kingdom courts to follow the case law of the European Court of Justice. That case law has established a doctrine of the primacy of Community law.[29] Thus a later provision of Community law falling within s 2(1) will override an earlier provision of English law which is in conflict with Community law on the ordinary principles of domestic statutory interpretation. Where a provision of English law is of a later date than the provision of Community law with which it is in conflict, it appears to be generally accepted that s 2(4) is effective to prevent inadvertent conflicts. Lord Denning has said that directly applicable Community law prevails over the internal law of a Member State whether passed before or after joining the Community.[30]

In the English House of Lords case of *Kirklees Metropolitan Borough Council v Wickes Building Supplies Ltd*[31] the local authority applied for an interlocutory injunction to restrain the defendant from using shop premises for Sunday trading in breach of s 47 Shops Act 1950. It was argued that s 47 was in conflict with Article 30 of the EC Treaty which, as between Member States, prohibited quantitative restrictions on imports and all measures having equivalent effect. The House of Lords held that a requirement that the plaintiff should give an undertaking had no justification in Community law since any obligation to make good any damage suffered by the defendants in the event of s 47 being found to be in breach of Article 30 of the Treaty would fall upon the United Kingdom government. In giving judgment Lord Goff restated the argument that s 47 cannot stand because it is inconsistent with Article 30, a provision having direct effect which prohibits between Member States' quantitative restrictions on imports and all measures having equivalent effect. It is said that the prohibition against Sunday trading in England had such an effect.[32]

The English courts have shown a tendency to try and construe English law as being in conformity with Community law. The House of Lords has held, for example, that the Transfer of Undertakings (Protection of Employment) Regulations 1981 were made for the express purpose of complying with Council Directive EEC 77/187 which provided for the safeguarding of employees' rights on the transfer of a business.

The courts of the United Kingdom are under a duty to give a purposive construction to the Regulations in a manner which would accord with the decisions of the European Court of Justice on the Directive. Where necessary, words can be implied which would achieve that effect. The House of Lords then implied in reg 5(3) after the words 'immediately before the transfer' the words 'or would have been so employed if he had not been unfairly dismissed in the

---

29 Case 6/64 *Costa v ENEL* [1964] ECR 585.

30 *Shields v E Coomes (Holdings) Ltd* [1979] 1 All ER 456, CA.

31 [1993] AC 227.

32 For a decision that Community law must be interpreted as meaning that a national court, which, in a case before it concerning Community law, considers that the sole obstacle which precludes it from granting interim relief is a rule of national law, must set aside such rule, see *R v Secretary of State for Transport, ex p Factortame Ltd (No 2)* [1991] 1 AC 603, HL. For construction of national law to provide an appropriate remedy see Case C-106/89 *Marleasing* [1990] 1 ECR 4135.

circumstances described by Regulation 8(1)'.[33] In another case the House of Lords held that the purpose for which s 1(2)(c) Equal Pay Act 1970 was enacted was to implement the United Kingdom's obligations of equal pay under Article 119 of the EEC Treaty and Council Directive EEC 75/117. Accordingly, if a female employee was employed on work of equal value to the work of a man doing another job for the employer, she was entitled under s 1(2)(c) to claim equal pay with that man notwithstanding that there was another man doing the same work as her for the same pay.[34]

---

33 *Litster v Forth Dry Dock and Engineering Co Ltd* [1990] AC 546, HL.
34 *Pickstone v Freemans plc* [1989] AC 66, HL.

CHAPTER 46

EUROPEAN PRINCIPLES

Unwritten principles

In ascertaining the intention of the wording of a legal instrument full effect must be given to the unwritten principles established by Community law. References to the spirit of the law provided the references are not to vague declarations but to clearly established principles can be regarded as a powerful tool to aid construction.[1]

It is well established that even if the wording appears not to be ambiguous, nonetheless it is regarded as appropriate to refer to the spirit, general scheme and context of the provision being construed.[2] If the wording is not clear then it is even more important to refer to the spirit, general scheme and context of the provision.[3]

Fundamental rights

A second principle is that where one is concerned with the interpretation of a concept defining the field of application of a fundamental freedom guaranteed by a Community treaty then such concept must not be given a restrictive interpretation.[4] It has thus been established that a restrictive interpretation cannot be given to a provision establishing a guarantee for the protection of a fundamental right to the detriment of the individual concerned.[5]

Where a legal instrument is silent on a matter which relates to the protection of the rights of individuals then such silence should not be called in aid to construe the text in a manner most unfavourable to individuals.[6]

Effet utile

Full effect must be given to the principle of *effet utile*. In Case 187/87 *Saarland and Others v Ministry of Industry and Others*[7] the Court was faced with the interpretation of Article 37 of the Euratom Treaty in the context of an authorisation by the French government for the disposal of radioactive waste

---

1   Case 43/75 *Defrenne v SA Belge de Navigation Aérienne* [1976] ECR 455, [1976] 2 CMLR 98.

2   Case 118/79 *Gebr der Knauf Westdeutsche Gipswerke v Hauptezollamt Hamburg Jonas* [1980] ECR 1183. See also Case 143/82 *Lipman v EC Commission* [1983] ECR 1301.

3   Case 136/80 *Hudig en Pieters BV v Minister Van Landbouw en Visserij* [1981] ECR 2233, [1983] 1 CMLR 582.

4   Case 53/81 *Levin v Staatssecretaris van Justitie* [1982] ECR 1035, [1982] 2 CLMR 454; Case 152/82 *Forcheri v Belgium* [1983] ECR 2323, [1984] 1 CMLR 334; Case 139/85 *Kempf v Staatssecretaris van Justitie* [1986] ECR 1741; and Case 316/85 *Centre Public d'aide Socialie de Courcelles v Lebon* [1987] ECR 2811, [1989] 1 CMLR 337.

5   Case 6/60 *Humblet v Belgium* [1960] ECR 559.

6   Joined Cases 8-11/66 *Cimenteries CBR Cementbedrijven NV v Commission* [1967] ECR 7; [1967] CMLR 77.

7   [1989] 1 CMLR 529.

from the nuclear power station at Cattenom. Article 37 appears in Chapter 3 of the Treaty headed 'Health and Safety', adopted to give effect to the fourth recital thereto to the effect that the Member States, whilst resolved to create the conditions necessary for the development of a powerful nuclear industry, were anxious to create the conditions of safety necessary to eliminate hazards to the life and health of the public. Advocate-General Slynn (later Lord Slynn of Hadley) in his Opinion concluded that, despite its wording, the intention of Article 37 was that the Commission's Opinion was to be received after consultation with the experts before the waste disposal operation began.

The principle of *effet utile* accepted in part of Community law as settled by Case 9/70 *Grad v Finanzamt Traunstein*,[8] Case 22/70 *Commission v Council*,[9] and Case 804/79 *Commission v United Kingdom*[10]and the principle of Community solidarity as explained by Joint Cases 6 and 11/69 *Commission v France*[11]and by Case 39/72 *Commission v Italy*[12], require, in the interests of health and safety efficiency and the protection of the environment, whilst not unduly encroaching on national procedures, that Article 37 requires that the Commission be notified and its Opinion be given and considered before the competent authorities of Member States authorise the disposal of radioactive effluents from a nuclear installation. The Court held that Article 37 can only achieve its purpose if it is interpreted to mean that it requires the Commission to be furnished with the general data concerning a plan for disposal of radioactive effluents before such disposal is finally authorised. Such an interpretation, which is able to safeguard the necessary effect of the pollution must be given priority in accordance with the court's settled case law in Cases 9/70, 22/70 and 804/79. The Court itself did not consider it necessary to call in aid the solidarity principle.

Solidarity

Full effect must be given to the principle of Community solidarity. Article 5 of the EC Treaty sets out this principle. Member States are obliged to take all appropriate measures, whether general or particular, to ensure fulfilment of the obligations arising out of the EC Treaty or resulting from action taken by the Institutions of the Community. They must facilitate the achievement of the Community's tasks. They must abstain from any measure which could jeopardise the attainment of the objectives of the Treaty. The actual tenor of this duty depends on the provisions of the Treaty or on legal instruments derived out of the scheme laid down by the Treaty.[13]

---

8   [1970] ECR 825, [1971] CMLR 1.

9   [1971] ECR 263, [1971] CMLR 335.

10   [1981] ECR 1045, [1982] 1 CMLR 543.

11   [1969] ECR 523, [1970] CMLR 43.

12   [1973] ECR 101, [1973] CMLR 439.

13   Case 78/70 *Deutsche Grammophon Gesellschaft mbH v Metro-SB-Grossmärkte GmbH and Co KG* [1971] ECR 487, [1971] CMLR 631.

Under the principle of solidarity national courts in construing legal instruments must ensure that citizens are given adequate protection derived from the direct effect of provisions of Community law.[14]

Human rights

The European Court of Justice looks at common constitutional traditions amongst the Member States and also at international treaties for the protection of human rights to which Member States are contracting parties. The court particularly has regard to the Convention for the Protection of Human Rights and Fundamental Freedoms signed in Rome in November 1950.[15] The Court of Justice has also referred to the European Social Charter signed in Turin in 1961.[16] In the *Defrenne*[17] case the European Court of Justice referred to the International Labour Organisation Convention signed in Geneva in June 1958.[18] Thus, in construing Community legislation the Court ensures that its construction respects fundamental rights such as equality between the sexes, freedom of religion, the right to pursue a trade or professional activity, the right to a fair hearing, the right to be granted an effective remedy and rights concerning the home such as privacy, peaceful enjoyment and inviolability of the home.

Equality of treatment

The principle of equality of treatment requires that construction of one clause in the treaty must not differ from construction of an identical clause in another treaty. It also requires that comparable situations must be treated similarly.[19] However, differences which arise from divergencies between the laws of the Member States are not necessarily contrary to the principle of equality of treatment so long as the provision of the national law in question affects all persons subject to it in accordance with objective criteria.[20]

Proportionality

The Court in construing a measure may examine whether such a measure is disproportionate, that is to say to establish whether such measure is compatible with the principle of proportionality. The Court is entitled to consider whether

---

14   Case 33/76 *Rewe-Zentralfinanz eG v Landwirtschaftskammer fur Saarland* [1976] ECR 1989, [1977] 1 CMLR 533; Case 5/67 *W Beus GmbH & Co v Hauptzollamt München* [1968] ECR 83, [1968] CMLR 131.

15   TS71 [1953], Cmnd 8969.

16   TS38 [1965], Cmnd 2643.

17   Case 149/77 *Defrenne v SA Belge de Navigation Aérienne Sabena* [1978] ECR 1365, [1978] 3 CMLR 312.

18   Cmnd 593.

19   Joined Cases 117/76 and 16/77 *Albert Ruckdeschel & Co v Hauptzollamt Hamburg-St Annen* [1977] ECR 1753, [1979] 2 CMLR 445; Joined Cases 198-202/81 *Micheli v Commission* [1982] ECR 4145, see in particular at 157.

20   Case 14/68 *Wilhelm v Bundeskartellamt* [1969] ECR 1, [1969] CMLR 100.

the means employed by a provision to achieve its aim correspond to the importance of the aim and whether those means are necessary in order to attain it.[21] The European Court of Justice must also apply the principle of proportionality to the construction of national measures.[22]

The principle of proportionality requires a derogation contained in a legal instrument to be within the boundaries of what is appropriate and necessary for achieving the objective of the legal instrument.[23]

Legal certainty

Under the principle of legal certainty, an interpretation adopted in one case is likely to be followed by the Court of Justice in another case in which the same point of construction arises for consideration. The Court, however, is not bound by the doctrine of precedent.[24] National courts, however, are bound not to give effect to a Community legal instrument which the Court of Justice has declared to be void.[25] In the *Deuka* case[26] the Court gave a somewhat liberal interpretation to certain provisions to allow traders to have time to comply with an amended regime in the interests of maintaining the principle of legal certainty which requires that the effect of the legal provision must be clear and predictable to persons subject to it.[27] Applications of the principle of legal certainty may justify imposing a time limit on the effect of a judgment.[28]

Legitimate expectations

The principle of the protection of legitimate expectations prevents the Community institutions from amending legislation setting out certain economic rules without at the same time setting out transitional provisions to give time for traders to adjust to the new rules, unless the adoption of traditional provisions would be contrary to an overriding public interest.[29] The Principle is

---

21 Case 266/84 *Denkavit France v FORMA* [1986] ECR 149, [1987] 3 CMLR 202; Case 56/86 *Société Pour L'Exportation Des Sucres v OBEA* [1987] ECR 1423.

22 Case 39/75 *Coenen v Sociaal-Economische Raad* [1975] ECR 1547, [1976] 1 CMLR 30; and *dicta* in various other cases. Contrast, however, Case 182/85 *Alfons Lüttiscke v Denkavit Futtermittel GmbH* [1987] ECR 3159 where it was held that the principle of proportionality was not offended where different methods of analysing a product were prescribed, in one case by a number of different methods and in another case by a single method of limited practical utility.

23 Case 222/84 *Johnston v RUC Chief Constable* [1986] ECR 1651.

24 Case 112/76 *Manzoni v Fonds Nationale de Retraite des Ouvriers Mineurs* [1977] ECR 1647, [1978] 2 CMLR 416.

25 Case 66/80 *International Chemical Corporation SpA v Amministrazione Delle Finanze Dello Stato* [1981] ECR 1191, [1983] 2 CMLR 593.

26 Case 78/74 *Deuka v Einfuhr-und Vorratsstelle Für Getreide und Futtermittel* [1975] ECR 421, [1975] 2 CMLR 28.

27 Joined Cases 212-217/80 *Amministrazione Delle Finanze Dello Stato v SRL Meridionale Industria Salumi* [1981] ECR 2735.

28 Case 43/75 *Defrenne v S A Belge de Navigation Aèrienne* [1976] ECR 455, [1976] 2 CLMR 98.

29 Case 81/72 *Commission v Council* [1973] ECR 575, [1973] CMLR 639.

based on the conduct adopted by a Community institution with regard to future events but in the *Mavridis* case[30] it was said that the administration's conduct led an individual to entertain reasonable expectations. The case of *Van Den Berg jen Jurgens*[31] was fought on the basis of justified hopes. The point is that the manner in which a provision has been implemented or not implemented should not support an interpretation which differs from a proper interpretation derived from a consideration of the wording, sense and purpose of the provision in question[32] although an investigation of this kind may find a legitimate expectation in the way in which a provision has been implemented continuing in a particular way by application of the principle of legitimate expectations.

Retrospective effect

A legal measure which provides for the withdrawal of a previous legal measure retrospectively is probably contrary to the general principles of European law.[33] As a general rule, therefore, one cannot retrospectively withdraw a legal measure which has conferred individual rights unless false or incomplete information has been provided by persons affected by the measure[34] or where the measure is otherwise illegal.[35] Thus the courts are unwilling to give any form of retrospective effect to Community legislation unless there is clear evidence from the terms of the legal instrument and from the objectives or scheme lying behind it that a retrospective effect was clearly intended.[36]

Where transitional provisions are introduced the general rule is that such transitional provisions only take effect after the non-transitional principal provisions have taken effect. It appears however that transitional rules could be made to apply to the period between the date of publication of a legislative instrument and its coming into full effect provided that the coming into force of such a transitional provision is clearly necessary to achieve objectives.[37]

Fairness

The application of the principle of equity or fairness is a guide in interpreting legislation. In the *Süddeutsche Zucker-AG* case[38] it was held that although Article 1(2) of Regulation 142/69 did not expressly mention 'sugar sweepings', both logic and equity drove one to the conclusion that it should have done. It was not

---

30 Case 289/81 *Mavridis v European Parliament* [1983] ECR 1731.

31 Case 265/85 *Van Den Bergh en Jurgens v Commission* [1987] ECR 1155 at para 44.

32 Case 43/75 *Defrenne v SA Belge de Navigation Aérienne* [1976] ECR 455, see 472 and 475.

33 Case 159/82 *Verli-Wallace v Commission* [1983] ECR 2711.

34 Joined Cases 42 and 49/59 *Société Nouvelle des Usines de Pontlieue-Aciéries du Temple v High Authority* [1961] ECR 53.

35 Case 111/63 *Lemmerz-Werke GmbH v High Authority* [1965] ECR 677, [1968] CMLR 280 – see especially at 301 and 302.

36 Joined Cases 212-217/80 *Amministrazione Delle Finanze Dello Stato v SRL Meridionale Inustria Salumi* [1981] ECR 2735 at 2751.

37 Case 278/84 *Germany v Commission* [1987] ECR 1.

38 Case 94/75 *Süddeutsche Zucker-AG v Hauptzollamt Mannheim* [1976] ECR 153 at 159 and 160.

appropriate to impose the production levy on the quantity of sugar corresponding to the amount lost during the refining process for sugar sweepings in disregard of the fact that this quantity was neither actually produced or indeed sold. Mr Advocate-General Warner in his opinion put it as follows:

> Equity certainly dictates that it should be held to be implicit in Article 1 (whether in paragraph (1) or paragraph (2) matters not) that, where sugar sweepings have already been included in a manufacturer's sugar production, the white sugar derived from them should not also be included. In Case 64/74 *Reich v Haumptzollamt Landau* [1975] ECR 274–75, I expressed the opinion that the principle of proportionality could, in an appropriate case, operate not to invalidate legislative provisions but to supplement them by requiring them to be interpreted as being, implicitly, inapplicable in circumstances where their application would infringe the principle. The Court, however, in that case, preferred to rest its judgment simply on 'reasons of equity' (*ibid* 268–69).

Firma Adolf Reich when importing into Germany from France two consignments of fodder maize had fixed in advance with the authority the rate of levy for September imports. Due it was said to the fault of the railways the goods did not reach their German destination until October. The Court had to examine whether and to what extent the exception of *force majeure*, allowed for by Regulation 87/62 in the field of trade with third countries, might equally apply to trade with Member States. Looking at the sixth and seventh recitals of Regulation 87/62, the Court concluded that the exception was justified by reasons of equity. The Court held that the fixed levy continued to apply when the delay was due to *force majeure*. In the *Johann Lührs* case[39] the Court held that in view of the uncertainties inherent in Regulation 348/76, natural justice demanded that for the purpose of converting a tax on exports into national currency the exchange rate which at the material time was less onerous for the taxpayer concerned should be applied.

---

39   Case 78/77 *Firma Johann Lührs v Hauptzollamt Hamburg-Jonas* [1978] ECR 169 at p 180.

CHAPTER 47

EUROPEAN CONSTRUCTION

General principles

The duty of the European Court of Justice under Article 164 of the EC Treaty is to ensure that, in the interpretation and application of the Treaty, the law is observed. The expression 'law' is not defined. The general principles of Community law are both written and unwritten. In general the written principles are to be found in Articles 1–7C of the EC Treaty, Articles 1–5 of the ECSC Treaty and Articles 1–3 of the Euratom Treaty. The unwritten general principles may also be found in the national laws of the Member States.

The law is to be found in Regulations, Decisions and Directives (as well as in Treaties) emanating from the European Parliament and the Council jointly, or the Council on its own or the Commission.

Legislation must be construed in the context of the general measure authorising it, such as a Treaty provision or a framework Directive setting out the general position which the detailed Directive or daughter Directive aims to implement. One must have regard to criteria for determining the legality of the provision and criteria relating to considerations for the proper exercise of powers. It is well established that a specific provision contained in a legal instrument must be construed in the light of the general principle or scheme established.[1] When interpreting Community legislation therefore the words or clause in question must be placed in an overall legal context and interpreted in the light of Community law as a whole.

The legislation in question must be studied to see what general rule can be derived[2] or to see whether a clear policy is revealed.[3] If there is no general rule then one might be able to find that the provision is an exceptional case[4] but one must always be on the lookout to see if there is in fact a general principle.[5] Clauses appearing in a Treaty must themselves be put in the context of the Treaty as a whole relating to the subject in question.[6] The Community

---

1 Case 152/73 *Sotgiu v Deutsche Bundespost* [1974] ECR 153; Case 93/81 *Institut National d'Assurance Maladie-Invalidité v Knoeller* [1982] ECR 951; Case 50/75 *Caisse de pension des employés privés v Massonet* [1975] EC 1473. See also Case 7/82 *GVL v Commission* [1983] ECR 483 at 502.

2 Cases 342/85 *Italy v Commission* [1987] ECR 4677 and 343/85 *Italy v Commission* [1987] ECR 4711 establish that particular provisions of secondary legislation may, when taken together, indicate the existence of a general rule applicable in the absence of a contrary provision, throughout a particular legislative or administrative scheme.

3 Case 94/86 *Maizena GmbH v Hauptzollamt Hamburg-Jonas* [1987] ECR 2941 which shows that other legislative measures may be looked at to establish whether or not the Community legislature would have used express words and given reasons for making a particular provision (see paras 11, 14, 15 and 16).

4 Case 222/84 *Johnston v RUC Chief Constable* [1986] ECR 1651; Case 198/86 *Conradi v Directeur de la Concurrence* [1987] ECR 4469 at paras 14 and 15.

5 Case 53/85 *AKZO Chemie BV and AKZ0 Chemie UK Ltd v Commission* [1986] ECR 1965.

6 Joined Cases 7,9/54 *Groupement des Industries Sidérurgiques Luxembourgeoises v High Authority* [1954-56] ECR 175 at 195.

instrument must not have a wider scope than that of its founding Treaty.[7] The principles to be taken into account include those derived from other Treaty provisions. Principles may also be taken into account derived from other secondary legislation.

Width of construction

Construction can be broad or narrow. Reference must certainly be made to the purpose or objective of the provision to determine whether the wording to be construed or the concepts referred to by it should be given a broad or narrow construction.[8]

Derogations from the Treaty must be strictly construed.[9]

Exceptions must be strictly construed.[10] Exceptions cannot take precedence over general and unconditional rules.[11] Exceptions to fundamental Treaty provisions cannot be given a scope which would exceed their objectives.[12]

Obligations imposed on national authorities in implementing Community rules relating to trade must be strictly construed.[13]

Provisions of Community law creating any right to benefits financed out of Community funds must be strictly construed.[14]

Where there are divergencies in texts then the narrowest meaning should be taken.[15]

In contrast, a broad construction may be appropriate to make sure that an

---

7   Case 24/68 *Commission v Italy* [1969] ECR 193, [1971] CMLR 611 at 625 which indicates that secondary legislation has the same scope as the EC Treaty where it implements the Treaty provision, has the same objective and uses the same form of words.

8   Case 13/84 *Control Data v Commission* [1987] ECR 275, para 16; Case 238/84 *Roser* [1986] ECR 795, para 25; Case 320/85 *Ministère Public v Maniglier* [1986] ECR 2917, para 9; Case 332/85 *Germany v Commission* [1987] ECR 5143, para 7 and Case 22/86 *Rindone v Allgemeine Ortskrankenkasse Bad Urach-Münsingen* [1987] ECR 1339, paras 13 and 21.

9   Case 127/73 *Belgische Radio EN Televisie (BRT) v SV SABAM* [1974] ECR 313, [1974] 2 CMLR 238; Case 67/74 *Bonsignore v Stadt Köln* [1975] ECR 297; Case 29/75 *Kaufhof AG v Commission* [1976] ECR 431; Case 95/81 *Commission v Italy* [1982] ECR 2187; Case 174/82 *Sandoz BV* [1983] ECR 2445 at 2464, [1984] 3 CMLR 43 at 58.

10 Case 176/73 *Van Belle v Council* [1974] ECR 1361; Case 24/76 *Estasis Salotti di Colzani Aimo v RUWA Polstereimaschinen GmbH* [1976] ECR 1831, [1977] 1 CMLR 345.

11 Case 25/76 *Galeries Segoura Sprl v Rahim Bonakdarian* [1976] ECR 1851, [1977] 1 CMLR 361.

12 Case 152/73 *Sotgiu v Deutsche Bundespost* [1974] ECR 153; Case 2/74 *Reyners v Belgium* [1974] ECR 631, [1974] 2 CMLR 305; Case 35/76 *Simmenthal SpA v Italian Minister for Finance* [1976] ECR 1871, [1977] 2 CMLR 1; Case 14/79 *Commission v Belgium* [1980] ECR 3881 at 3900 and 3901; Case 124/81 *Commission v United Kingdom* [1983] ECR 203 at 235, [1983] 2 CMLR 1 at 26.

13 Case 61/72 MIJ *PPW Internationaal NV v Hoofdproduktschap Voor Akkerbouwprodukten* [1973] ECR 301; Case 55/74 *Unkel v Hauptzollamt Hamburg-Jonas* [1975] ECR 9, [1975] 2 CMLR 76.

14 Joined Cases 146, 192 and 193/81 *BayWa Ag v Bundesanstalt für Landwirtschaftliche Marktordnung* [1982] ECR 1503; Case 278/84 *Germany v Commission* [1987] ECR 1, [1988] 1 CMLR 632.

15 Case 295/81 *International Flavors and Fragrances IFF (Deutschland) GmbH v Hauptzollamt Bad Reichenhall* [1982] ECR 3239 at 3248.

administrative scheme works without a hitch.[16] Such a construction may not, however, introduce a formalism which goes beyond what is necessary for the effective operation of such a scheme.[17]

Literal meaning

The literal meaning is the clear meaning.[18] The analysis may, however, be different if there are divergencies between the various language texts and consequently no uniform version available for consultation.[19]

A literal interpretation is hardly possible where there are so many divergencies between the different language versions of a provision that it is impossible to get a clear and uniform interpretation.[20] In such circumstances the Court has to refer to the purpose, general scheme and context of the provision in question in order to ascertain its meaning because it is impossible to construct any sensible argument based on linguistic discrepancies.[21]

Uniformity

One objective of the Community laws relating to construction is that a uniform interpretation should prevail.[22] None of the three Acts of Accession allowing new Member States to join the Community can be construed as validating measures which are themselves incompatible with the three Treaties establishing the three Communities.[23] It follows that, although there is no doctrine of precedent, where a provision similar to that to be construed has already been construed then the Court should try and ensure an identical construction in the interests of creating uniform interpretation.[24]

---

16 Case 32/72 *Wasaknäcke Knäckebrotfabrik GmbH v Einfuhr-Und Vorratsstelle für Getreide und Futtermittel* [1972] ECR 1181.

17 Case 94/71 *Schluter und Maack v Hauptzollamt Hamburg-Jonas* [1972] ECR 307.

18 Case 67/79 *Fellinger v Bundesanstalt für Arbeit, Nuremberg* [1980] ECR 535 at 550, [1981] 1 CMLR 471 at 478 and 479; Case 40/64 *Sgarlata v Commission* [1965] ECR 215 at 226 and 227, [1966] CMLR 314 at 323 and 324; Joined Cases 146,192 and 193/81 *Bay Wa AG v Bundesanstalt für Landwirschaftliche Marktordnung* [1982] ECR 1503 at 1529.

19 Case 6/74 *Maulijn v Commission* [1974] ECR 1287 at 1293.

20 Case 11/76 *The Netherlands v Commission* [1979] ECR 245 at 278; Case 18/76 *Germany v Commission* [1979] ECR 343 at 383; Case 80/76 *North Kerry Milk Products Ltd v Minister for Agriculture and Fisheries* [1977] ECR 425 at 435, [1977] 2 CMLR 769 at 781.

21 Case 143/82 *Lipman v Commission* [1983] ECR 1301 at 1310.

22 Case 49/71 *Hagen OHG v Einfuhr-und Vorratsstelle für Getreide und Futtermittel* [1972] ECR 23, [1973] CMLR 35; Case 50/71, *Wünsche OHG v Eihfuhr-und Forratsstelle für Getreide and Futtermittel* [1972] ECR 53, [1973] CMLR 35.

23 Case 185/73 *Hauptzollamt Bielefeld v König* [1974] ECR 607.

24 Case 101/63 *Wagner v Fohrmann and Krier* [1964] ECR 195, [1964] CMLR 245.

Footnotes

Footnotes in whatever form and any other kind of annotation are an integral part of a legal instrument. They have the same legal force as the provisions to which they relate.[25]

Plural

The use of the plural indicates both the singular and the plural.[26]

Implication

Where there is a lacuna in the text and the Court thinks that it is appropriate to fill that lacuna then it can do so by implication of a provision applied by analogy,[27] notwithstanding the fact that a provision usually applies only to the situations actually envisaged by it.[28] However if an appropriate analogy cannot be discovered or if the Court thinks that it is not appropriate to imply a provision on the basis of analogy then no such implication can be made.[29]

Three examples can be given where the European Court of Justice has dealt with a lacuna situation by implication based on analogy. In the *Brouwer-Kaune* case[30] the Court did so where secondary legislation made no express provision because it was thought appropriate to give effect to a mandatory principle. In the *Union Francaise de Céréals* case [31] the Court was prepared to make an implication to preserve an overriding principle of Community law. In the case of *Germany v Commission*,[32] the Court did so in order that persons concerned would have effective protection for their rights.

Member States in implementing Directives are not allowed to imply additional listing requirements. For example Article 6(1) of Directive 76/768 on cosmetic products lists the information which the packaging, containers or labels relating to cosmetic products are to bear. That list does not include information as to the quality and quantity of the substances mentioned in the presentation of those products. The Court has held that a list of information is

---

25 See Case 80/72 *Koninklijke Lassiefabrieken NV v Hoofdproduktschap voor Akkerbrouwprodukten* [1973] ECR 635 at 650; Case 38/75 *Douaneagent Der NV Nederlandse Spoorwegen v Inspecteur der Invoerrechten en Accijnzen* [1975] ECR 1439 at 1448; Case 94/86 *Maizena GmbH v Hauptzollamt Hamburg-Jonas* [1987] ECR 2941 at para 14.

26 Case 32/74 *Friedrich Haaga GmbH* [1974] ECR 1201 at 1207.

27 Joined Cases 15/64 and 60/65 *Moreau v EAEC Commission* [1966] ECR 459; Case 64/74 *Reich v Hauptzollamt Landau* [1975] ECR 261 at 268.

28 Case 21/64 *Macchiorlati Dalmas e Figli v High Authority* [1965] ECR 175 at 190 and 191; Case 48/70 *Bernard v European Parliament* [1971] ECR 175 at 184.

29 Case 137/77 *Frankfurt-am-main City v Neumann* [1978] ECR 1623 at 1637; Case 7/81 *Sinatra v Fonds National de Retraite des Ouvriers Mineurs* [1982] ECR 137 at 145.

30 Case 180/78 *Brouwer-Kaune v Bestuur van de Bedrijfsverenging Voorhetkledingbedrijf* [1979] ECR 2111 at 2120 and 2121.

31 Case 6/78 *Union Francaise de Céréals v Hauptzollamt Hamburg-Jonas* [1978] ECR 1675 at 1683 and 1684.

32 Case 44/81 *Germany v Commission* [1982] ECR 1855 at 1875.

exhaustive and that a Member State may not require the indication, where this is not expressly provided for in the Directive, of particulars as to the quality and substances mentioned in the presentation of cosmetic products. This is sometimes called the exhaustiveness principle.

The Court would not imply a provision if such provision enables conditions to be imposed which are not in accord with the objectives of the legal instrument concerned and which are a source of discrimination.[33]

Amendments

Directives are frequently amended by the replacement of words, phrases, sentences or whole Articles or by the repeal of Articles or parts of Articles. In such circumstances the text of the Directive being amended may be referred to, to ascertain the precise nature of the amendment[34].

If different words are used then this may raise a presumption that it was intended that the interpretation of the revised Directive should be different. It can happen that a word with a precise meaning is replaced by a word with a less precise meaning. In such circumstances the meaning conveyed by the original Directive is to be replaced with the meaning conveyed by the amended Directive.[35]

On the other hand if it were the other way round, namely a meaning with wording which is somewhat ambiguous being replaced by a much clearer provision, then it may not necessarily be possible to use the amended version as an aid to construction to give meaning to the original version.[36]

Where a term used in an amended Directive is the same as in the original Directive the Court will probably conclude that no change of meaning is intended but before arriving at such a conclusion other sources such as those referred to in the preamble to the Directive will be consulted to support such an approach. The Court will come to a different conclusion if references to other documentation indicates an intention to change the meaning of the word in question.[37]

Decisions

Decisions of the Council of Ministers are addressed to Member States.

They are subject to a special rule of construction that where there is some discrepancy or divergence between the different language versions then the most liberal interpretation must be given to the Decision consistent with its declared objectives. The reason for this is that it cannot be said that one

---

33 Joined Cases 275/80 and 24/81 *Krupp Stahl AG v Commission* [1981] ECR 2489 at 2514.

34 Case 15/60 *Simon v Court of Justice* [1961] ECR 115.

35 Case 15/60 *Simon v Court of Justice* [1961] ECR 115 at 124 and 125.

36 Case 283/82 *Papierfabrik Schoellershammer Schoeller & Söhne GmbH & Co KG v Commission* [1983] ECR 4219 at 4225.

37 Case 84/85 *United Kingdom v Commission* [1987] ECR 3765.

language version of a Decision was intended to impose a stricter obligation upon the Member State concerned than obligations placed on other Member States through the use of a different language.[38]

Direct effect

The European Court of Justice has found no difficulty in construing legal instruments addressed to Member States as creating rights for the benefit of individuals who may have an interest in the carrying out of duties placed on Member States in such instruments.

As explained in *Humblet v Belgium*[39] a substantive right has as its corollary a means of enforcement by an individual benefited by the provision by proceedings before the Courts.

The doctrine of direct effect applies when four conditions are satisfied namely the obligation in the Directive must be clear and precise, the obligation must not be accompanied by conditions, no discretion must be left to the Member State in respect of how the Article of the Directive is to be implemented and time for implementation specified in the Directive must have passed. It is based on the premise that it should not be open for a Member State which has not adopted the implementing measures required by a Directive in the prescribed period to rely on its own failure, as against individuals, to perform the obligations which the Directive imposes. Thus it was decided in one case on a reference for a preliminary ruling that the first paragraph of Article 95 produced direct effects and created individual rights which national courts must protect.[40]

Precedent

The doctrine of precedent does not apply to the European Court of Justice. It is not bound by its previous decisions.[41] It is however bound by the principle of legal certainty mentioned above. The national court making a reference is bound by the interpretation of Community law by the European Court of Justice.[42]

---

38 Case 29/69 *Stauder v Ulm* [1969] ECR 419 at 425, [1970] CMLR 112 at 118.

39 Case 6/60 *Humblet v Belgium* [1960] ECR 559 at 571; Case 43/75 *Defrenne v SA Belge de Navigation Aérienne* [1976] ECR 455 at 475.

40 Case 28/67 *Firma Molkerei-Zentrale Westfalen/Lippe GmbH v Hauptzollamt Paderborn* [1968] ECR 143.

41 Case 112/76 *Manzoni v Fonds National de Retraite des Ouvriers Mineurs* [1977] ECR 1647 at 1662.

42 Case 29/68 *Milch-Fett-Und Eirkontor GmbH v Hauptzollamt Saarbrücken* [1969] ECR 165 at 179 and 180.

CHAPTER 48

AIDS TO CONSTRUCTION

Objectives

The European Court ascertains the objectives behind the making of a legislative provision. As an aid to interpretation the Court first of all ascertains the relevant Treaty and then looks at the objectives of that Treaty.[1] The Court then considers the objectives of the instrument containing the relevant provisions. The Court then reviews the objectives to see if there is any ambiguity in them. The Court will also look at the general scheme to which the legislation in question relates. The scheme is an important guide to construction provided that it is clearly expressed.[2] An examination of the general scheme may well disclose the purpose for which the legislation is promulgated and this should enable the Court to put the provision being construed into an appropriate context.[3] In order to understand fully the scheme it may be necessary for the Court to look at the origins of the development of the legislation including all preparatory documents.

Surrounding circumstances

The surrounding circumstances may be taken into account as an aid to construction where the wording is not clear. If surrounding circumstances point to the true construction of a legal instrument affecting trading ventures then they must clearly not be disregarded.[4] It might well be relevant to look at the circumstances in which the provision in question was adopted.[5]

---

1   Case 6/72 *Europemballage Corpn and Continental Cam Co Inc v Commission* [1973] ECR 215 at 243–45; Case 15/81 *Gaston Schul Douane Expediteur BV v Inspecteur der Invoerrechten en Accijnzen, Roosendaal* [1982] ECR 1409 at 1431 and 1432; Case 384/85 *Borrie Clarke v Chief Adjudication Officer* [1987] ECR 2865.

2   Case 9/70 *Grad v Finanzamt Traunstein* [1970] ECR 825; Case 23/70 *Haselhorst v Finanzamt Dusseldorf-Alstadt* [1970] ECR 881; Case 67/79 *Fellinger v Bundesanstalt für Arbeit, Nuremberg* [1980] ECR 535; Case 89/81 *Staatssecretaris van Financien v Hong Kong Trade Development Council* [1982] ECR 1277.

3   Case 6/74 *Maulijn v Commission* [1974] ECR 12/87 at 1293; Case 30/7 *R v Bouchereau* [1977] ECR 1999 at 2010.

4   Case 215/85 *Bundesanstalt für landwirtschaftliche Marktordnung v Raiffeisen Hauptgenossenschaft eG* [1987] ECR 1279.

5   Case 342/82 *Cohen v Commission* [1983] ECR 3829 at 3841 and 3842.

Social developments

General social developments may be taken into account as an aid to construction.[6] However it should be noted that social considerations do not operate so as to override the objectives of the legislation.[7]

Preamble

Community legislation contains as a general rule a large number of recitals. These explain the background, objectives, scheme and purpose of the legislation. Reference to documents referred to in the recitals may well assist to confirm the court's interpretation.[8] In no circumstances will the contents of the preamble or any document referred to in the preamble be allowed to override the Court's proper construction of a legal provision.[9]

Minutes of Council meetings

Reference to minutes of Council meetings as an aid to construction is not generally allowed[10] A practice has now however developed of publishing extracts or summaries of important points.

Opinion of officials

References to an opinion given by officials in dealing with the matter is not regarded by the Court as an appropriate aid to construction.[11]

Informal documents

It appears that reference to informal documents prepared by the Commission for the purposes of consultation between Commissioners and for other internal purposes is not regarded as appropriate as an aid to construction.[12]

---

6   Case 59/85 *Netherlands v Reed* [1986] ECR 1283.

7   Case 61/82 *Italy v Commission* [1983] ECR 655; Case 234/87 *Casio Computer Co GmbH Deutschland v Oberfiananzdirektion München* [1989] ECR 63.

8   Case 29/69 *Stauder v Ulm* [1969] ECR 419; Case 107/80 *Adorno v Joint Commission* [1981] ECR 1469; Case 38/81 *Effer SpA v Kantner* [1982] ECR 825. Joined Cases 424-425/85 *Frico v Voedselvorrzienings In-en Verkoopbureau* [1987] ECR 2755; Case 232/86 *Nicolet Instrument GmbH v Hauptzollamt Berlinpackhof* [1987] ECR 5025.

9   Joined Cases 154 and 155/83 *Hoche v De Beste Boter v BALM* [1985] ECR 1215.
    See further Chapter 45, The nature of the preamble.

10 Case 38/69 *Commission v Italy* [1070] ECR 47 at 57; Case 429/85 *Commission v Italy* [1988] ECR 483 at paras 1–9.

11 Joined Cases 53 and 54/63 *Lemmerz-Werke GmbH v High Authority* [1963] ECR 239 at 247.

12 Case 74/69 *Hauptzollamt Bremer-Freihafen v Waren-Import-Gesellschaft Krohn & Co* [1970] ECR 451 at 459.

Negotiating documents

Reference to negotiating documents is allowed as an aid to construction to disclose the purpose of the legislation. In the case of *Netherlands v Commission*[13] preparatory material was used as an aid for the construction of certain secondary legislation. In another case[14] preparatory material was used as an aid in the construction of a Convention. Working documents can be examined to ascertain intention but in the absence of any working documents it appears that a literal interpretation must be given.[15] To enable the Court to gain a full understanding of the scheme it is necessary to look at the origins for the provision in question and this inevitably involves an examination of all preparatory documents. Unpublished notes of preparatory meetings are probably not admissible but secondary legislation can be looked at to see if this adds anything to establishing the general picture.[16] Preparatory documents recording negotiations between the various Member States are not regarded to an aid to construction.[17] However recorded events which lead to the preparation of proposals may be admissible[18].

Implemented legislation

The way in which a provision has been implemented by a Member State does not give any assistance to the Court who must interpret the meaning of a provision from its wording, sense and purpose.[19]

Public international law

Where a Directive is based on an international Convention then public international law can be called in aid to assist in interpretation. International agreements can be effective aids to construction.[20] However, where a provision being construed exceeds the requirements of international law, then such a provision must receive a strict construction.[21] The General Agreement on Tariffs and Trade (GATT) has been referred to for assistance in interpreting the

---

13 Case 11/76 *Netherlands v Commission* [1979] ECR 245 at 278.

14 Case 201/82 *Gerling Konzern Speziale Kreditversicherungs-AG v Amministrazione del Tesoro Dello Stato* [1983] ECR 2503, [1984] 3 CMLR 638.

15 Case 15/60 *Simon v Court of Justice* [1961] ECR 115.

16 Case 11/76 *Netherlands v Commission* [1979] ECR 245.

17 Case 201/82 *Gerling Konzern Speziale Kreditversicherungs-AG v Amministrazione del Tesoro Dello Stato* [1983] ECR 2503; Cases 305/85 and 142/86 *United Kingdom v Commission* [1988] ECR 467.

18 Case 90/85 *Mikx v Minister van Economische Zaken* [1986] ECR 1695; Case 131/86 *United Kingdom v Council* [1988] ECR 905, [1988] 2 CMLR 364.

19 33/69 *Commission v Italy* [1970] ECR 93 at 101; Case 43/75 *Defrenne v SA Belge de Navigation Aérienne* [1976] ECR 455 at 472 and 475, [1976] 2 CMLR 98 at 123 and 124.

20 Case 6/60 *Humblet v Belgium* [1960] ECR 559.

21 Case 20/59 *Italy v High Authority* [1960] ECR 325 at 339; Case 25/59 *Netherlands v High Authority* [1960] ECR 355 at 374–75.

classification rules applicable to the Common Customs Tariff.[22] It should be noted however that the interpretation of a provision of one of the three Community treaties is not necessarily decisive as to the interpretation of a similar provision contained another Community treaty.[23]

Member State laws

Member State laws are not applied in the construction of Community law because a Community view is taken, not a Member State view. The Community has developed its own legal terminology and its own legal concepts which are applied. Community principles are therefore not defined upon the basis of any one Member State's national legal concept.[24] By way of comparison one could look at cases[25] dealing with the interpretation of the Brussels Convention on Jurisdiction and the Enforcement of Judgments in Civil and Commercial Matters.[26] Such cases show that in relation to each provision of the Brussels Convention a choice must be made between giving an independent meaning to the words and concepts used or interpreting them as to referring to the applicable national law. The principles common to the laws of the Member States may be called in as aids to construction.[27] It would be inappropriate,

---

22 Case 92/71 *Interfood GmbH v Hauptzollamt Hamburg–Ericus* [1972] ECR 231 at 241; [1973] CMLR 562 at 564 and 565.

23 Case 9/56 *Meroni & Co, Industrie Metallurgiche, SpA v Higher Authority* [1957–58] ECR 133; Case 15/57 *Compagnie des Hauts Fourneaux de Chasse v High Authority* [1957–58] ECR 211; Case 108/63 *Officine Elettromeccaniche Ing A Merlini v High Authority* [1965] ECR 1.

24 Case 51/76 *Verbond Van Nederlandse Ondernemingen v Inspecteur Der Invoerrechten En Accijnzen* [1977] ECR 113 at 124 and 125; Case 154/80 *Staatssecretaris Van Financen v Co-operative Aarlappelenbewaatplaats G A* [1982] ECR 445 at 453; Case 64/81*Nicolaus Corman & Fils SA v Hauptzollamt Gronau* [1982] ECR 13.

25 Case 12/76 *Industrie Tessili Italiano Como v Dunlop AG* [1976] ECR 1473; Case 144/86 *Gubisch Maschinenfabrik v Palumbo Handels* [1987] ECR 4861. In Case 21/76 *Handelswekerij GJ Bier NV v Mines de Potasse d'Alsace SA* [1976] ECR 1735 at paras 24 and 25 and Case C-68/93 *Shevill v Presse Alliance SA* (1995) Times, 6 April; [1995] 2 AC 18, para 20, the European Court of Justice held that where the place of the happening of the event which might give rise to liability in tort, delict or quasi delict and the place where that event resulted in damage were not identical, the term 'place where the harmful event occurred' in Article 5(3) of the 1968 Brussels Convention covered both the place where the damage occurred and the place of the event giving rise to it. The Court, however, decided in Case C-364/93 *Marinari v Lloyds Bank plc and Another* (1995) Times, 19 October, that this interpretation could not be extended beyond the particular circumstances which justified it and in this case held that the 'place where the harmful event occurred' was to be interpreted as not referring to the place where the victim claimed to have suffered financial loss consequential upon initial damage arising and suffered by him in another contracting State.

26 The Brussels Convention of 1968, see Cmnd 7395.

27 Case 155/79 *AM & S Europe Ltd v Commission* [1982] ECR 1575 at 1610–12.

however, to have a reference to any national interpretation of rules.[28] Such a reference might lead to a restricted interpretation.[29] Such a reference could well result in giving effect to a purely local judgment.[30]

Laws of a third country

Laws of a third country are not relevant for construction purposes unless in the document being construed there is an express reference to the laws of such third country.[31]

Languages

All the European languages are equally authentic. There is one exception in the case of the text of the ECSE Treaty where the Treaty provides that only the French text is the official text. Where there are discrepancies in different language versions of Directives then the normal meaning of language can be looked at. This was established in the *North Kerry Milk Products* case.[32] This case decided that no preference should be given to any particular language version. On the other hand, it was established in the case of *Stauder v Ulm*[33] that all the different language versions must be taken into account. The EC Treaty originally provided that there would be four language versions, namely Dutch, French, German and Italian but this was changed as other countries joined the Community by Acts of Accession. Reliance can, however, be placed on the text which provides the most clarity. There may be more than one text which is particularly clear.[34] A mis-translation in the language version of a Directive does not affect the validity of the Directive itself.[35] It is perfectly proper to refer to the various language versions in order to check the objectives to see if there are any ambiguities.[36]

28 Case 75/63 *Hoekstra (née Unger) v Bestuur der Bedrijfsvereniging Voor Detailhandel En Ambachten* [1964] ECR 177; CMLR 319; Case 149/85 *Wybot v Faure* [1986] ECR 2391.

29 Case 149/79 *Commission v Belgium* [1980] ECR 3881; Case 118/85 *Commission v Italy* [1987] ECR 2599.

30 Case 1/77 *Robert Bosch GmbH·v Hauptzollamt Hildesheim* [1977] ECR 1473; [1977] 2 CMLR 563.

31 Case 12/73 *Muras v Hauptzollamt Hamburg-Jonas* [1973] ECR 963.

32 Case 80/76 *North Kerry Milk Products Limited v The Minister of Agriculture and Fisheries* [1977] ECR 425; [1977] 2 CMLR 769.

33 Case 29/69 *Stauder v Ulm* [1969] ECR 419, [1970] CMLR 112.

34 Case 316/85 *Centre Public d'aide Sociale de Courcelles v Lebon* [1977] ECR 2811; [1989] 1 CMLR 337.

35 Case 424/85 *Frico v Voedselvoorzienings In-en Verkoopbureau* [1987] ECR 2755

36 Case 16/65 *Schwarze v Einfuhr-Und Vorratsstelle Für Getreide Und Futtermittel* [1965] ECR 877, [1966] CMLR 172; Case 9/79 *Wörsdorfer v Raad van Arbeid* [1979] ECR 2717; [1980] 1 CMLR 87.

Member State opinions

When implementing national legislation has been discussed in a Member State parliament it is not unusual for the government of the Member State concerned to explain why the legislation is being promoted or why a Treaty is being entered into. In two cases the European Court of Justice has referred to the stated opinions of Member State governments for the purposes of either trying to discern their common intention[37] or to confirm the Court's interpretation.[38]

---

37 Case 6/60 *Humblet v Belgium* [1960] ECR 559 at 575 and 576.
38 Joined Cases 2-3/60 *Niederrheinische Bergwerks-AG v High Authority* [1961] ECR 133 at 147.

CHAPTER 49

NOW READ ON

Highlights and history

The Act of Parliament has a history extending back over more than 700 years. As should only be expected, that history has its highlights and its humour. The reader who finds pleasure in the curiosities of the law can gain pleasure from reading such long titles as that of:

'An Act to repeal the Act of Parliament of Ireland, of the Sixth Year of Anne, Chapter Eleven, for explaining and amending the several Acts against Tories, Robers and Raparees,'[1]

or

'An Act for improving the Dublin Police,'[2]

or from the Act which provided for the appointment of a local government officer to be known as a 'garbler'. That interesting Act provided that a garbler

'at the request of any person or persons owner or owners of any spices drugs or other wares of merchandise garbleable and not otherwise shall garble the same.'[3]

These and many other curiosities of the law are set out in interesting fashon in Sir Robert Megarry's book, *Miscellany-at-Law.*

Further reading on the rules for finding the meaning of Acts of Parliament

The object of the present book has been to set out as simply as possible the basic rules that the courts have laid down for the reading of Acts of Parliament. The footnotes in this book have given references to the decisions of the courts in which the reader can find the judges' statements of the rules set out in the text of the book. Those references have been designed to help the reader who wants to take the study of these rules further, but it has not been the intention to provide a full scale textbook on the intricacies of what is known to the lawyer as statutory interpretation. The reader who desires to pursue those intricacies in their full technical detail should turn to the following books:

Additional sources for law students

The Digest (Butterworths & Co Publishers Ltd, London, 1985) vol 45.

Halsbury Laws of England (4th edn, Butterworths, London, 1983) vol 44.

Vaughan, *Law of the European Communities Service*, Butterworths, London, 1990–95) vol 1.

1　Act 28 & 29 Vict c 33, quoted in Megarry, Sir Robert, QC (formerly Megarry V-C), *Miscellany-at-Law* (5th imp) (Stevens & Sons Ltd, London, 1975), p 339.

2　Referred to in Megarry, p 365.

3　6 Anne c 68, 3, quoted in Megarry, p 337.

Textbooks

Craies on Statute Law (7th edn, by SGG Edgar, Sweet & Maxwell, London, 1971).

Maxwell, *The Interpretation of Statutes* (NM Tripathi Private Ltd, 1969).

Odgers, *The Construction of Deeds and Statutes* (5th edn, Sweet and Maxwell, 1967).

INDEX